Women in America

FROM COLONIAL TIMES TO THE 20TH CENTURY

Women in America

FROM COLONIAL TIMES TO THE 20TH CENTURY

Advisory Editors
LEON STEIN
ANNETTE K. BAXTER

A Note About This Volume

Changing concepts of the role of sex in society are reflected in the nineteenth-century writings assembled in this book. Hannah Crocker (1752-1829) was descended from Cotton and Increase Mather. Her observations were published on subscription in 1818. They draw directly on her own experiences and her deep faith in the equality of the sexes under Christianity. Margaret Fuller Ossoli (1810-1850) made her home the center for Boston's transcendentalists and joined Emerson in publishing the *Dial* where her 1843 article appeared with tremendous impact. Ezra Heywood, who was editor of the New England anarchist publication *The Word*, attacked all social restraints including marriage as well as private property and, as a result, suffered imprisonment. Ida Craddock, toward the end of the century, conducted a sex clinic in Philadelphia, and as her pamphlet shows, used remarkable frankness in seeking to lessen nuptial night traumas. Thorstein Veblen's article is a fine example of the style in which he toppled sham.

Sex

and

Equality

ARNO PRESS
A New York Times Company
NEW YORK – 1974

Reprint Edition 1974 by Arno Press Inc.

Observations on the Real Rights of Women
    was reprinted from a copy in The State
    Historical Society of Wisconsin Library

WOMEN IN AMERICA
From Colonial Times to the 20th Century
ISBN for complete set: 0-405-06070-X
See last pages of this volume for titles.

Publisher's Note: This volume was
reprinted from the best available copies.

Manufactured in the United States of America

———◆———

Library of Congress Cataloging in Publication Data

Main entry under title:

Sex and equality.

    (Women of America: from colonial times to the 20th
century)
    Reprint of Observations on the real rights of
women, by H. M. Crocker, first published in 1818; of
The great lawsuit, by M. F. Ossoli, first published
in 1843; of Uncivil liberty, by E. H. Heywood, first
published in 1877; of Cupid's yokes, by E. H. Heywood,
first published in 1887; of Letter to a prospective
bride, by I. C. Craddock, first published in 1897; and
of The barbarian status of women, by T. Veblen, first
published in 1899.
    1. Women in the United States—Addresses, essays,
lectures. 2. Women's rights—United States—
Addresses, essays, lectures. 3. Sex instruction for
women—Addresses, essays, lectures. I. Series.
HQ1418.S48   301.41'2'0973   74-3986
ISBN 0-405-06121-8

CONTENTS

Crocker, H[annah] Mather
OBSERVATIONS ON THE REAL RIGHTS OF WOMEN, With Their
Appropriate Duties Agreeable to Scripture, Reason and Common Sense.
Boston, 1818

[Ossoli, Margaret Fuller]
THE GREAT LAWSUIT: Man versus Men, Woman versus Women (Reprinted from *The Dial,* Vol. IV, No. 1, July 1843)

Heywood, E[zra] H.
UNCIVIL LIBERTY: An Essay to Show the Injustice and Impolicy of
Ruling Woman Without Her Consent. Princeton, Mass., 1877

Heywood, E[zra] H.
CUPID'S YOKES; Or, The Binding Forces of Conjugal Life. Princeton,
Mass., 1887

Craddock, Ida C.
LETTER TO A PROSPECTIVE BRIDE. Philadelphia, 1897

Veblen, Thorstein
THE BARBARIAN STATUS OF WOMEN (Reprinted from *The American Journal of Sociology,* Vol. 4, No. 4, Jan. 1899)

0

OBSERVATIONS
ON THE
REAL RIGHTS OF WOMEN

H[annah] Mather Crocker

OBSERVATIONS

ON THE

REAL RIGHTS OF WOMEN,

WITH THEIR

APPROPRIATE DUTIES,

AGREEABLE TO

SCRIPTURE, REASON AND COMMON SENSE.

BY H. MATHER CROCKER.

And God saw it was not good for man to be alone; and he made him an help meet for him.—And Adam said she is bone of my bones, and flesh of my flesh, therefore she shall be called woman.

BOSTON :
PRINTED FOR THE AUTHOR.
1818.

DEDICATION.

—

TO MISS H. MORE.

Madam,

Your writings on moral and religious subjects are held in the highest estimation by one, who thinks your Comparative View of the Sexes is indeed worthy of yourself.

To your patronage allow me to devote the following pages. Your approbation of the sentiments will be the most distinguished palm the author wishes to obtain.

Though personally unknown, permit me to subscribe myself, with sentiments of the highest esteem and respect,

Yours,

H. M. Crocker.

AUTHOR'S PREFACE.

———

PROPOSALS for printing the following pages were issued more than a year since. The author, having been afflicted with sickness, has unavoidably been unable to collect subscriptions till the present time.

The publishing has therefore been suspended. To those who first subscribed let me say, I hope when they receive the work, they will have reason to say, patient waiters are no losers; and she sincerely wishes those who peruse the work may find reason to say, the author has not spent her strength for nought, neither have they spent their time in vain, who have read the work.

With this wish the work is now devoted to the public notice; with a hope, that the work will receive the candour and patronage of a free, enlightened, independent, federal nation.

CONTENTS.

—◆—

CHAP. VII.

CHAP. VIII.

INTRODUCTION.

THIS little work is not written with a design of promoting any altercation or dispute respecting superiority or inferiority, of the sexes;
but the aim will be to prove, in a pleasant manner, and, we hope, to even demonstration, that
though there are appropriate duties peculiar
to each sex, yet the wise Author of nature has
endowed the female mind with equal powers
and faculties, and given them the same right
of judging and acting for themselves, as he
gave to the male sex; although it is plain, from
scripture account, that the woman was the
first in the transgression, she justly forfeited
her original right of equality for a certain space
of time, and a heavy and humiliating sentence
was past upon her, that her sorrow should be
multiplied, and that under the Jewish dispensation, the man should rule over her; and she
was under the yoke of bondage, till the birth
of our blessed Saviour, which, according to
the promise given, was the seed of the woman,
that should bruise the serpent's head.

We shall consider woman restored to her
original right and dignity at the commence-
ment of the christian dispensation, although
there must be allowed some moral and physi-

cal distinction of the sexes agreeably to the order of nature, and the organization of the human frame, still the sentiment must predominate, that the powers of mind are equal in the sexes. We shall produce examples, both from sacred and profane history, of the great abilities and exertion of many females, when called into action, either on political or religious account. For the interest of their country, or in the cause of humanity, we shall strictly adhere to the principle and the impropriety of females ever trespassing on masculine ground : as it is morally incorrect, and physically improper.

We shall therefore state in a plain manner the beauty and order that must arise, from each sex performing their appropriate duties with mutual fidelity and harmony; a plan or theory, or a christian system will be drawn, by which means the mutual happiness of the sexes may be promoted; and the rights, liberties, and independence of a brave and free people shall continue secure to them, by the mutual virtues and integrity of the sexes; the plan must be reduced to practice, by mutual agreement, and the mantle of charity be drawn over every little imperfection, that peace and harmony may prevail.

May the same mantle be extended to the following pages by the candid reader.

RIGHTS OF WOMAN, &c.

—•—

CHAP. I.

Of the creation and fall of our first parents.

THE foundation stone of the present work must be laid in the first creation of the human race. When the great Jehovah had created the earth, and all things therein, he created man; male and female created he them, in his own image, so far as he endowed him with intellectual powers and faculties, and gave him an immortal and rational soul, and powers of mind capable of reasoning on the nature of things.   And the Lord God said, it is not good for man to be alone; I will make him an help meet, for him : And the Lord God caused a deep sleep to fall upon Adam, and he slept: and he took one of his ribs, and closed up the flesh instead thereof.   And the rib, which the Lord God had taken from man, made he a woman: and brought her unto the man, and Adam said, this is now bone of my bone, and flesh of my flesh : she shall be called woman, because she was taken out of man; as she partakes of my original nature, she shall therefore partake of my name; therefore shall a man leave his father and his mother, and shall cleave unto his wife, and they shall be one flesh: See Gen. ii. 24.

It seems, says an able commentator,* to have been the Creator's design to have inculcated the lesson of perfect love and union, by forming the woman out of the man's body, and from a part of it so near the heart, as well as to make woman of a more refined and delicate nature, by thus causing the original clay to pass, as it were, twice through his refining hand. Now it is consistent to say, if they are become one flesh, there should be but one and the same spirit operating equally upon them both, for their mutual happiness. Adam, having given her a name, and placed himself as her guardian, became in some measure, responsible for her conduct, as the rightful protector of her innocence. It should be recollected, as a small palliative for Eve, that the command, respecting the tree of knowledge and forbidden fruit, was before the woman was made: see Gen. ii. 16 and 17. And the Lord God commanded the man, saying, of every tree of the garden thou mayest freely eat; but of the tree of knowledge, of good and evil thou shalt not eat, for in the day thou eatest thereof, thou shalt surely die. She must therefore have received her information from Adam, if she knew of any command; as she probably had heard of it, by her answer to the serpent. Perhaps Adam communicated it to her as the injunction of their Maker, but possibly with such mildness and indifference, that she was not fully impressed with the importance of the command.

* Lord Coke.

It seems, that, in an unfortunate hour, these then pure and happy beings, were separated. Oh, fatal hour! Oh, inconsiderate Adam! How couldst thou leave the friend of thy affection to wander in the garden, unaided by the support and strength of thy arm, and the pleasure of thy conversation. Didst thou for one moment feel the supreme dignity and full consequence of being placed lord of the lower creation? Didst thou walk forth to survey the animals created for thy use, and subjected to thy dominion? No, no; we say pride had not then polluted the human heart. Thou wast not then puffed up with the idea of knowing good and evil; but thou might have had tenderness enough for thy 'rib, that was taken from thy side,' to have kept near enough to her to protect her innocence from the wiles of the tempter. Nothing can justify Eve's imprudence in parlying with the serpent at all; and she is condemnable for holding any converse, or supposing knowledge was ever desirable, that must be obtained in any clandestine or dishonorable manner. No one can approve of the asperity of Adam's answer to his maker, when called on to answer how he knew that he was naked. He answered evidently with a very indignant air: The woman thou gavest to be with me, gave me of the fruit of the tree, and I did eat. It does not appear, from his own account, that Adam withstood the temptation with more fortitude than Eve did; for she presented the fruit, and he received it without hesitation; but it is plain she did not yield im-

*2

mediately, though the most subtle agent of the
devil told her that her eyes should be opened,
and that she should be like a god. When indeed she saw that the tree was good for food,
and that it was pleasant to the eyes, and a tree
to be desired to make one wise, she took of
the fruit thereof, and did eat. It appears her
desire was to obtain knowledge, which might
be laudable, though her reason was indeed
deceived.

And reason is quickly deceived, says the eloquent Saurin, when the senses have been se-
duced. It was already yielding to the temptation, to hearken so long to the tempter.

By the joint transgression of our first parents, sin, misery and death were introduced into this present world: They appear equally
culpable; yet God, who is ever wise and just
in his dealings, passed the most severe sentence
on the woman, as she was told her sorrows
should be multiplied. And a still harder fate
attended her. She was reduced, from a state
of honorable equality, to the mortifying state
of subjection: Thy desire shall be to thy husband, and he shall rule over thee. Heaven
never intended she should be ruled with a rod
of iron; but drawn by the cords of the man,
in the bonds of love. It is however evident,
Adam was placed over her as her lord and
master, for a certain period, and by the express
will of his maker, and was taught to appreciate his own judgment, as every creature was
brought to him to give them names; and what-
soever names he gave them, they were called:

And he gave his rib the name of woman, and displayed some judgment in the reason given for calling her woman: For she is bone of my bone, and flesh of my flesh, and therefore she shall be my equal. She shall have equal right to think, reason and act for herself, with my advice corroborating. He should therefore have resisted the temptation with manly fortitude, and, not only by precept, but by example, strengthened her resolution to resist the evil spirit: but he fell a prey to his own credulity, and sunk his posterity in depravity.

However strange their conduct may appear to the human understanding, we fully believe, in the great scale of divine providence, it was perfectly just they should be left to commit sin and folly, to convince the human race of their insufficiency, when left to act for themselves; and, from their example, shew to their posterity, the propriety of placing their dependence on Him, who alone is able to keep us from falling.

There is a very beautiful description of our primeval parent's first interview, in Miss Akin's epistles on women. We give the extract in her own style:

" See where the world's new master roams along,
Vainly intelligent, and idly strong ;
Marks his long listless steps and turpid air,
His brow of densest gloom, and fix'd infantile stare;
No mother's voice has touch'd that slumb'ring ear,
Nor glist'ning eye beguiled him with a tear.
Love nurs'd not him with sweet endearing wiles,
Nor woman taught the sympathy of smiles.
Ah ! hapless world, that such a wretch obeys,
Ah ! joyless Adam, though a world he sways.

But see they meet, they gaze, the new born pair,
Mark now the youth, and now the wond'ring fair.
Sure a new soul that moping idiot warms,
Dilates his statue, and his mein informs.
A brighter crimson tints his gloomy cheeks,
His broad eye kindles, and his glances speaks."

From this description, there appears to commence a sympathy of nature, or mutual affection, inherent in nature, which perhaps might operate on Adam's sensibility, and cause him insensibly to partake of the forbidden fruit that proved their fatal fall, and her deepest humiliation; as she is placed under subjection to the man: And the command was put into full force under the old Jewish dispensation, as they bought and sold their wives and daughters, and made trafficks of them as they did their cattle. But, blessed be God, the bonds are dissolved, the snare is broken, and woman has escaped by the blessing of the gospel.

CHAP. II.

Woman is restored to her original rights of equality under the christian dispensation.

HERE, indeed, is the love of God manifested to the disobedient children of men. Though by the fall of our first parents misery and death was the consequence; yet the promise is made good to man, that the seed of the woman should bruise the serpent's head, and that in her seed, all mankind should be restored to peace and happiness. And at the appointed time Jehovah was pleased to over-shadow the espoused wife of Joseph : and there was more than a common presence of the divine eradiator attending at his birth. The wise men or astrologers of the east, had calculated a new star that would appear about that time, and it forboded some great event to take place. Agreeably to their calculation, at the very time they were gazing for the stranger, behold it did appear agreeable to their expectation, and by the bright and effulgent light of this new and till now unknown star, the wise men of the east were directed till the star reflected on the menial place of the birth of our Saviour. And here was the degraded woman found; exalted to the highest honour of embracing in her maternal arms the Son of God himself in human nature. What an interesting scene it must have been to the wise men that had been looking for some great event to take place! What a scene it must have been to the man of sensibility! The amiable, the devout Mary, apparently degraded, is now exalted to the highest honour among men ; and life and immortality are brought to light, by the divine influence of the gospel, under the dispensation of grace. She, who was condemned to servitude, is now, by the blessing of the dispensation, restored to her original privileges : As the woman was first in the transgression, and, in some measure, the cause of their fall, she is now, by divine goodness, made the instrument of bringing life and future happiness to mankind.

The prophecy is accomplished, that in her seed all nations shall be blessed: Herein she is exalted, and fully restored to her original dignity, by being the mother of our blessed Lord and Saviour Jesus Christ, according to his human nature. This, surely, must place her equal with man, under the christian system. Since the christian era she is no longer commanded to be the slave to man, and he is no longer commanded to rule over her.

The offers of divine grace are equally tendered to both male and female; and all have equal right to accept the blessing; and if any judgment can be formed from the visible church, there is reason to conclude that women embrace the privileges of the gospel, with as much, or more energy, than men. If we trace throughout the known world, it will be found that there are more open professors of religion amongst women, than there are amongst men. And they have an undoubted right to this distinction, as their powers of mind are not inferiour, and their sensibilities are certainly greater, or as keen. There must be a moral and physical distinction of sexes, from the organization of the human frame, as well as from their different modes of life and education, as from their different appropriate duties; and women for the most part are not called to make the same exertions in life; yet there are frequent instances of women, when called in providence to the trial, have made as great exertions as men; and have stemmed the torrent of human misery, with equal fortitude to any man, under like circumstances. They can claim no superiority of opinion, only an equal right of judgment with the bolder sex. They are not called to plough on masculine grounds, from the moral distinction there is in nature.

It must be the appropriate duty and privilege of females, to convince by reason and persuasion. It must be their peculiar province to sooth the turbulent passions of men, when almost sinking in the sea of care, without even an anchor of hope to support them. Under such circumstances women should display their talents by taking the helm, and steer them safe to the haven of rest and peace, and that should be their own happy mansion, where they may always retire and find a safe asylum from the rigid cares of business. It is woman's peculiar right to keep calm and serene under every circumstance in life, as it is undoubtedly her appropriate duty, to sooth and alleviate the anxious cares of man, and her friendly and sympathetic breast should be found the best solace for him, as she has an equal right to partake with him the cares, as well as the pleasures of life.

It was evidently the design of heaven, by the mode of our first formation, that they should walk side by side, as mutual supports in all times of trial. There can be no doubt, that, in most cases, their judgment may be equal with the other sex; perhaps even on the subject of law, politics or religion, they may

form good judgment, but it would be morally
improper, and physically very incorrect, for
the female character to claim the statesman's
birth, or ascend the rostrum to gain the loud
applause of men, although their powers of mind
may be equal to the task.

We find among men, that their powers of
mind are not equal in all cases; if the wise
author of nature has been graciously pleased
to endow all men with the same powers of
mind, they do not all improve them to the
same advantage; or from some imperfection
in the organization of the human frame, the
powers or faculties cannot operate on all alike.
Some minds are so enfeebled that they are
rendered incapable of judging right from
wrong; therefore it appears necessary, from
the very order of nature, that there should be
a distinction in society, and that those whose
minds are more expanded should be looked up
to, as guides, to the general mass of the citizens. Females have equal right with the male
citizen, to claim the protection, friendship and
the approbation of such a class of men. As
she is now restored to her original right by
the blessing of the christian system, no longer
is she the slave, but the friend of man. From
the local circumstances, and the domestic cares
in which most females are involved, it cannot
be expected they should make so great improvement in science and literature, as those
whose whole life has been devoted to their
studies. It must not be expected that the
reputable mechanic will rival the man of let-

ters and science, neither would it well suit
the female frame or character, to boast of her
knowledge in mechanism, or her skill in the
manly art of slaughtering fellow-men. It is
woman's appropriate duty and peculiar privilege to cultivate the olive branches around her
table. It is for her to implant in the juvenile
breast the first seed of virtue, the love of God,
and their country, with all the other virtues
that shall prepare them to shine as statesmen,
soldiers, philosophers and christians. Some
of our first worthies have boasted that they
imbibed their heroic principles with their mother's milk; and by precept and example were
first taught the love of virtue, religion, and
their country. Surely they should have a
right to share with them the laurel, but not the
right of conquest; for that must be man's prerogative, and woman is to rejoice in his conquest. There may be a few groveling minds
who think woman should not aspire to any
further knowledge than to obtain enough of
the cymical art to enable them to compound a
good pudding, pie, or cake, for her lord and
master to discompound. Others, of a still
weaker class, may say, it is enough for woman
scientifically to arrange the spinning-wheel
and distaff, and exercise her extensive capacity in knitting and sewing, since the fall and
restoration of woman these employments have
been the appropriate duties of the female sex.
The art of dress, which in some measure produced the art of industry, did not commence
till sin, folly and shame, introduced the first in-

3

vention of dress, which ought to check the modest female from every species of wantonness and extravagance in dress; cultivate the mind, and trifling in dress will soon appear in its true colours.

To those who appear unfriendly to female literature let me say, in behalf of the sex, they claim no right to infringe on any domestic economy; but those ladies, who continue in a state of celibacy, and find pleasure in literary researches, have a right to indulge the propensity, and solace themselves with the feast of reason and knowledge; also those ladies who in youth have laid up a treasure of literary and scientific information, have a right to improve in further literary researches, after they have faithfully discharged their domestic duties. With maternal affections, when her olive branches have spread forth to form new circles in society, the maternal mind has become satiated with the common concerns of life, and the real christian wishes for peace and retirement, for contemplation; and this is the most convenient season for to take a retrospect of past scenes, and this is a fully ripe season to read, write, meditate and compose, if the body and mind are not enfeebled by infirmities. The well informed mind, if still in full vigour, is now fully ripe for composing; and females of that class must have a right to unbend their minds in well digested thoughts for the improvement of the rising generation; and if they can by well digested sentiments, implant in the youthful breast, by precept and their

example, the seeds of virtue and religion, it
will fully compensate, for a long life of toil and
study. The furrows of age shall be cheered
with the expectation of a rich harvest of mental improvement and satisfaction; and where
religion sways, the whole deportment will be
calm, serene and placid, and the infirmities
natural to the decline of life, will be alleviated
in the bright prospect of immortality, to which
both sexes are equally entitled to aspire.

Women have an equal right, with the other
sex, to form societies for promoting religious,
charitable and benevolent purposes. Every
association formed for benevolence, must have
a tendency to make man mild, and sociable to
man; an institution formed for historical and
literary researches, would have a happy effect
on the mind and manners of the youth of both
sexes. As the circulating libraries are often
resorted to after novels by both sexes for want
of judgment to select works of more merit,
the study of history would strengthen their
memory, and improve the mind, whereas novels have a tendency to vitiate the mind and
morals of the youth of each sex before they
are ripe for more valuable acquisitions. Much
abstruse study or metaphysical reasoning seldom agrees with the natural vivacity or the
slender frame of many females, therefore the
moral and physical distinction of the sex must
be allowed; if the powers of the mind are fully
equal, they must still estimate the rights of men,
and own it their prerogative exclusively to
contend for public honours and preferment.

either in church or state, and females may console themselves and feel happy, that by the moral distinction of the sexes they are called to move in a sphere of life remote from those masculine contentions, although they hold equal right with them of studying every branch of science, even jurisprudence.

But it would be morally wrong, and physically imprudent, for any woman to attempt pleading at the bar of justice, as no law can give her the right of deviating from the strictest rules of rectitude and decorum. No servile dependence on men can be recommended under the christian system, for that abolished the law of slavery, and left only a claim on their friendship; as the author of their nature originally intended, they should be the protectors of female innocence, and not the fatal destroyers of their peace and happiness. They claim no right at the gambling table, and to the moral sensibility of females how disgusting must be the horse-race, the bull-bate, and the cock-fight. These are barbarous scenes, ill suited to the delicacy of females.

It must be woman's prerogative to shine in the domestic circle, and her appropriate duty to teach and regulate the opening mind of her little flock, and teach their juvenile ideas how to shoot forth into well improved sentiments. It is most undoubtedly the duty and privilege of woman to regulate her garrison with such good order and propriety, that the generalissimo of her affection, shall never have reason to seek other quarters for well disciplined and

regulated troops, and there must not a murmur
or beat be heard throughout the garrison, except that of the heart vibrating with mutual
affection, reciprocally soft. The rights of woman displayed on such a plan, might perhaps
draw the other sex from the nocturnal ramble
to the more endearing scenes of domestic
peace and harmony. The woman, who can
gain such a victory, as to secure the undivided
affection of her generalissimo, must have the
exclusive right to shine unrivalled in her garrison. There is no distinction of sexes in heav-
en, which may be found agreeable to scripture in our blessed Master's answer to the
Sadduces when they interrogated him respecting the woman who had been the wife of seven
brethren, Matthew xxii. 29, 30. Jesus answered and said unto them, ye do err, not
knowing the scriptures, nor the power of God.
For in the resurrection they neither marry nor
are given in marriage, but are as the angels of
God in heaven.

It is a pleasant and most sublime idea, that
we shall know and be known to each other
in this state of bliss and happiness, and perhaps agreeably to Dr. Watts' enlarged ideas,
though there is no marriage, nor giving in marriage, nor any distinction of sex, yet those who
have lived in a state of celibacy here, may, in
the expansion of the celestial regions, find the
twin soul that, though lost upon the road, had
joined the general choir of perfected spirits;
and that may account for some continuing single in the present world.

*3

The following extract from Watts' Indian Philosopher, perhaps, he intended should be a handsome apology for his own living in a state of celibacy.

" The mighty power, that form'd the mind,
One mould for every two design'd,
    And bless'd the new-born pair ;
This be a match for this, he said,
Then down he sent the souls he made,
    To seek them bodies here.

But parting from their warm abode,
They lost their fellows on the road,
    And never join'd their hands ;
Ah, cruel chance, and crossing fates,
Our eastern souls have lost their mates,
    On Europe's barren lands."

This possibly may account for some cross matches, or be a sufficient reason for some continuing single, which the sexes have a right to do. It must be left to their mutual decision. There is reason to suppose the mental powers of the sexes are about equal, though their bodily habits, from constitution or mode of living, are different; and both moral and physical causes may be ascribed for it. Alexander, in his history of women, says, the notion of woman's being addicted to witchcraft, had taken deep root, and spread itself all over Europe; it had been gathering strength from the days of Moses, and had subsisted till the inquiring spirit of philosophy demonstrated by the plainest experiments, that many things supposed supernatural, were really the effects of natural causes, though it was always old women most suspected.

This idea of the inferiority of female nature has drawn after it several others most humiliating to the sex, as well as absurd and unreasonable; but such is the pride of man, that wherever the doctrine of immortality has obtained footing he has confined that immortality to his own genus, and has considered it much too exalted for any other being, and only their prerogative. Where this opinion first began is uncertain; it could not however be of very ancient date, as the belief of the immortality of the soul never obtained much footing till it was revealed in the gospel. The mahometans both in Asia and Europe, and a great variety of writers, have entertained this general opinion. Lady Montague has opposed this general opinion, in her letters, of the writings concerning the mahometans: She says, they do not absolutely deny the existence of the female soul, but only hold them, inferior to men, and that they enter not into the same, but an inferior paradise, prepared for them on purpose. But the religion of the gospel teaches better things; and shews plainly our God is no respecter of persons or sex.

My respected Miss H. More observes in her comparative view of the sexes, " whatever characteristical distinction may exist, whatever inferiority may be attached to women from the slighter frame of her body, or the more circumscribed powers of her mind, or from a less systematical education, or from the subordinate station she is called to fill in life, there is one leading circumstance, which raises her im-

portance, and even establishes her equality.
Christianity has exalted women to true and
undisputed dignity in Christ Jesus. As there
is neither rich nor poor, bond nor free, there
is neither male nor female, in the view of that
immortality which is brought to light by the
gospel.

"Woman has no superiour. To borrow the
idea of an excellent prelate, women make up
one half of the human race, equally redeemed
by the blood of Christ. In this their true dignity consists; here their best pretensions rest,
and here their claims are allowed. All the
disputes for preeminence between the sexes
have only a few short years, the attention of
which would be better devoted to the duties
of life, and the interest of eternity. As the
final hopes of the female sex are equal, so are
the present means perhaps more favourable,
and their opportunities less obstructed than
those of the other sex. In the christian warfare, women have every superiour advantage,
though it is the main object of this little work
rather to lower, than raise any desire of celebrity in the female heart, yet I would awaken
it to a just sensibility for honest fame. I would
call on women to reflect, that our religion has
not only made them heirs of a blessed immortality hereafter, but has raised them to an em-
inence in the scale of beings unknown to the
most polished ages of antiquity. The religion
of Christ has bestowed a degree of renown on
the sex, beyond what any other religion ever
did. Perhaps there are hardly so many vir-

tuous women, (as I reject the whole catalogue
of those whom their vices have transferred to
infamy, and who are named in all the pages of
Greek and Roman history) as those handed
down to eternal fame, in a few of those short
chapters with which the great Apostle of the
gentiles has concluded his epistles to his converts of devout and honourable women. The
sacred scriptures record not a few. Some of
the most affecting scenes, the most interesting
transactions, and the most touching conversa-
tions which are recorded of the Saviour of the
world past with women : They are the first
remarked as having administered to him of
their substance ; they appear to be the last at
his tomb, and the first in the morning, when
he arose from it. Theirs was the praise of not
abandoning their despised Redeemer when he
was led to execution ; and under all the hopeless circumstances of his ignominious death,
they left him not a moment : and theirs was
the privilege of receiving the earliest consolation from their risen Lord. Theirs was the
honour of being first commissioned to announce
the glorious resurrection, to the world, and
even to furnish heroic confessors, devoted
saints, and unshrinking martyrs to the church
of Christ, which has not been the exclusive
honour of the bolder sex."—*Miss More.*

There is a natural desire in women to be
agreeable, and they no doubt would wish to
model themselves to what they think will
please. If, therefore, those who take the lead
in society would set the fashion to be wise and

virtuous, others would follow. Villamont says in his friend to women, Wisdom and reason are found much oftener united with the graces, than the detractors of the sex conceive them to be endowed with. As well as us with a soul and heart, they ought to labour to enlighten one, and regulate the other. The mind, to perfect itself, only requires a moderate degree of study, which may be ranked among the class of pleasures. A woman of real good sense, only makes herself noticed by that which deserves to be so; she is independent of all those trifles which cause to weak minds a joy or affliction equally ridiculous. Free from those alterations of good and bad humour that disconcert friendship, she preserves a continual pleasing gaiety, which sets her charms off better than the most studied decoration. The empire of beauty is short, but the dominion of virtue, and triumphs of religion, are great and eternal; and since the promulgation of the gospel, it has been fairly proved, even to demonstration, that the female powers and faculties are equal with the men; but their mode of education often checks their progress in learning.

There appears a chasm in the history of women till the time of Moses; and he speaks of singing men and singing women. Among a variety of the nations, the Egyptians, however, were in this respect, different and singular. The same reason that determined other nations to teach women that pleasing art, determined the Egyptians to debar them from it.

because, said they, it softens and relaxes the mind, as it was found that music would often soothe even the savage breast. Therefore it was probably the opinion of the legislator, that too much softness and delicacy would disqualify them for managing the affairs of trade and commerce, and that certain softness of sex, which was encouraged in other nations, would ill suit the Egyptian women, who were generally employed in the same manner as was destined to the men. However, when we survey the account given by the ancients, of the arts, sciences, laws, and above all, the culture and wisdom of the Egyptians; and when we consider the high estimation in which women were held, and the powers with which they were invested; when to this we add the literary fame of the nation, there is the strongest reason to conclude, that though we are at this period unacquainted with their opinion of female education, it certainly must have been such as suited the dignity of so wise a people, and of a sex, so beloved and respected. Whatever moral or physical distinction they allowed is uncertain; but there is no doubt they fully appreciated the judgment of the female sex. In any region a superior genius will soar above the common level. Even two women, grinding at the same mill, will rise or soar above each other, not only in their mode of work, but in their mental powers and faculties. These kind of mills are in use, at this very day, all over the Levant, and in the north of Scotland, where they have a song composed on purpose to divert their attention from thinking of their hard fate, and to alleviate the female mind.

It has been observed, that men, secluded from women, have become more slovenly in their persons and manners; but women secluded from men are generally more neat and particular than other women are. If the observation is just, men must reap most advantage from the company of women. In former times, the greatest philosophers were seldom fit company for women, or enjoyed their conversation. Sir Isaac Newton hardly ever conversed with any of the sex, though he allowed each sex were equally subject to the power of custom, and civil and religious compacts were equally binding on the sexes.

Therefore, with Watts, we say, the mind must be the standard of the man or woman. And shall proceed to give some account of illustrious females and their writings, which have appeared in almost every age of the world.

CHAP. III.

Of the strength of mind, and writings of many illustrious females, both in sacred and profane history.

From Dr. Hunter's Sacred Biogrophy, which places females in a very desirable point of light, the following character of Deborah is extracted:

He says, And whither are our eyes turned or directed at this time? To behold the Saviour of a sinking country, behold the residue of the spirit is on the head of a woman: The sacred flame of public spirit smothered and dead in every manly breast, yet glows in a female's bosom ; and the tribunal of justice, deserted by masculine virtue and ability, is honourably and usefully filled by feminine sensibility, discernment, honesty and zeal.

Deborah was a prophetess, the wife of Lepidoth, she judged Israel at that time. She was a wife and mother in Israel; and such a wife is a crown to her husband, and the pride and glory of her children; but her capacious soul, embraced more than her own family; she aimed at the happiness of thousands; she sweetly blended public, with private virtue. It is not unreasonable to suppose, the discreet and wise management of her own household first procured her the notice and esteem of the public ; and the prudent deportment of the matron past by an easy transition to the sanctity of a prophetess, and the gravity of a judge. Certain it is that the reputation which is not established on the basis of personal goodness, is like a house built on the sand, which must soon sink and fall. Hitherto we have seen only holy men of God speaking as they were moved by the Holy Spirit. But the great Jehovah is no respecter of persons or sex: The secrets of the Lord are with them that fear him, and he sheweth unto them his holy covenant. The simple dignity of her unadorned and unassuming state is beautifully represented.

4.

She dwelt under the palm tree of Deborah, between Ramah and Bethel, in mount Ephraim, and the children of Israel came up to her for judgment. Behold a female mind exalted, above the pageantry and pride of external appearance, not deriving consequence from the splendour of her attire, the charms of her person, or the number of her retinue: but from the affability of her manners, the purity of her character, and sacredness of her office; the impartiality of her conduct, the importance of her public services; not wandering from place to place, panting after little empty applause, but sought unto of all Israel, from the eminency and extensive ability of her talents and virtue.

Her canopy of state was the palm tree, her rule of living God, her motive the inspiration of the Almighty, her aim and end the glory of God, and the good of his people, her reward, the testimony of a good conscience and the respect of a grateful nation, the admiration of future generations, and the smiles of approving heaven. In her, united poety and musical skill, fervent devotion, heroic intrepidity, and prophetic inspiration.

A combination how rare! how instructive! how respectable! To her life is affixed an historical note, short indeed, but highly interesting and important. And the land had rest forty years. This is the noblest eulogium of Deborah, and the most honourable display of her talents and virtues. If there are feelings worthy of envy, they are those of this exalted woman. How lasting and extensive is the influence of real worth! There is one way by which every person may be the saviour of his country, that is, by cultivating the private virtues.

I now proceed to illustrate the female character, its amiableness, usefulness, and importance, in persons and scenes of a very different complexion; in the less glaring, but not less instructive history of Ruth the moabitess, and Naomi her mother. Let us wait her appearance in silent expectation, and muse on what is past.

She had a soul capacious and capable of fond respect for departed worth and living virtue : She had magnanimity to sacrifice every thing the heart held dear to decency, friendship, and religion. In Ruth we have this higher principle likewise beautifully exemplified, rational, modest, and unaffected piety.

We proceed to unfold from sacred history, the character and conduct of Hannah. Every thing, of any importance for us to know respecting Hannah, is what related to her son Samuel, and to that, accordingly, the scripture account is confined. She is the fourth, as far as we can recollect, recorded in the same similar case ; and she is not the least respectable.

The manner in which Elkanah and Hannah lived together was exemplary and instructive. They have one common interest, they have one darling object of affection, they express one and the same wish, in terms of mutual kindness and endearment Hannah's song of praise, possesses all the majesty, grace, and beauty of ancient oriental poetry. It is one of the happiest effusions of an excellent female heart, labouring under a grateful sense of the highest obligation.

From the sacred records in the New Testament, we find many females celebrated for virtue, religion and true holiness; and some were admitted to the highest dignity and honour, in attending on, and having the friendship and blessing of their Lord and Saviour Jesus Christ.

Russel says, The courage of the christian women was founded on the noblest principles and motives, and animated by the glorious hopes of immortality. Those to whom the church assign the compound title of saint and orator, recommended to admiration the christian women.

But he who speaks of them with most zeal, is St. Jerome, who, born with a soul of fire, spent twenty-four years in writing, combating and conquering himself. The manners of this saint were probably more severe than his thoughts. He had a number of illustrious women at Rome, among his disciples. But, though surrounded with beauty, he escaped weakness without slander, and flying the world, the women, and himself, he retired to Palestine, where all which he had quitted pursued him, and still tormented him, under the penitential sackcloth, and in the midst of solitary deserts, reechos in his ears the tumults of Rome.

Such was St. Jerome, the most eloquent panegyrist of the christian women, of the fourth century. That warm and pious writer, though harsh and austere, softens his style in a thousand instances, to praise the Marcelas, the Paulas, and many other Roman women, who, at the capital had embraced christianity, and studied in Rome the language of the Hebrews, to read the books of Moses.

When the Roman empire, like some venerable column, was pushed from its basis, and broken in pieces by the myriads of the north, christianity passed from the conquered to the conqueror by the zeal of the women, who at the same time, diffused the gospel, and softened the manners of the savages. It has been observed in every age, that christian women have been more anxious to make proselytes, than men have been. However just this observation may have been, or from what motive they were actuated, the world has been obliged to them for their ardour. It was woman, who, making the charms of their sex subservient to religion, raised to thrones by their beauty, drew over their husbands to their opinion, and spread christianity over the greatest part of Europe. It was by their means that France, Germany, Bavaria, Hungary, Lithuania, Poland and Russia, and for some time, that Persia, received the gospel. By the same influence Lombardy renounced the opinion of Arius ; women were then desirous of attaining every species of learning, and some have succeeded in every age of the world. In former

*4

ages what has since been called society, was
not then known. Luxury and the want of occupation had not introduced the fashion of sitting five or six hours at the glass to invent
fashions. Some use was then made of time,
and hence the languages and sciences were acquired by females. If the women of those
ages were ambitious of arraying themselves in
the knowledge of men, the men were at all
times ready with their panegyricks to return
the compliment.

It was the sequel of the general spirit that
carried gallantry into letters, as it had introduced it into arms. Greece was governed by
eloquent men, and the influence courtezans
had held in public affairs was by the influence
of the celebrated courtezans held over the orators. There was not one, but they had some
influence over; even the thundering, the in-
flexible Demosthenes, so terrible to tyrants,
was subjected to their sway. Of that great
master of eloquence, it has been said, what he
had been a whole year in erecting, a woman
overturned in one day.

The illustrious Zenobia, though not of Roman extraction, presents herself to view, as a
widow who reigned in great glory for some
time. The celebrated Longinus was her pre-
ceptor and secretary. Not being able to
brook the Roman tyranny, she declared war
against the emperor Aurelian, who took her
prisoner and led her in triumph to Rome, and
butchered her principal nobility, and among
others the excellent Longinus, who taught her

to write as well as to conquer. She was afterwards unfortunate with dignity, and she
consoled herself for the loss of a throne with
the sweets of solitude and the joys of reason.

Jane of Flanders is highly celebrated by
Rapin and other historians. When John was
taken prisoner and sent to Paris, which misfortune must certainly have ruined his party,
had not his interest been supported by the extraordinary abilities of his wife, Jane of Flanders, a lady who seems to possess all the excellent qualities of both sexes. Bold, daring and
intrepid, she fought like a hero in the field;
shrewd, sensible and sagacious, she spake like a
politician in the council; and endowed with the
most amiable manners, and winning address,
she was able to draw the minds of her subjects
by the force of her eloquence, and mould them
to her pleasure. She happened to be at Rennes
when she received the news of her husband's
captivity. But that disaster instead of depres-
sing, raised her native courage and fortitude.
She assembled the citizens, and holding her
infant son in her arms, recommended him to
their care and protection, in the most pathetic
terms, as the male heir of their ancient dukes,
who had governed them with lenity and indulgence, and to whom they had ever profes-
sed their zealous attachment. She declared
herself willing to run all hazards with them in
so just a cause. She pointed out to them the
resources that yet remained in the alliances
with England, earnestly beseeching them to
make one vigorous effort against the usurper,

who being forced on them by the intrigues of France, would, as a mark of gratitude, sacrifice the liberties of Britanny to his protector. The people, moved by the affecting appearance of the princess, vowed to live and die with her in defence of the rights of her family.

There has been many eminent and distinguished writers in almost every age of the world. In 1643, a piece appeared at Paris, under this title, The Generous Woman; who shews her sex are more noble, more patriotic, more brave, more learned, more virtuous and economical than men. In 1665, another lady published at Paris, a book entitled The Illustrious Dames, where, by good and strong reasoning it is fairly proved that women surpass the men. In 1673, a performance appeared, entitled, The Equality of the Sexes, shewing the importance of divesting ourselves of prejudices. These discourses, were philosophical and moral. Madam De Gournay wrote upon her sex; but being more modest, she confined herself and pretensions, and was contented with equality.

Mary Shurman, born at Calona, is extolled for extraordinary capacity in learning. She was a painter, musician, engraver, sculptor, philosopher, geometrician, and understood nine different languages.

Elizabeth, queen of England, is noticed by some historians, for the great strength of mind she discovered in her youth. Mr. Ascham, her tutor, in a letter to his friend Sturminus, says, I am reading Greek with the princess.

The orations she understood at first; not only
the meaning of the orator, but the whole force
of the language, and the whole system of the
laws, customs, and manners of the Athenians.
Some historians say, the reign of Elizabeth
was justly esteemed as one of the most shining
periods of English history; and for purity of
manners, vigour of mind, vigour of character,
and personal address, it is perhaps unequalled.
The magnificent entertainments which that illustrious princess so frequently gave her court,
and at which she generally appeared in person,
with a most engaging familiarity, rubbed off the
ancient reserve of nobility, and increased the
taste of society, and even of gallantry.

Some historians assert that the reign of
queen Anne was the summer, of which William was only the spring. Every thing was
ripe and nothing was corrupted. It was a
short, but glorious period of heroism, and national capacity of taste and science, learning
and genius, gallantry without licentiousness,
and politeness without effeminacy.

Lady Jane Gray is described by Dr. Fuller,
as possessing the innocency of childhood, the
beauty of youth, the solidity of maturity, and
the gravity of age.

In the character of Sir Thomas More are
found blended the perfections of the male sex,
as neither his religion, or learning, blunted or
soured his temper, or his taste for society. His
love, affections, and ideas of the female character would do honour to any gentleman of the
present day. In an elegant latin piece to a

friend on the choice of a wife, he writes, May
you meet with a woman not stupidly silent,
nor always prattling nonsense. May she be
learned, if possible, or at least capable of being made so. A learned and accomplished
woman will be always drawing sentiments out
of the best authors. She will be herself in all
the vicissitudes of fortune, neither blown up
by prosperity, or broken down by adversity.
She will be your friend at all times. You will
spend your time in her company with delight.
You will be always finding out new beauties
in her mind. She will keep your soul in continual serenity, agreeably to these delicate sentiments. It is virtue, learning, and religion,
which constitute the real felicity of the connubial relation.

From history we shall furnish a few more
instances of exalted characters that have shone
as bright luminaries, in different ages, for virtue, learning, religion, and for filial and maternal affection.

Cornelia, the illustrious mother of the
Gracchi, after the death of her husband, who
left her twelve children, applied herself to the
care of her family, with a wisdom and prudence, that acquired her universal esteem;
only three lived to maturity, one daughter
named Semphronia, who was married to the
second Scipio Africanus; two sons, Tiberius
and Caius, whom she brought up with so much
care, that, though they were generally acknowledged to have been born, with natural
talents and happy dispositions, it was judged

that they were still more indebted to education, than nature. The answer she gave a
Campanian lady concerning them, is very famous, and includes in it great instructions for
ladies and mothers. That lady who was very
rich, and still fonder of pomp and shew, after
having displayed in a visit to her, her diamonds,
pearls, riches, and jewels, earnestly desired
Cornelia to let her see her jewels also. Cornelia turned the conversation to another subject, to wait the return of her sons, who were
gone to the public school. When they return-
ed and entered their mother's apartment, she
said to the Campanian lady, pointing to them
with her hand, these are my jewels and the
only ornaments I admire. And such ornaments
are the strength and support of society, and
add a brighter lustre to the fair, than all the
jewels of the east.

Valerius Maximus relates a singular fact of
a woman of illustrious birth, who had been
condemned to be strangled. The Roman
prætor delivered her to the triumvir, who
caused her to be carried to prison in order to
her being put to death. The goaler who was
ordered to execute her, was struck with com-
passion, and could not resolve to kill her ; he
chose therefore to let her die of hunger, besides which he suffered her daughter to see
her in the prison, taking care however that she
brought nothing for her to eat. As this continued many days, he was surprised that the
prisoner lived so long without eating; and sus-
pecting the daughter, upon watching her, he

discovered that she nourished her mother with her own milk. Amazed at so pious, and at the same time so ingenious an invention, he told the fact to the triumvir, and the triumvir to the prætor, who believed the thing merited relating in the assembly of the people. The criminal was pardoned. A decree was passed that the mother and daughter should be supported for the rest of their lives at the expense of the public, and that a temple sacred to piety should be erected near the prison.

The same author gives a similar instance of filial piety, in a young woman named Xantippe, to her aged father Cimonus, who was also condemned to die, and in prison, and which is universally known by the name of the Roman charity. Both these instances appear so extraordinary and uncommon to that people, that they could only account for them, by supposing, that the love of children was the first law of nature.—*Plin. Hist.* 1, 7, 36.

Lady Burleigh is noticed in English history as an amiable example of beneficence. She was wife of the famous Lord Burleigh, lord high treasurer of England, and privy counsellor to queen Elizabeth.

Madam Maintenon, Madam de Severns and Madam Chapon, rank high in history, as letter-writers, in their day. Miss Wolstonecraft mentions some ladies with energy. Of Mrs. Chapon she says, I only mention her letters, as they are wrote with such good sense and unaffected humility, and contain so many useful observations, that I notice them to pay the worthy writer a tribute of respect. The word respect, reminds me of Mrs. Macauly, a woman undoubtedly of the greatest abilities this country ever produced, and yet this woman has been suffered to die without sufficient respect having been paid to her memory ; posterity will be more just, and remember Catharine Macauly was an example of intellectual acquirements, supposed to be incompatible with the weakness of her sex. In the style of her writing, indeed no sex appears, for it is like the sense it conveys, strong and clear. Her judgment is the profound mature fruit of thinking ; she writes with sober energy.

Mary Wolstonecraft was a woman of great energy and a very independent mind ; her Rights of Women are replete with fine sentiments, though we do not coincide with her opinion respecting the total independence of the female sex. We must be allowed to say, her theory is unfit for practice, though some of her sentiments and distinctions would do honour to the pen, even of a man. Her distinction between modesty and humility is certainly very ingenious. She says, modesty, sacred offspring of sensibility and reason, true delicacy of mind, may I unblamed presume to investigate thy nature, and trace to its covert the mild charms, that, mellowing each harsh feature of character, renders what would only inspire admiration, lovely.

Milton was not arrogant when his suggestion of judgment suffered that to escape, which proved a prophecy. Nor was General Washington, when he accepted the command of the American forces. The latter has always been characterised a modest man. Had he been merely modest, he would have probably shrunk back irresolute ; and afraid to trust himself with the direction of an enterprize on which so much depended. A modest man is steady, a humble man is timid, a vain man is presumptuous ; this is the observation many characters have led me to form. Jesus Christ himself was modest, Moses was humble, Peter was vain.—*Vol. II. p.* 314.

These questions are put to the higher class of ladies, who have been weak enough to consult old gypsies for the knowledge of future events. Do you believe that there is but one God, and that he is powerful, just, and good? Do you believe that all things were created by him, and that all things are dependent on him? Do you rely on his wisdom, so conspicuous in his works, and in your own frame; and are you convinced, that he has ordered all things, that do not come under the cognizance of your senses, in the same perfect harmony, to fulfil his designs? Do you acknowledge that the power of looking into futurity and seeing things that are not as if they were, is an attribute of the Creator? And should he see fit, by any impression on the mind of his creatures, to impart any event hid in the shades of time, to whom would he reveal the secret by immediate inspiration? The opinion of ages will answer this question—To reverend old men, distinguished for eminent piety.

Impressed by their solemn, devotional parade, a Greek or Roman lady might be excus-
able to inquire of the oracle, when she was anxious to pry into futurity.—*Wolstonecraft's Observation.*

In this enlightened age, it seems almost impossible that any one, either in Europe or
America, can be so infatuated as to encourage
such a class of artful vagrants, who pretend to
reveal future events. Be not deceived by their
juggling tricks, but put your trust in the All-
wise Disposer of the affairs of human life, and
know that it is not in man that walketh to direct his steps, neither is it wise or prudent tor
any person to pry into the hidden mysteries of
futurity, but trust in Providence, that what we
know not in this state, shall be revealed to us
in another.

There are few females at the present day,
that would wish to claim the Otaheite's
strength, as represented by Capt. Wallis. He
says, that Oberach, queen of Otaheite, lifted
him over a marsh with as much ease, as he
could a little child.

For strength of mind, and real virtue and
dignity, we must now introduce queen Isabella,
whose influence in the court of Spain determined them to support Columbus, in his voyage
to America. Had it not been for her energy,
the plan must have been frustrated, and perhaps the continent not discovered till this present time. She offered to pawn her jewels to
defray the expenses, rather than the voyage
should fail. The court were so impressed

with the magnanimity of her conduct, that they resolved to support the cause without the aid of her jewels.

It certainly is not beneath the dignity of the female character, to aid, assist or advise, when any thing of importance labours, either in church or state. They have a right to even pawn their jewels, or any other ornament, for the general good of the community.

CHAP. IV.

The female character and writings are equal in the present day to any former period; and some miscellaneous sentiments respecting the sex.

MADAM DE STAAL, for strength of mind, true magnanimity, patriotism and independence, as well as her literary talents and acquirements, shines unequalled. Her late work of the Influence of Literature on Society, would do honour to the able pen of a man. She can have no rival.

For poetic fancy and genius few have ever excelled Lucy Akin. Her Epistles on Women, and other poems, do honour to her pen. We give a further specimen of the general spirit of the author.

"Does history speak; drink in her loftiest tone
And make Cornelia's virtues all thy own.
Thus self endow'd, thus arm'd for every state,
Improve, excel, surmount, subdue your fate;
So shall enlighten'd man at length efface,
That slavish stigma, sear'd on half the race;
His rude forefather's shame, and pleas'd confess.
Tis your's to elevate, tis your's to. bless.

> Your interest, one with his, your hope the same, }
> Fair peace on earth, in death undying fame, }
> And bliss in words, beyond the species general aim. }
> Rise shall he say, O woman, rise, be free,
> My life's associate, now partake with me.
> Rouse thy keen energies, expand thy soul,
> And see and feel, and comprehend the whole.
> My deepest thoughts intelligent divide ;
> When right confirm me, and when erring guide ;
> Sooth all my cares, in all my virtues blend,
> And be my sister, be at length my friend."
> *Epist. on Women.*

Many other authors could be produced who have done honour to the female pen and character in their writings.

We must now say of the amiable Miss H. More, " many daughters have done virtuously, but thou hast excelled them all." Her works from the smallest grade to the most important, are all calculated to improve the mind, and mend the heart.

American Character noticed.

America, though as yet but young in the arts and sciences, will not long remain in the back ground, as she can now claim the birth-right of many respectable female writers, both in prose and verse.

The lovely Morton may vie with many in Europe for her sublime and poetic fancy. She, with many other respectable writers, who have not been sufficiently appreciated, still shine with the lustre of the aurora borealis in the northern hemisphere.

Among the most distinguished historians are seen a Warren, and an Adams, who have done

*5

honour to themselves, their country and sex, as faithful compilers of history. Mrs. Warren, in her History of the American Revolution, (vol. I. page 4) observes, There are appropriate duties assigned to each sex, and surely it is the peculiar province of masculine strength, not only to repulse the bold invader of his country's rights, but in the nervous style of manly eloquence, describe the blood stained field, and relate the story of slaughtered armies.

In vol. II. page 30, she mentions Mrs. Ackland, who was a British officer's lady, as a pattern of female heroism and conjugal affection: She came with her husband to America, and shared with him all the hardships of the camp life ; he was badly wounded and taken prisoner by the Americans ; she knew his situation, and left him not a moment, but joins herself a prisoner, and by her fortitude supported him, as she lost not her resolution or usual spirits. The American commander, pleased with her firmness, gave orders that she should have every attention paid to her rank, character, and sex.

There might now be recorded a number of American ladies, who left domestic peace and retirement, to share with the partners of their affections, all the trials and fatigue of a camp life ; suffice it to notice two in particular, Mrs. Washington, and Mrs. Jackson, who with six little boys, left her rural retreat to accompany the Colonel to the field of battle. She partook with him in the fatigues and inconveniences of the camp life ; he was soon

commissioned as a general officer : Under her
own guardian eye she had these sons trained
and disciplined, till they were efficient to become respectable officers, which they all were
in the American army.

Mrs. Washington shone a bright example of
female excellence ; she followed the foot paths
of her beloved hero, by her firmness and christian fortitude ; with affection she soothed every
care of his long war-worn life. She has left
a bright example, of every virtue that adorns
the christian or female character. Mrs. Warren says, Having personally known her I can
say, her whole deportment was blended with
such a sweetness of manners, that she not only
engaged the affection of her intimates, but of
all who had the felicity of knowing her, and
even strangers were captivated with her mild
and affectionate address. To every child of
sorrow and affliction, she lent a listening ear,
and often extended the hand of meek charity,
to alleviate the cruel anguish of poverty. She
shone as the patriotic wife, the meek christian,
and the truly upright in heart. She was like
her Fabius, modest, but not timid. She may
with propriety be esteemed a model of female
perfection, and highly worthy the imitation of
the American fair. May her memory, with
her virtues, be engraven on the tablet of every
female's heart. She has erected a temple of
virtue and fame, for the female standard.

By the mutual virtue, energy, and fortitude
of the sexes, the freedom and independence of
the United States were attained and secured.

The same virtue, energy, and fortitude, must be called into continual exercise, as long as we continue a free, federal, independent nation. The culture and improvement of the female understanding will strengthen the mental faculties, and give vigour to their councils, which will give a weight to any argument used for their mutual defence and safety. No nation nor republic ever fell a prey to despotism, till by indolence and dissipation, it neglected the arts and sciences, and the love of literature. They then became effeminate and degraded; and by them the female character was degraded. As long as the German women were free and honoured by the men, it acted as a stimulous to their ambition. On the value and integrity of both sexes their success and independence very much depended.

If we take a retrospect of the world, from the creation, it will be found, that in every age where ignorance prevailed most, women were most degraded. Before the christian era, and through the dark ages, very little light was thrown upon their characters. They were supposed to have the command of Pandora's iron box, which contained all the accumulated evils incident to human nature. Some authors say, from the circumstance attending this box, at that period, that age was called the iron age, and has been known by that name ever since.

There are some excellent sentiments respecting women in a small treatise, entitled, The Friend of Women, by De Villamont, in French, translated by Maurice. He says, every one speaks of women according to the disposition of his heart; and the most vicious men are most disposed to paint them in the most odious colours. He says, whatever we meet with in the different opinions of men with regard to women, the lively interest they regard them with, is always the principal.

Every thing which this lovely half of the human race does, has a right to interest us; we are born the friends of women, and not their rivals, still less their tyrants. Let women then, who lead in our first circles, condescend to cultivate their minds, and encourage useful reading; their merit will cause a swarm of thoughtless beaux to disappear from their presence, and men of more merit will form a circle about them, more worthy the name of good company; in this new circle they will join on the score of friendship, without losing any thing in point of cheerfulness; merit is not naturally gloomy, on the contrary, there is generally found among polite people, who are well bred, a mild serenity far preferable to bursts of stupid and ignorant merriment. Happily for us, the day is past that condemned women, as well as the nobility, to rustic ignorance, though there has always been some women found, who dared to think, and speak reasonably. We have in the present day, many who do not blush to be better informed than many of our court gentry, or petit-maitres are.

But of all studies most necessary and most natural to women is the study of men, as their government must be that of persuasion; it is

necessary for them to know the main springs
by which men are actuated. If any thing can
add to the pleasure derived from a select society, it is the charms of friendship. The injustice they have done women by excluding
them the privilege of being friends, they cannot account for on any principle, as women are
born with more sensibility than men, and are
as capable of being friends.

I shall not enlarge on the advantage of
friendship, which may be called a double life,
as each lives in his friend. I shall give you
Pliny's receipt for making friendship. From
Pliny's Natural History we find this curious
receipt, for making a Roman friendship.

The principal ingredients were, union of
hearts, a flower that grew in several parts of
the empire, sincerity, frankness, disinterested-
ness, pity and tenderness, of each an equal
quantity; these made up together with a rich
oil, which they called perpetual good wishes,
and serenity of temper, and the whole was
strongly perfumed with the desire of pleasing,
which gave it a most grateful smell, and was
a sure restorative against vapours of every
kind. The cordial thus prepared was of so
durable a nature, that length of time could
not waste it. What is more remarkable, says
our author, it increases in value the longer it
is kept.

That women are capable of friendship there
can be no doubt. There is no deficiency in
the female mind, either as to talent or disposition. Women are more sensible than men to

all moral distinction : They do not indeed class the virtues in the same order, but they give the highest importance to the comprehensive virtue of temperance. But it is christianity, undoubtedly, which has seated woman on her true throne. Bound to the same duties, and candidates for the same happiness, as soon as a woman wishes to raise herself above all the trifling objects that debase her, her mind will find itself capable of the same strength as that of men. Mind has no sex, and women cannot be made too frequently to recollect this truth, to preserve them from all those frivoloties in which they place too much happiness. Oh, that women would but keep their rights, and improve them to their and our advantage. For women have not degenerated; there are many among us at this time, whose success has made them sufficiently known, without my naming them; and who comparatively with us, have reaped the golden harvest in the fertile field of history and philosophy. Their powers and intellects are equal with the men, but their mode of education often checks their progress in learning.—*So says Villamont.*

We must join with him in thinking their powers of mind are very equal. Still it might be thought an unequal right, to profess or claim any knowledge of the masonic art; for it seems really man's prerogative to bear the hod, or mould the mortar.

But females may erect a temple of fame, and support it by virtue, wisdom, strength, and beauty, and perfect rectitude. Let then the

mysteries of the craft remain profoundly secret to the female ken, till time shall unfold
the hidden mysteries of all ancient knowledge
and science. Then may the master mason display his skill and talent in architecture, and
lay the corner-stone in rectitude and justice,
and by his skill draw the parallel line correct,
that shall encompass the views of the sexes
to their mutual satisfaction and happiness. It
cannot be expected the views of females will
exactly correspond with the men, respecting
the masonic art, as they are debarred the investigation of its principles in some measure.
Yet in the present day, there ought to be that
harmony and mutual confidence, respecting
the system, as shall effectually eradicate any
old prejudices respecting the powers of females being unequal to comprehend the in-
comprehensible mysteries of the masonic art.
Let females then retire within the vail, and in
the Sanctum Sanctorum, study the beauty of
holiness, and endeavour to follow the example
of their king and master, Solomon, by praying
for an understanding heart, and seeking that
wisdom which is from above, and can direct
our moral and religious course through life.

CHAP. V.

From observation on characters sacred and profane may
be drawn a theory, or plan of rights and duties as
agreeable to scripture, reason and common sense.

AGREEABLY to scripture, the corner stone
for permanent happiness must be laid in vital

piety, or heart religion, reduced to practice. As much of the happiness of nations depends on the domestic economy of individuals, oftentimes the trials and perplexities of families arise from the trifling way some women spend their time, and gratify their eyes and ears only, instead of improving their mental faculties. It may be said the same of some men. There are triflers of both sexes, who do not consider time is a jewel that every one bids largely for, when they want it, and often spend it very foolishly when they have it. They are indeed to be pitied, who spend themselves and mispend their time in doing nothing. For the most part ceremonious visits are an intolerable consumption of time, unless regulated with more than common prudence. They are often spent in vain and frivolous conversation, or a pack of cards must fill up the vacancy of time; whereas, if the mental faculties were cultivated, the mind would be enriched and capable of communicating mutual information and pleasure, of the most rational kind, from sex to sex. Let those who move in the first circles shew the sacred right they have to set an example of purity of manners, mutual harmony of sentiments and reciprocal union of soul. There can be no doubt but the same harmony, and good order will extend itself throughout all classes of society, as the force of example has much greater effect than precept. Nothing can contribute more to the happiness of mankind than a well regulated community, which must commence in personal

6

agreement, and mutual compact, founded on love and friendship; for love is the life and soul of every relative duty—the powerful enlivening principle, which alone can inspire us with vigour and activity in the execution of it.

Without love even diligence is ungrateful, and submission itself has the air of disobedience. Mutual trust and confidence are the great bonds of society, without which it cannot possibly subsist. Mutual love must be founded on the basis of mutual friendship, without which life will have but few charms. The only things which can render friendship sure and lasting, are virtue, purity of manners, and perfect integrity of heart. With an elevated soul, it is highly proper that we should distinguish the friend from the companion. A conformity of taste for pleasure, and for any thing besides virtue, may constitute a club, but cannot make a society of friends. We must commence life with a religious determination, that " as for me and my house, we will serve the Lord" ; and by a mutual agreement and sympathy, cemented by friendship, secure the right of mutual affection, on which connubial happiness very much depends.

The surest foundation to secure the female's right, must be in family government, as without that, women can have no established right. This must be the touchstone of the matrimonial faith; and on this depends very much the safety and happiness of a free republic. Family government should, in some measure, resemble a well regulated garrison ; there should be sentinels continually on the watch-tower, and general orders should be given for the day, and these should be attended with the morning and evening orisons, that should ascend like holy incense, with gratitude of soul, for the divine care and protection. Women have a right to join in the family prayer and praise. Family worship must be mutual, as any jar or animosity will disorder the whole garrison, and a mutiny may ensue and throw the whole into confusion, and thus frustrate the cause of religion and virtue, and the demon of discord may enter, with all the accumulated miseries of Pandora's box, and perhaps storm and carry the garrison. For want of mutual skill and judgment to defend the fortress, there must be a fixed principle in the mind, that no real happiness can be attained, but in a religious course of life, and that will give a calm serenity, and peace of mind, that will afford us real satisfaction in every situation of life. We must believe there is no situation so permanent but it may have some alloy; and there is no one so happy, as might warrant our changing with them at all hazards; for what would make one person apparently happy, might not suit another. Our ideas are so very different, that what would consummate one person's happiness, would prove to another complete misery.

I must think the wise Author of our nature has distributed human happiness much more equally than the generality of mankind will allow: therefore they must determine in their own minds what sort of happiness they are in pursuit of, and what use they intend to make of it, when their desires are obtained. It is to be feared, we may say, without pretending to much superior sagacity, that few people know themselves. The only sure resource for real happiness, is to obtain peace of mind, arising from a pure conscience, with principles founded on real vital religion. The christian hope has always sustained the christian women, and reconciled them to their many privations, which they always sustained with christian fortitude. Many instances might be produced of both sexes, who have stemed the torrent of human misery in support of christian principles. In support of the rights of women, the only wish is to analyze, harmonize and equalize the sexual rights, as far as the human organization will admit.

There can be no doubt but there is as much difference in the powers of each individual of the male sex, as there is of the female; and if they received the same mode of education, their improvement would be fully equal. All mankind are not born to be heroes or heroines. The constitution and habit of body has a very great effect on the mind of either sex, allowing for the moral and physical distinction. A morbid, or bilious habit of body, will have pretty much the same effect on the constitution. Those, who are much afflicted with a bilious complaint, are often of a gloomy turn of mind, and view the dark side of every event that happens in the course of divine providence : On the contrary, those who are more free from such complaints, are generally more vigorous and animated, and for the most part cheerful, and willing to make the best of even a bad bargain.

From the gloomy habits of the ancient monks, may be traced all the austerities of the monastic life ; when disappointed in life, many poor females have immured themselves in the solitary cell of a convent. But this is not the pure vital religion of the heart, which works by love, and is pure and peaceable ; which produces good fruits and is replete with good works. A gloomy religion generally originates in the gall of bitterness, and is seated in an affection of the liver; real religion expands the heart with every sentiment of affection for our fellow-creatures. This is the religion our blessed Saviour taught, and exemplified in his own life. This religion is not confined to any particular party or sect. It is extended to all who will accept the offered blessing. There will be no distinction of sex. There will be no distinction of climate or religion, in another and better world. As all mankind do not look alike, neither can they think or act, exactly the same. Still in essential points all may unite. Women have an undoubted right, agreeable to scripture, to think, reason and determine on all points relating to religious principles; that by a union of sentiments, they may lay the foundation for mutual peace, and assist each other in the christian warfare to eternal bliss and happiness. This is the christian plan, and real right of woman.

*6

CHAP. VI.

Reason dictates that a regular christian course of life
will have a tendency to promote future happiness, and
is but a reasonable service.

REASON surely must dictate to common
sense, that women have a right to join in every reasonable service, for the mutual security and happiness of the female compact. As
the care of children naturally devolves on the
women, and is one of the important duties an-
nexed to the female character, this relative
duty may afford forcible arguments in favour of
female education. To strengthen their understanding, and fit them, if necessary, to obtain
their own living, only let it be properly considered. How much more respectable is the
woman, who earns her own living, than the
most accomplished beauty, who depends on
her friends for support? Heaven has bestowed on all its rational creatures the faculty or
power of reasoning; the reflecting mind will
reason on the nature of men and things; females have a right to study the ways of man,
and the dispensation of divine providence, in
its dealings towards the children of men,
agreeable to the dictates of reason. Men will
act or forbear; many of the evils of this life
might be prevented was reason always at the
helm. To guide the fractured bark through
the stormy sea of human life, reason is undoubtedly a good director; but without the

divine guide of religion to pilot our frail bark, the earthly vessel may founder for want of proper ballast. It is religion alone that can direct and guide us safe to the haven of bliss and perfect happiness.

There must be a reasonable allowance made for the moral and physical distinction there is in nature, as well as constitution and habit of body; as also different climate. It is plain a very warm climate has a great effect on the human constitution, and has a tendency to produce a general debility of the whole animal system, which often degenerates into a complete lassitude of body and mind, which prevents any mental improvement.

Let these very same persons remove into a colder climate, they will soon recover strength, and find themselves renovated, animated, and able to engage in making further mental improvement. So nearly are the body and soul allied, that when the whole head is sick, the whole heart is faint.

So nearly are the soul and body connected, that it requires a constant supply of rational christian philosophy to balance the scale, and poise a proper equilibrium. The powers of the human mind have often been weakened, by a continual pain of the body, and vice versa, the body has often been greatly emaciated and even crumbled to dust, from some secret affliction of the soul, concealed in the human heart. From the preceding suggestions may be seen the many advantages that may accrue from having a rational companion; not only a

help meet, but a woman capable of reasoning
and giving advice for mutual happiness. This
is woman's reasonable right.

As there is a sympathy between the human
frame and soul, there is also a natural, or mutual sympathy of the sexes. There is a natural affection, implanted in the human breast,
by the wise Author of our nature, which gives
the sexes equal right to partake with each other, in the cares and trials, as well as the pleasures of this life. There cannot be a doubt
that many of the serious squabbles in the matrimonial life might be prevented, by the woman's showing her right, and by giving up the
point contended for in a reasonable manner;
but never assent merely to please a tyrant, for
that betrays a servile mind; nor ever contra-
dict merely to vex, for that shews an ill temper, and bad breeding. There should be not
only love, but that mutual friendship and confidence in each other's fidelity, that nothing
ought to be concealed from each other but the
secrets of another friend.

The necessary advantages of friendship are
mutual confidence and benevolence; the purse
and the heart ought to be open for the use of
a bosom friend. There can be no hazard in
trusting a well chosen friend with your secrets,
or your strong box; for where true friendship
subsists, their mutual interest is one and the
same; and as it is the lot of mankind to be
happy or unhappy by turns, and divine wisdom sees fit it should be so for our mutual advantage, that by the mediation of this mixture

we have the comfort to support us in affliction, and the apprehension of change to keep a check on us in the height of our grandeur; so by this vicissitude of good and evil we are kept steady in our philosophy and religion; as one puts us in mind of God's omnipotence and justice, the other of his goodness and mercy; the one tells us there is no trusting to our own strength, the other preaches faith and resignation in the government of divine providence.

It is woman's reasonable right to partake with man in all the vicissitudes and changes of life, and faithfully support their mutual interest, as by the reciprocal exchange of kind attentions they will secure that love and affection, which will eventually constitute the permanent love of our neighbour as ourselves, agreeably to the golden rule of equity, which implies that love, which will produce the affection of benevolent and generous sympathy, that shall interest the heart in the misfortunes of our fellow-creatures.

It must be allowed that these fine feelings are most particular traits in the female character; every habit of their lives incline them to a generous sympathy for other's woes. Very few women have ever been wanting in commiseration for the patient sufferer; and there is reason to believe, very few men of any sensibility have ever been unwilling to aid and assist them in their benevolent intentions. The mutual and reasonable right of the sexes may be handsomely displayed, by the males supplying the means to help the needy; and the females, who were the first susceptible of the fine feelings of benevolence for the sufferer, shall have the right and privilege to distribute relief and comfort to the destitute and afflicted.

From the same principle of benevolence, women may reasonably become equal with men in patriotism and disinterested love of country, which embraces all its citizens, and produces that universal benevolence and philanthropy, which extends its influence to all nations. This idea leads us to an important subject, that is, the moral and political, which Russel says, consists in regulating ourselves and others. He says, to compare the advantages and disadvantages of the sexes, with regard to this object, it would be necessary to observe the same talent in society, and as applied to government, the women in society being continually upon the look-out. From the motive of curiosity and policy they must have perfect knowledge of men; they must be able to disentangle all the folds of self-love, and discover all their secret weaknesses; the false modesty, and the false grandeur; what man is, and what he should be. They must know and distinguish character. They must know the diffidence which proceeds from character or vice; from misfortune or from the mind; in short, they must know all their sentiments and all their shades. As women set a high value on opinion, they must reflect much on what will produce it: They must know how far one can direct without appearing to be interested, and how far one may presume upon that art after it is known; in what estimation they are held by those with whom they live, and to what degree it is necessary to serve them, that they may govern them, in all cases of business. Women know the great affairs which are produced by little causes; they know how to captivate by praises those who deserve them, and sometimes raise a blush by bestowing them where they are not due.

These delicate sciences are the leading strings by which women conduct the men; men have less time for observation and can hardly be possessed of such a crowd of little notices, and those polite attentions, which are every moment necessary in the commerce of life. Therefore men's calculations in society must be more slow and less sure than women's, as applied to government. It seems, in consequence of the character of women, that their religion must be more tender, and the men's more sincere, as one consists more in practice, the other more in principle. The women are more liable to superstition; and the men are liable to fanaticism. The domestic virtues are intimately connected with religion, and doubtless common to both sexes; but the advantage seems still to be in favour of women; at least they have more need of virtue, which they have more call to practice. He says, these are some of the subjects, which should be considered in settling the dispute respecting the superiority or equality of the sexes. To treat the subject properly, it would be necessary to be at the same time a philosopher, a physician, an anatomist; and to be equally rational and sentimental, and above all these singular attainments, we must be perfectly disinterested. —*Russel's Hist. of Women.*

The writer of this little work cannot pretend to attain to the stated qualification here mentioned, but hopes to be so singular and disinterested, as to convince the reader she has the mutual interests of the sexes very much at heart, in drawing the line of equality as impartially as the nature of the subject will admit, after consulting the most approved authors who have wrote on the subject.

As a philosopher we would wish to reason on the nature of men and things, the nature, causes, and effects of all moral distinction of every created being; as a physician would consult, advise, prescribe and administer rational, quiet, and pacific medicine, as best for all rational beings; and as an anatomist would dissect the brain, and analyze every fibre of the human heart, to harmonize the sexual right, to the mutual satisfaction of the sexes. Certainly scripture and reason appear to be on the side of the just equality of the sexes.

This orthodox doctrine can be proved by plain philosophical reasoning on the nature of men, and may be demonstrated as clearly as any problem in Euclid.

CHAP. VII.

Treats of the beauty and good order that may accrue to society, by the united fidelity of the sexes in performing their appropriate duties.

As it appears from scripture and reason there is a just, and right equality of the sexes, common sense must teach the propriety of a union of the sexes in sentiments and opinions respecting the rights of women. Very little has been written on the subject in America; and perhaps it has not been necessary in a land where the rights of women have never appeared a bone of much contention. It may naturally be supposed, the ideas of a free independent people, will be more liberal and expanded respecting the sexual rights.

Under this impression, the writer has ventured to pen this small system or statement of the mutual rights and appropriate duties of the sexes with the most philanthropic wish, that the parties concerned may mutually agree to support the real orthodox principle of a mutual dependence on each other, which will promote peace, harmony and happiness; for without harmony and affection subsist between the sexes, society must soon become a mere nuisance to itself.

Our venerable ancestors, soon after they came to this country, framed laws and regulations for the general utility, and made ample provision for the happiness of every class of the citizens, including equal rights for the female sex. They soon as possible instituted schools, churches, and colleges, as the best mode of promoting the interest of their country ; and females partook of the advantage of education, and some made a wise improvement of it.

Among some of the early instructors of writing may be found Mrs. Sarah Knights, in the year 1706. She was famous in her day for teaching to write. Most of the letters on business, and notes of hand, and letters on friendship were wrote by her. She was a smart, witty, sensible woman, and had considerable influence at that period.

The first characters for learning and knowledge at that time certainly had an exalted opinion of the female character and abilities, and fully appreciated their rights and judgment, as they were often consulted on important subjects both in church and state. From that time they have often been consulted on important occasions.

In the important struggle for the independence of the American States, some females embarked in the cause of freedom, both by their writings and advice; and ever since the establishment of independence, it has been an invariable fixed principle in the female character to pray for the peace of our American Israel. And they must have an equal right to enjoy, with mutual satisfaction, all the blessings, tranquillity, freedom, and peace can bestow on a free and happy people.

It is almost impossible that those, who reside under a despotic or monarchical government, can imbibe as liberal sentiments as those, who reside under the more temperate zone of a free, federal republican government, which admits of free discussion of sentiments among all classes of the citizens. Such a government requires more sense and judgment to preserve it from disorder and disunion; therefore the union and right understanding of the sexes will have a tendency to strengthen, confirm and support such a government, and common sense must allow women the right of mutual judgment, and joining with the other sex in every prudent measure for their mutual defence and safety.

It may be seen by the fatal fall of Greece and Rome how much depends on public faith and confidence in the government, which must commence in the private faith and confidence of individuals.

From the universal benevolence, conspicuous in every section of the union, there is reason to anticipate our future greatness and respectability. The various institutions, for benevolent and charitable purposes, have a tendency to promote the kind affections, and make man mild and sociable to man; women shine preeminent in most of them, and have an equal right to establish schools of industry and economy, which must have a happy effect on the community. There is nothing can make better subjects for a republican government, than to give children an early education, and

train them in habits of prudence and industry.
Every day produces some proofs how much we
are the creatures of habit; the juvenile mind
requires continual occupation, for the vivacity
of youth is such, that if not constantly employed in some valuable pursuit, there is danger of
their resorting to some evil propensity, for
want of regular occupation; for such is the
natural depravity of the human heart. As
women generally have the forming of the infant mind, it is necessary their own minds
should be cultivated, that they may be capable of enlarging the mind of their pupils; as the
first seeds implanted in their breast, if virtuous
and noble, will prepare them for some important station in life. Children's constitution and
capacities differ so very much, that it requires
the affection, tenderness and care of a prudent
woman to mould and model the tender olive-
branch, as there is hardly a human being,
though of very inferior abilities, but will discover a genius for some particular employment, and that ought to be cultivated, and the
bent of their genius should be always consistent; for of those, who set out wrong in life, there
are few who ever clear the rocks and ledges,
and very seldom arrive at plain sailing; the
whole voyage of life will prove rough and boisterous, if it is not commenced right. This may
often be seen in the common course of human
life, if the compass of genius is not regulated
by learning, prudence, discretion and religion.

A religious, steady, rational course of living
will be found the safest pilot to the haven of

rest and perfect happiness. It is faith in the divine promises that can alone give peace of mind and great joy in believing. It is that which only can give that calm serenity of mind, which will support us under all the vicissitudes of this transitory state. There is no path can be pursued more likely to promote this calmness and serenity of mind, than to appropriate a certain space of our time every day for meditation; as every rational being, who reflects at all, must be sensible there is a wise governing providence that superintends the affairs of men, kingdoms, nations and states. It is most undoubtedly the duty of every individual to commit every event of their lives to his care and disposal, for he who can take into view and comprehend the whole plan of creation, must know what is best for his dependent creatures.

Therefore unerring wisdom can do no wrong. We may safely trust in his protecting care, and when called to affliction in the course of divine providence, if we receive the chastisement with the spirit of meekness, and bear it with christian fortitude, it may prove the brightest epoch in human life.

The minds of the sexes are equally capable of making a wise improvement of the various dispensations of divine providence; they all have equal need, and equal right, to seek the divine favour, aid, protection and consolation; and without the support, hope, trust and confidence in the promises of divine grace, they must both be equally unhappy. How vain and

*7

inconsistent are those, who flee from trouble to drown sorrow in dissipation! Oh foolish and inconsiderate mortals, why will you involve yourselves in greater troubles and tenfold misery, by adding to your sorrow the bitter sting of perhaps a too late death-bed repentance!

But let us turn the scene, and view the calm sedate christian, who, through the whole passage of life, is resigned to the divine direction and guidance, in the firm faith, that all the dispensations of providence are perfectly consistent with divine rectitude, and goodness. Under such impressions, the real christian will most fervently say, not my will, but thine be done, heavenly Father.

Scripture, reason and common sense dictates the divine right is in women, to promote those fine sympathetic affections that will have a tendency to assist, harmonize and sweeten a religious course of life. The power of friendship can sooth the cares of this transitory state, and meliorate the greatest miseries of human woe. Love is the sacred bond of mutual friendship, and promotes a reciprocal intercourse of kind affection.

Good humour, Dr. Johnson says, may be defined a habit of being pleased; a constant and perennial softness of manners, easiness of approach, and serenity of disposition, like that which every man perceives in himself, when the first transports of new felicity have subsided, and his thoughts are only kept in motion by a slow succession of soft impulses.

Good humour is a state between gayety and unconcern, the act or emanation of mind at leisure to regard the gratification of another.

It has been justly observed that discord generally operates in little things. It is inflamed to its utmost vehemence by contrariety of talk oftener than of principle; and might therefore commonly be avoided by innocent conformity, which, if it was not at first the motive, ought always to be the consequence, of indissoluble union.

The great remedy which heaven has put in our hands is patience; by which, though we cannot lessen the torments of the body, we can in a great measure, preserve the peace of the mind, and shall suffer only the natural and genuine force of an evil, without heightening its acrimony or prolonging its effects. When patience has performed its perfect work, it is the right of every female to have ready the mantle of meek charity, to gently cover the faults of her domestic circle.

CHAP. VIII.

Let the mantle of charity make allowance for, and shield every human imperfection.

THE hand of meek charity should be extended to every object of our affections. It is the soft hand of an affectionate female that can best soothe the pillow of dissolving nature, and meliorate the passage to the grave, by constant expressions of that love and mutual friendship, which never shall be dissolved.

Although the king of terrors shall arrest this earthly frame, yet the friendly spirit, still hovering over the pensive brow, shall kindly whisper in the ear, thy friend and lover is not dead, but only sleepeth. The spirit must ascend to the realms of bliss, where we shall meet again, and be renovated and prepared to join the sacred lodge, where the refined soul shall partake of love, friendship and uninterrupted happiness, never to suffer change, or any mixture or alloy.

As there is no spiritual distinction of sexes, the twin soul shall there join the general choir of all those who are equally redeemed by the precious blood of Jesus Christ, the Lamb of God. Such will be the advantage of forming sacred love and friendship here, that it shall be the foretaste of our future bliss, and temporal death will not dissolve the sacred tie, and there the sexual rights will be mutual; our God is no respecter of persons or sexes.

From what has been here offered on behalf of female rights, it appears plainly, virtue, harmony, love and friendship, religiously improved, will be the surest passport to the realms of bliss and happiness. And may the voice of philanthropy unite to embrace in the arms of her affection the whole human race, which the sexes have equal right to extend to every individual person throughout the whole order of society.

It is hoped this treatise or small system of the sexual rights will meet the mutual approbation of the sexes. Allow the author to say, it was written with the best intention ; of communicating some pleasure with instruction to the candid reader. Let the philanthropic peruser then, gently draw the mantle of charity over all its imperfections.

APPENDIX.

TO shew real impartiality, it is but just to give some account of illustrious men, as a sequel to illustrious women, as our wish is the mutual happiness of the sexes, for the well being and good order of society.

In every age of the world, from creation to the present day, there has been recorded many illustrious characters, both in sacred and profane history. Moses was the first legislator and law-giver, and he was a wise one, as he received his laws from Jehovah himself. His mother, it seems, shewed great prudence in concealing him in the ark of bulrushes, and she was blessed of heaven for her faith in the preserving care of a gracious providence, and he was preserved and made an instrument in the divine hands to lead his people Israel through all the Egyptian bondage, and conduct them safely through the Red Sea, as on dry land. We find many great and illustrious characters among the kings and prophets of ancient times. Job is recorded for patience, Solomon for wisdom, and he asked that of the Almighty. Isaiah, among the prophets, stands preeminent, as giving the most correct prophecy respecting the Messiah. Isaiah and Daniel, more especially, seem rather to describe the past, as historians, than to anticipate the future as prophets. We know that multitudes of the Jews, who had diligently studied the prophecies from their youth, and acknowledged their divine authority, felt the force of their application to our Lord, and were converted to his religion. And not to appeal to other instances, we know the fifty-third chapter of Isaiah, so circumstantially descriptive of the suffering Messiah, effected the conversion of the Eunuch of Ethiopia mentioned in the acts of the apostles, and contributed greatly to produce a conviction in the mind of the profligate Lord Rochester. This fact is recorded by Bishop Burnet. To him Lord Rochester held open with great freedom the tenor of his opinion and the course of his life, and from him he received such conviction of the reasonableness of moral duty, and truth of christianity, as produced a total change both in his manners and opinions. The account of those salutary conferences is given by Burnet in a book, entitled, Some passages of the life and death of John, Earl of Rochester. The critic ought to read it for its eloquence, the philosopher for its argument, and the saint for its piety.—*Johnson's Life of Rochester.*

Christians can appeal to an independent train of witnesses, to Jewish and profane writers, for circumstantial accounts of the fulfilment of his and our Lord's predictions. The historian Josephus descended from the family which bore the sacred office of high priest. A distinguished general in the early part of the last Jewish war has given a particular and exact confirmation of every circumstance. With singular care he has avoided to mention the name of Christ, and yet with singular precision he has illustrated his prediction relative to the destruction of Jerusalem. The important service he has thus rendered to christianity is wholly unintentional. What he relates is drawn from him by the power of irresistible truth, and is a testimony far more unexceptionable than an explicit mention of the name of Christ, and a laboured encomium of his words and actions. Josephus' history of the wars of the Jews is confirmed by Tacitus, Philostrates and Dion Cassius. It is probable they were all of them unacquainted with the works of the Jewish historian, and yet they all corroborate his account, and all unite to illustrate the prophecies of our Lord; and when we contemplate on the character of our Lord and his apostles, we are lost in wonder and admiration at the strength of mind and energy of the apostle Paul, after his conversion. We cannot help exclaiming, surely he must have been inspired with divine grace. But if the infidel will not believe Moses and the prophets, neither will he be persuaded though one come to him from the dead.

A due attention to ancient history might have a good effect on many, who are wavering in mind. Where can we find persons of such profound understandings and inquisitive minds as Bacon, Lock and Newton; where of such sublime genius as Milton; where of such extensive learning, exhausting all the literary treasures of the eastern as well as western literature, as Sir William Jones, who at the close of life recorded his conviction of the truths of divine revelation, and celebrated the excellency of the holy scriptures. To compare the race of modern infidels in point of genius; to compare Voltaire, Hume, Gibbons, Godwin and Paine, with such men as these, were surely idle, and as absurd as to compare the weakness of infancy with the maturity of manhood, or the fluttering of a butterfly with the vigour and soaring of a eagle, or the twinkling of a star with the glory of the sun, illuminating the world with his meridian brightness.—*See Kett's Elements.*

We wish to give an impartial account of illustrious characters that have been conspicuous in different ages of the world, both male and female, as the author's wish is to equalize the mutual rights of the sexes, and to harmonize the whole by the bright examples of the most amiable and virtuous of both sexes, as collected from sacred and profane history.

Pliny is recorded as one of the most finished gentlemen and the politest writer of the age in which he lived; and one of the best husbands in the whole Roman empire. He did not think it below him to treat his wife as a friend, companion and counsellor. He has left us in his letter to Hispulla, his wife's aunt. one of the most agreeable family pieces I ever met with ; conjugal love is drawn with a delicacy which makes it appear an ornament as well as a virtue. The following extract is from the letter, and we refer the reader to the Beauties of History for the whole.

Pliny to Hispulla.

As I remember the great affection which was between your excellent brother, and know you loved his daughter as your own, so as not only to express the tenderness of the best of aunts, but even to supply that of the best of fathers, I am sure it will give you pleasure to hear that she proves worthy of you, and of yours, and her ancestors; accept, therefore, our united thanks : mine, that you have bestowed her on me, her's as a mutual grant of joy and felicity.

The same amiable disposition and conjugal tenderness is seen in his letters to his wife, when he was at a distance from her.—*See Beauties of H. Ist. vol.*

Cicero was in all respects as good a man as Pliny, and has written whole books of letters to his wife. They are full of beautiful simplicity, which is altogether natural, and is the distinguished character of the best ancient writers. Some of his letters to his wife were written when he was banished from his country by a faction that then prevailed at Rome. After reading them, it gives pleasure to see this great man in his family, who makes so different a figure in the forum, or senate of Rome.

Every one admires the orator and the consul,
but for my own part I esteem the husband and
the father. His private character, with all
the little weaknesses of humanity, is as amiable, as the figure he makes in public is awful
and majestic. The writer says it would be
ill-nature not to acquaint the English reader
that his wife was successful in her solicitations
for this great man, and saw her husband return to the honours of which he had been deprived, with all the pomp and acclamation that
usually attended the greatest triumph.

From the foregoing example, it appears
incontestably evident, that a happy marriage
has in it all the pleasures of friendship, and all
the enjoyments of sense and reason, and indeed all the sweets of life ; and to make it so,
nothing more is required than discretion, virtue and good nature. The poet says,

"They know a passion, still more deeply charming,
Than favour'd youth e'er felt, and that is love,
By long experience mellow'd into friendship."

The character of a good husband, may not
come amiss after the foregoing account. A
good husband is one, who, not wedded by interest but by choice, is constant, as well from
inclination as from principle ; he treats his wife
with delicacy as a woman, with tenderness as
a friend. He attributes her follies to her weakness ; her imprudence to her inadvertency.
He passes them over therefore with good nature, and pardons them with indulgence ; all
his care and industry are employed for her

welfare; all his strength and power are exerted for her support and protection; he is more anxious to preserve his own character and reputation, because her's is blended with it. Lastly, the good husband is pious and religious that he may animate her faith by his practice, and enforce the principles of christianity by his own example, that, as they join to promote each other's happiness in this world, they may unite to secure eternal joy and felicity in that which is to come.

To equalize, we give the character of a good wife, from the same author. The good wife is one, who, ever mindful of the solemn contract which she hath entered into, is strictly, conscientiously virtuous. Constant and faithful to her husband, chaste, pure and unblemished in every thought, word and deed, she is humble, modest from reason and conviction, submissive from choice, and obedient from inclination; what she acquires by love and tenderness, she preserves by prudence and discretion. She makes it her business to serve, and her pleasure to oblige her husband, conscious that every thing that promotes his happiness must in the end contribute to her own; her tenderness relieves his cares, her affection softens his distress, her good humour and complacency lessen and subdue his afflictions. " She openeth her mouth," as Solomon says, " with wisdom, and in her tongue is the law of kindness. She looketh well to the way of her household, and eateth not the bread of idleness; her children rise up and call her

*8

blessed, her husband also, and he praiseth her." As a pious and good christian, she looks up with an eye of gratitude to the great dispenser and disposer of all things, as the husband of the widow, and the father of the fatherless, entreating his divine favour and assistance in this, and every other moral duty, well satisfied that if she punctually discharges her several offices in this life, she shall be blessed and rewarded for it in another. " Favour is deceitful, and beauty is vain, but a woman that feareth the Lord she shall be praised."

We here see drawn the character of a good husband and a good wife on a plan worthy of imitation. It may not be amiss to mention some traits of a good father. The good father is ever tender, humane and affectionate to his children ; he treats them with lenity and kindness, corrects with prudence, rebukes with temper, and chastises with reluctance. He is prudent that they may be happy ; industrious that they may be rich ; good and virtuous that they may be respected. He instructs by his life, and teaches by his example. Parents repeat their lives in their offspring, and their concerns for them is so near, that they feel all their sufferings, and taste all their enjoyments, as much as if they regarded their own persons. However strong the fondness of a father for his children, yet they will find more lively marks of tenderness in the bosom of a mother. There are no ties in nature to compare with those that unite an affectionate mother to her children, when they repay her tenderness with obedience and love, which has been seen in some of the most exalted characters in every age of the world. Some of the ancient fathers have owned they loved a mother, and some have wrote in praise of the sex. Jerome has been noticed.

All Europe have had their great and good men. Calvin, Luther, and Melancthon, were all great in the reformation. Great Britain can boast of her great and good men. A Baxter, Howe, Owen and Burroughs, were great and good. They all rank high in theology. In our own time we call to mind an Erskine, an Ogilvie, with half a score more, too many to mention. Our respected Watts must yet bring up the mighty rear. To equalize the sex allow us to say, he jointly with Mrs. Steel we hear resounding with praises in our churches. As statesmen, politicians, and as heroes, Great Britain has her best and wisest men. Who ever rivalled a Pitt, Burke, or an Erskine; and for literary fame, no period ever exceeded that of Dryden, Pope, Prior, Addison, and Johnson. For purity of style, harmony, blended with taste, chasteness, piety, and sweetness, none ever exceeded Addison; for strength of mind, and profound learning, and critical knowledge, few ever exceeded Johnson. It may be said he was a great man, with many eccentricities. See his life for proof. For law knowledge, they boast of a Coke, Bacon, Hale, and many others, who were great indeed. Their warriors and seamen rank high in the annals of fame.

America has her worthies yet to claim. Columbus, to thee we owe the discovery of this vast region; and to those venerable sires, who sprang from British root, and branched forth into this then howling wilderness, do we owe all our gratitude for their unbounded zeal and perseverance, under all the difficulties they had to combat with. The names of many great and worthy men could be collected. We shall only mention a few of the first worthies, among whom stands a Bradford, Winthrop, Bradstreet, an Allen, with the good old Brewster, and the enterprizing Standish, brave and daring. America can boast of her great and good men throughout the union. New England can glory in her worthies, divines, statesmen and heroes. In theology and piety who ever excelled a Hooker, a Partridge, an Eliot, a Cotton, with the fourfold line of Mathers; a Chauncy too we name, for ancient learning, piety and virtue, all renowned in the annals of America. Of more recent date, for purity of manners, meekness and piety, who can we name to excel our venerable Sewall; Prince stands the faithful chronologer of his country; in the elegant Colman we view the good man and the gentleman; and whoever surpassed the accomplished Coopers, predecessors to our respected friend Dr. Thacher; the harmonious voice of a Stillman yet vibrates on our ears. As the friend, christian and gentleman he lived and died unrivalled. We might add a Pemberton and a Lathrop to the list, with a whole score of worthy divines, but we wish not to enlarge. We are led to say, our fathers, where are they?

As statesmen, politicians and heroes, we have our boast; for philosophers our Franklin might be styled a Newton; for literary and law knowledge, who can vie with our Paine and Parsons; as historians, we may boast a Belknap and Minot, with many others; as statesmen, we have had an Adams, a Bowdoin, an Ames, and a Dexter. Ames and Dexter have been compared by strangers to a Chatham and an Erskine, the pride of England.

The United States can claim a Washington as their father, friend, protector, and saviour of his country. Here we might name a host of heroes, but he was indeed an host himself. Gratitude demands the names of Warren, Lincoln, Hamilton and Knox, with many more whom we revere, but it will enlarge our work too much to name. Should we name the catalogue of old Harvard, and the other Universities, it would swell our work to the frightful size of a huge folio; which, as a late elegant critic observes, few men dare combat with, though a recent female writer has had the hardihood to wade through folio after folio from Josephus, Basnage, and Turkish history, even to the Magnalia of America, and all to compile a Compendious History of the Jews, for the benefit of those who dare not, or cannot wade through a folio. In this day of duodecimos, the writers have reason to acknowledge with gratitude, that they have their ancient learning to assist them in their abridgements, and

from them we can collect sentiments worthy
to be handed down to the latest posterity.

Miscellaneous Sentiments, moral and religious,
From various authors.

Give me, says Quintillian, among his excellent rules for instructing youth, a child that is
sensible of praise and touched with glory, and
that will cry at the shame of being outdone,
and I will keep him at his business by emulation; reproof will afflict and honour will encourage him, and I shall not fear to cure him
of idleness. None can be eminent without
application and genius. To become an able
man in any profession three things are necessary, nature, study, and practice.

The Hon. Mr. Boyle was a man of extensive learning, and one of the most exact inquirers into the works of nature that any age
has known; and what reflects the greatest
honour on himself and upon christianity is, that
while he was an accurate reasoner, he was a
firm believer in the christian religion.—*See*
Life of Boyle.

Marcus Aurelius tells us, that he could not
relish a happiness that nobody shared in but
himself.

When Cato was drawing near the close of
life, he declared to his friend, that the greatest
comfort of his old age, and that which gave
him the highest satisfaction, was the pleasing
remembrance of the many benefits and friendly offices he had done to others.

There is more satisfaction in doing good than receiving. To relieve the oppressed is the most glorious act a man is capable of! It is in some measure doing the business of Providence, and is attended with a heavenly pleasure, unknown but to those who are beneficent and liberal. Men of the noblest dispositions think themselves happiest when others share with them in their happiness. We ought to consult the worth of the person whom we have chosen for our liberality. Let a present be ever so considerable, the manner of conferring it is the noblest part.

The uncertainty of our duration ought at once to set bounds to our designs, and add incitements to our industry; and when we find ourselves inclined either to immensity in our schemes, or sluggishness in our endeavours, we may either check or animate ourselves, by recollecting, with the father of physick, that art is long, and life is short.—*Johnson.*

When Lee was once told by a critic that it was very easy to write like a madman, he answered, that it was difficult to write like a madman, but easy enough to write like a fool; and I hope to be excused if in imitation of this great author I presume to remind my kind contributers, that it is much easier not to write like a man than to write like a women.—*See Rambler.*

Johnson says, as every writer has his use, every writer ought to have his patrons; and since no man, however high he may now stand, can be certain that he shall not be thrown

down from his elevation by criticism or ca-
price, the common interest of learning requires
that her sons should cease from intestine hostilities, and instead of sacrificing each other to
malice and contempt, endeavour to avert persecution from the meanest of their fraternity.

Seneca has attempted not only to pacify
us in misfortune, but almost to allure us to it
by representing it as necessary to the pleasures
of the mind. He that never was acquainted
with adversity, says he, has seen the world but
on one side, and is ignorant of half the scenes
of nature. It was the wisdom, says Seneca,
of ancient times, to consider what is most useful as most illustrious. Johnson says, if this
rule be applied to works of genius, scarcely
any species of composition deserves more to
be cultivated than the epistolary style, since
none is of more various or more frequent use
through the whole subordination of human life.
The man whose genius qualifies him for great
undertakings, must at least be content to learn
from books the present state of human knowledge.

Constancy of mind gives a man reputation,
and makes him happy in despite of all misfortunes. There is not on earth a spectacle more
worthy the regard of the Creator intent on his
works, than a brave man superior to his sufferings. What can be more honourable than
to have courage enough to execute the commands of reason and conscience, to maintain
the dignity of our nature, and the station assigned us, to be proof against poverty, pain

and death. To do this is to be great above title and fortune. This argues the soul of heavenly extraction, and is worthy the offspring of the Deity.

"He lives in fame, who dies in virtue's cause."

From the many illustrious characters and sentiments we have before us, arises this reflection; it must be for the mutual happiness of the sexes to unite in sentiments, and endeavour to follow the precepts and examples of the wise and good of every age, and thus promote the equality and happiness of the sexes, agreeably to scripture, reason and common sense.

To conclude: we shall give our readers a short account of Aurelius and Prudencia, from recent observation in real life.

Aurelius was the son of an eminent clergyman, possessed with a natural, amiable disposition, and strong powers of mind. He soon made progress in his learning; at an early age entered the seat of science, and passed through with great honour, and soon after obtained a handsome settlement. At the age of twenty-five, he formed a connexion in life with the daughter of an opulent merchant. Prudencia was only eighteen when they commenced life in the marriage state. She was a lady of a strong and well improved mind, which had been well cultivated by a mother's prudent mode of education. They commenced life with the same views. They had but one mind and but one heart, vibrating the same cord, and that was philanthropy to all mankind.

Aurelius was a great scholar, a hard stu
dent, a christian philosopher, but the truly polite gentleman. He could unbend himself from
the most abstruse studies, and in the most engaging manner enjoy the society of his friends
in the circle of domestic life, with the pleasing
gayety of the man of gallantry ; but he always
blended instruction with morality and religion,
in his conversation. He was easy of access
to every fellow-creature and nation, as he was
often heard to say, " He hath made of one
blood all the nations of the earth." Being
asked by an Irish soldier, in the time of the
revolutionary war, if he was a Roman Catholic, he observed to him, he could not say he
was a Roman, but he could say he was a Catholic, and wished every order of men well and
happy. He was always happy in the bosom
of his family. That he might have full scope
for his literary pursuits, his prudent and amiable wife took from his mind every domestic
care. She was a wife and mother indeed.
Such an one as Solomon describes, for she
looked well to the ways of her household, and
never eat the bread of idleness. Prudencia
was rather tall, and possessed all the dignity
of ancient nobility ; but with the utmost familiarity and kindness, she could accommodate
herself to the most menial objects that often
surrounded her. In her intercourse with society, she was an agreeable companion. She
loved her friends, and would descend to the
most menial duty, to assist a poor neighbour.
He was often seeking objects of distress, and

she was ever ready to aid and assist them.
They had several sons and daughters. Their
sons were called to fill places of respectability
at a distance from home ; their daughters continued near them. Though several of them
married, they settled near enough to be a blessing to them, in the decline of life. The worthy old gentleman and lady mutually aided
and supported each other through all the various changing scenes of this life : they had
their mutual trials and comforts, though they
appeared to have but one general sentiment
prevailing in their hearts ; and that was, the
interest and happiness of all around them
They lived to communicate happiness to their
friends.. With a talent to please, and a heart
ever open to generous acts, who could be more
happy than this amiable and virtuous couple.
They were guided by religious principles and
practised its precepts. They passed through
life as ornaments to society to quite an honorable old age. Ever resigned to the various
dispensations of divine providence, their life
on earth might be said to be a foretaste of bliss
in heaven. After living nearly fifty years together, Prudencia departed this life. We cannot say she closed her eyes in death, for she
gently fell asleep in Jesus. Aurelius supported the trying scene with christian fortitude and philosophy. He continued a few
years after her, and then a short illness ter-
minated his valuable life, when, like a shock
of corn fully ripe, he quited his clay, and like a
triumphant saint, he was heard to articulate

this sentence, " Now lettest thou thy servant depart in peace :" then he gently closed his eyes to sleep and wake with Jesus, as we believe, to hear that blessed sentence, " Well done thou good and faithful servant, enter thou into the presence of your Lord and Saviour."

The design of giving the account of this virtuous, happy and wise pair, drawn from a known couple in real life, is with the most ardent wish it may have a happy effect on those who are commencing life, and all who peruse the account may determine and say, let me live the life of the righteous, that my end may be like their's, peace and future bliss, and happiness in another, better, and more permanent world than the present.

Here ends the mutual rights of all,
Attend the summons and obey the call;
Let reason govern, and religion guide,
For soul and body are most near allied.
Rise then to virtue, quickly rise,
To join with saints beyond the skies.

THE GREAT LAWSUIT

[Margaret Fuller Ossoli]

THE DIAL.

Vol. IV.   JULY, 1843.   No. I.

THE GREAT LAWSUIT.

MAN *versus* MEN. WOMAN *versus* WOMEN.

This great suit has now been carried on through many
ages, with various results. The decisions have been numerous, but always followed by appeals to still higher
courts. How can it be otherwise, when the law itself is
the subject of frequent elucidation, constant revision?
Man has, now and then, enjoyed a clear, triumphant hour,
when some irresistible conviction warmed and purified the
atmosphere of his planet. But, presently, he sought repose
after his labors, when the crowd of pigmy adversaries bound
him in his sleep. Long years of inglorious imprisonment
followed, while his enemies revelled in his spoils, and no
counsel could be found to plead his cause, in the absence
of that all-promising glance, which had, at times, kindled
the poetic soul to revelation of his claims, of his rights.

Yet a foundation for the largest claim is now established.
It is known that his inheritance consists in no partial sway,
no exclusive possession, such as his adversaries desire. For
they, not content that the universe is rich, would, each one
for himself, appropriate treasure; but in vain! The many-
colored garment, which clothed with honor an elected son,
when rent asunder for the many, is a worthless spoil. A
band of robbers cannot live princely in the prince's castle;
nor would he, like them, be content with less than all,
though he would not, like them, seek it as fuel for riotous
enjoyment, but as his principality, to administer and guard
for the use of all living things therein. He cannot be satisfied with any one gift of the earth, any one department of
knowledge, or telescopic peep at the heavens. He feels

himself called to understand and aid nature, that she may, through his intelligence, be raised and interpreted ; to be a student of, and servant to, the universe-spirit; and only king of his planet, that, as an angelic minister, he may bring it into conscious harmony with the law of that spirit.

Such is the inheritance of the orphan prince, and the illegitimate children of his family will not always be able to keep it from him, for, from the fields which they sow with dragon's teeth, and water with blood, rise monsters, which he alone has power to drive away.

But it is not the purpose now to sing the prophecy of his jubilee. We have said that, in clear triumphant moments, this has many, many times been made manifest, and those moments, though past in time, have been translated into eternity by thought. The bright signs they left hang in the heavens, as single stars or constellations, and, already, a thickly-sown radiance consoles the wanderer in the darkest night. Heroes have filled the zodiac of beneficent labors, and then given up their mortal part* to the fire without a murmur. Sages and lawgivers have bent their

---

* Jupiter alloquitur,
　　　　Sed enim, ne pectora vano
Fida metu paveant, Œteas spernite flammas,
Omnia qui vicit, vincet, quos cernitis, ignes ;
Nec nisi maternâ Vulcanum parte potentem
Sentiet. Aeternum est, à me quod traxit, et expers
Atque immune necis, nullaque domabile flamma
Idque ego defunctum terrâ cœlestibus oris
Accipiam, cunctisque meum lætabile factum
Dis fore confido. Si quis tamen, Hercule, si quis
Fortè Deo doliturus erit, data prœmia nollet ;
Sed meruisse dari sciet, invitusque probabit.
Assensêre Dei.

Ovid, Apotheosis of Hercules, translated into clumsy English by Mr. Gay, as follows.

Jove said,
　　　　Be all your fears forborne,
Th' Œtean fires do thou, great hero, scorn ;
Who vanquished all things, shall subdue the flame ;
The part alone of gross *maternal* frame,
Fire shall devour, while that from me he drew
Shall live immortal, and its force renew ;
That, when he 's dead, I'll raise to realms above;
May all the powers the righteous act approve.
If any God dissent, and judge too great
The sacred honors of the heavenly seat,
Even he shall own his deeds deserve the sky,
Even he, reluctant, shall at length comply.
Th' assembled powers assent.

whole nature to the search for truth, and thought themselves happy if they could buy, with the sacrifice of all
temporal ease and pleasure, one seed for the future Eden.
Poets and priests have strung the lyre with heart-strings,
poured out their best blood upon the altar which, reared
anew from age to age, shall at last sustain the flame which
rises to highest heaven. What shall we say of those who,
if not so directly, or so consciously, in connection with the
central truth, yet, led and fashioned by a divine instinct,
serve no less to develop and interpret the open secret of
love passing into life, the divine energy creating for the
purpose of happiness ; — of the artist, whose hand, drawn
by a preëxistent harmony to a certain medium, moulds it
to expressions of life more highly and completely organized than are seen elsewhere, and, by carrying out the
intention of nature, reveals her meaning to those who are
not yet sufficiently matured to divine it; of the philosopher, who listens steadily for causes, and, from those obvious, infers those yet unknown; of the historian, who, in
faith that all events must have their reason and their aim,
records them, and lays up archives from which the youth
of prophets may be fed. The man of science dissects the
statement, verifies the facts, and demonstrates connection
even where he cannot its purpose.

Lives, too, which bear none of these names, have yielded
tones of no less significance. The candlestick, set in a
low place, has given light as faithfully, where it was needed,
as that upon the hill. In close alleys, in dismal nooks, the
Word has been read as distinctly, as when shown by angels
to holy men in the dark prison. Those who till a spot of
earth, scarcely larger than is wanted for a grave, have deserved that the sun should shine upon its sod till violets answer.

So great has been, from time to time, the promise, that,
in all ages, men have said the Gods themselves came down
to dwell with them ; that the All-Creating wandered on the
earth to taste in a limited nature the sweetness of virtue,
that the All-Sustaining incarnated himself, to guard, in space
and time, the destinies of his world ; that heavenly genius
dwelt among the shepherds, to sing to them and teach them
how to sing. Indeed,

"Der stets den Hirten gnädig sich bewies."

"He has constantly shown himself favorable to shepherds."

And these dwellers in green pastures and natural students of the stars, were selected to hail, first of all, the holy child, whose life and death presented the type of excellence, which has sustained the heart of so large a portion of mankind in these later generations.

Such marks have been left by the footsteps of man, whenever he has made his way through the wilderness of men. And whenever the pigmies stepped in one of these, they felt dilate within the breast somewhat that promised larger stature and purer blood. They were tempted to forsake their evil ways, to forsake the side of selfish personal existence, of decrepit skepticism, and covetousness of corruptible possessions. Conviction flowed in upon them. They, too, raised the cry; God is living, all is his, and all created beings are brothers, for they are his children. These were the triumphant moments; but, as we have said, man slept and selfishness awoke.

Thus he is still kept out of his inheritance, still a pleader, still a pilgrim. But his reinstatement is sure. And now, no mere glimmering consciousness, but a certainty, is felt and spoken, that the highest ideal man can form of his own capabilities is that which he is destined to attain. Whatever the soul knows how to seek, it must attain. Knock, and it shall be opened; seek, and ye shall find. It is demonstrated, it is a maxim. He no longer paints his proper nature in some peculiar form and says, " Prometheus had it," but " Man must have it." However disputed by many, however ignorantly used, or falsified, by those who do receive it, the fact of an universal, unceasing revelation, has been too clearly stated in words, to be lost sight of in thought, and sermons preached from the text, " Be ye perfect," are the only sermons of a pervasive and deep-searching influence.

But among those who meditate upon this text, there is great difference of view, as to the way in which perfection shall be sought.

Through the intellect, say some; Gather from every growth of life its seed of thought; look behind every symbol for its law. If thou canst *see* clearly, the rest will follow.

Through the life, say others; Do the best thou knowest to-day. Shrink not from incessant error, in this gradual, fragmentary state. Follow thy light for as much as it will show thee, be faithful as far as thou canst, in hope that faith presently will lead to sight. Help others, without blame that they need thy help. Love much, and be forgiven.

It needs not intellect, needs not experience, says a third. If you took the true way, these would be evolved in purity. You would not learn through them, but express through them a higher knowledge. In quietness, yield thy soul to the causal soul. Do not disturb its teachings by methods of thine own. Be still, seek not, but wait in obedience. Thy commission will be given.

Could we, indeed, say what we want, could we give a description of the child that is lost, he would be found. As soon as the soul can say clearly, that a certain demonstration is wanted, it is at hand. When the Jewish prophet described the Lamb, as the expression of what was required by the coming era, the time drew nigh. But we say not, see not, as yet, clearly, what we would. Those who call for a more triumphant expression of love, a love that cannot be crucified, show not a perfect sense of what has already been expressed. Love has already been expressed, that made all things new, that gave the worm its ministry as well as the eagle; a love, to which it was alike to descend into the depths of hell, or to sit at the right hand of the Father.

Yet, no doubt, a new manifestation is at hand, a new hour in the day of man. We cannot expect to see him a completed being, when the mass of men lie so entangled in the sod, or use the freedom of their limbs only with wolfish energy. The tree cannot come to flower till its root be freed from the cankering worm, and its whole growth open to air and light. Yet something new shall presently be shown of the life of man, for hearts crave it now, if minds do not know how to ask it.

Among the strains of prophecy, the following, by an earnest mind of a foreign land, written some thirty years ago, is not yet outgrown; and it has the merit of being a positive appeal from the heart, instead of a critical declaration what man shall *not* do.

" The ministry of man implies, that he must be filled from the divine fountains which are being engendered through all eternity, so that, at the mere name of his Master, he may be able to cast all his enemies into the abyss; that he may deliver all parts of nature from the barriers that imprison them; that he may purge the terrestrial atmosphere from the poisons that infect it; that he may preserve the bodies of men from the corrupt influences that surround, and the maladies that afflict them; still more, that he may keep their souls pure from the malignant insinuations which pollute, and the gloomy images that obscure them; that we may restore its serenity to the Word, which false words of men fill with mourning and sadness; that he may satisfy the desires of the angels, who await from him the development of the marvels of nature; that, in fine, his world may be filled with God, as eternity is." *

Another attempt we will give, by an obscure observer of our own day and country, to draw some lines of the desired image. It was suggested by seeing the design of Crawford's Orpheus, and connecting with the circumstance of the American, in his garret at Rome, making choice of this subject, that of Americans here at home, showing such ambition to represent the character, by calling their prose and verse, Orphic sayings, Orphics. Orpheus was a lawgiver by theocratic commission. He understood nature, and made all her forms move to his music. He told her secrets in the form of hymns, nature as seen in the mind of God. Then it is the prediction, that to learn and to do, all men must be lovers, and Orpheus was, in a high sense, a lover. His soul went forth towards all beings, yet could remain sternly faithful to a chosen type of excellence. Seeking what he loved, he feared not death nor hell, neither could any presence daunt his faith in the power of the celestial harmony that filled his soul.

It seemed significant of the state of things in this country, that the sculptor should have chosen the attitude of shading his eyes. When we have the statue here, it will give lessons in reverence.

> Each Orpheus must to the depths descend,
> For only thus the poet can be wise,
> Must make the sad Persephone his friend,
> And buried love to second life arise;
> Again his love must lose through too much love,
> Must lose his life by living life too true,
> For what he sought below is passed above,

---

* St. Martin.

Already done is all that he would do;
  Must tune all being with his single lyre,
Must melt all rocks. free from their primal pain,
  Must search all nature with his one soul's fire,
Must bind anew all forms in heavenly chain.
  If he already sees what he must do,
Well may he shade his eyes from the far-shining view.

Meanwhile, not a few believe, and men themselves have expressed the opinion, that the time is come when Euridice is to call for an Orpheus, rather than Orpheus for Euridice; that the idea of man, however imperfectly brought out, has been far more so than that of woman, and that an improvement in the daughters will best aid the reformation of the sons of this age.

It is worthy of remark, that, as the principle of liberty is better understood and more nobly interpreted, a broader protest is made in behalf of woman. As men become aware that all men have not had their fair chance, they are inclined to say that no women have had a fair chance. The French revolution, that strangely disguised angel, bore witness in favor of woman, but interpreted her claims no less ignorantly than those of man. Its idea of happiness did not rise beyond outward enjoyment, unobstructed by the tyranny of others. The title it gave was Citoyen, Citoyenne, and it is not unimportant to woman that even this species of equality was awarded her. Before, she could be condemned to perish on the scaffold for treason, but not as a citizen, but a subject. The right, with which this title then invested a human being, was that of bloodshed and license. The Goddess of Liberty was impure. Yet truth was prophesied in the ravings of that hideous fever induced by long ignorance and abuse. Europe is conning a valued lesson from the blood-stained page. The same tendencies, farther unfolded, will bear good fruit in this country.

Yet, in this country, as by the Jews, when Moses was leading them to the promised land, everything has been done that inherited depravity could, to hinder the promise of heaven from its fulfilment. The cross, here as elsewhere, has been planted only to be blasphemed by cruelty and fraud. The name of the Prince of Peace has been profaned by all kinds of injustice towards the Gentile whom

he said he came to save.   But I need not speak of what
has been done towards the red man, the black man.   These
deeds are the scoff of the world ; and they have been ac-
companied by such pious words, that the gentlest would not
dare to intercede with, " Father forgive them, for they know
not what they do."

Here, as elsewhere, the gain of creation consists always
in the growth of individual minds, which live and aspire,
as flowers bloom and birds sing, in the midst of morasses ;
and in the continual development of that thought, the
thought of human destiny, which is given to eternity to
fulfil, and which ages of failure only seemingly impede.
Only seemingly, and whatever seems to the contrary,
this country is as surely destined to elucidate a great moral
law, as Europe was to promote the mental culture of man.

Though the national independence be blurred by the
servility of individuals ; though freedom and equality have
been proclaimed only to leave room for a monstrous display of slave dealing, and slave keeping ; though the free
American so often feels himself free, like the Roman, only
to pamper his appetites and his indolence through the
misery of his fellow beings, still it is not in vain, that the
verbal statement has been made, "All men are born free and
equal."   There it stands, a golden certainty, wherewith to
encourage the good, to shame the bad.   The new world
may be called clearly to perceive that it incurs the utmost
penalty, if it reject the sorrowful brother.   And if men are
deaf, the angels hear.   But men cannot be deaf.   It is inevitable that an external freedom, such as has been achieved for
the nation, should be so also for every member of it.   That,
which has once been clearly conceived in the intelligence,
must be acted out.   It has become a law, as irrevocable as
that of the Medes in their ancient dominion.   Men will privately sin against it, but the law so clearly expressed by a
leading mind of the age,

> " Tutti fatti a sembianza d' un Solo ;
>   Figli tutti d' un solo riscatto,
>   In qual ora, in qual parte del suolo
>   Trascorriamo quest' aura vital,
>   Siam fratelli, siam stretti ad un patto :
>   Maladetto colui che lo infrange,

Che s' innalza sul fiacco che piange,
Che contrista uno spirto immortal." *

" All made in the likeness of the One,
   All children of one ransom,
In whatever hour, in whatever part of the soil
   We draw this vital air,
We are brothers, we must be bound by one compact,
   Accursed he who infringes it,
Who raises himself upon the weak who weep,
   Who saddens an immortal spirit."

cannot fail of universal recognition.

We sicken no less at the pomp than the strife of words. We feel that never were lungs so puffed with the wind of declamation, on moral and religious subjects, as now. We are tempted to implore these " word-heroes," these word-Catos, word Christs, to beware of cant above all things ; to remember that hypocrisy is the most hopeless as well as the meanest of crimes, and that those must surely be polluted by it, who do not keep a little of all this morality and religion for private use.† We feel that the mind may " grow black and rancid in the smoke" even of altars. We start up from the harangue to go into our closet and shut the door. But, when it has been shut long enough, we remember that where there is so much smoke, there must be some fire ; with so much talk about virtue and freedom must be mingled some desire for them ; that it cannot be in vain that such have become the common topics of conversation among men ; that the very newspapers should proclaim themselves Pilgrims, Puritans, Heralds of Holiness. The king that maintains so costly a retinue cannot be a mere Count of Carabbas fiction. We have waited here long in the dust ; we are tired and hungry, but the triumphal procession must appear at last.

Of all its banners, none has been more steadily upheld, and under none has more valor and willingness for real sacrifices been shown, than that of the champions of the

---

* Manzoni.
  † Dr. Johnson's one piece of advice should be written on every door ; " Clear your mind of cant." But Byron, to whom it was so acceptable, in clearing away the noxious vine, shook down the building too. Stirling's emendation is note-worthy, " Realize your cant, not cast it off."

enslaved African. And this band it is, which, partly in consequence of a natural following out of principles, partly because many women have been prominent in that cause, makes, just now, the warmest appeal in behalf of woman.

Though there has been a growing liberality on this point, yet society at large is not so prepared for the demands of this party, but that they are, and will be for some time, coldly regarded as the Jacobins of their day.

"Is it not enough," cries the sorrowful trader, "that you have done all you could to break up the national Union, and thus destroy the prosperity of our country, but now you must be trying to break up family union, to take my wife away from the cradle, and the kitchen hearth, to vote at polls, and preach from a pulpit? Of course, if she does such things, she cannot attend to those of her own sphere. She is happy enough as she is. She has more leisure than I have, every means of improvement, every indulgence."

"Have you asked her whether she was satisfied with these indulgences?"

"No, but I know she is. She is too amiable to wish what would make me unhappy, and too judicious to wish to step beyond the sphere of her sex. I will never consent to have our peace disturbed by any such discussions."

"'Consent'—you? it is not consent from you that is in question, it is assent from your wife."

"Am not I the head of my house?"

"You are not the head of your wife. God has given her a mind of her own."

"I am the head and she the heart."

"God grant you play true to one another then. If the head represses no natural pulse of the heart, there can be no question as to your giving your consent. Both will be of one accord, and there needs but to present any question to get a full and true answer. There is no need of precaution, of indulgence, or consent. But our doubt is whether the heart consents with the head, or only acquiesces in its decree; and it is to ascertain the truth on this point, that we propose some liberating measures."

Thus vaguely are these questions proposed and discussed at present. But their being proposed at all implies much thought, and suggests more. Many women are considering within themselves what they need that they have not, and what they can have, if they find they need it. Many men are considering whether women are capable of being and having more than they are and have, and whether, if they are, it will be best to consent to improvement in their condition.

The numerous party, whose opinions are already labelled and adjusted too much to their mind to admit of any new light, strive, by lectures on some model-woman of bridal-like beauty and gentleness, by writing or lending little treatises, to mark out with due precision the limits of woman's sphere, and woman's mission, and to prevent other than the rightful shepherd from climbing the wall, or the flock from using any chance gap to run astray.

Without enrolling ourselves at once on either side, let us look upon the subject from that point of view which to-day offers. No better, it is to be feared, than a high house-top. A high hill-top, or at least a cathedral spire, would be desirable.

It is not surprising that it should be the Anti-Slavery party that pleads for woman, when we consider merely that she does not hold property on equal terms with men; so that, if a husband dies without a will, the wife, instead of stepping at once into his place as head of the family, inherits only a part of his fortune, as if she were a child, or ward only, not an equal partner.

We will not speak of the innumerable instances, in which profligate or idle men live upon the earnings of industrious wives; or if the wives leave them and take with them the children, to perform the double duty of mother and father, follow from place to place, and threaten to rob them of the children, if deprived of the rights of a husband, as they call them, planting themselves in their poor lodgings, frightening them into paying tribute by taking from them the children, running into debt at the expense of these otherwise so overtasked helots. Though such instances abound, the public opinion of his own sex is against the man, and when cases of extreme tyranny are made known, there is private action in the wife's favor. But if woman be, indeed, the weaker party, she ought to have legal protection, which would make such oppression impossible.

And knowing that there exists, in the world of men, a

tone of feeling towards women as towards slaves, such as is expressed in the common phrase, " Tell that to women and children ;" that the infinite soul can only work through them in already ascertained limits ; that the prerogative of reason, man's highest portion, is allotted to them in a much lower degree ; that it is better for them to be engaged in active labor, which is to be furnished and directed by those better able to think, &c. &c.; we need not go further, for who can review the experience of last week, without recalling words which imply, whether in jest or earnest, these views, and views like these ? Knowing this, can we wonder that many reformers think that measures are not likely to be taken in behalf of women, unless their wishes could be publicly represented by women?

That can never be necessary, cry the other side. All men are privately influenced by women ; each has his wife, sister, or female friends, and is too much biassed by these relations to fail of representing their interests. And if this is not enough, let them propose and enforce their wishes with the pen. The beauty of home would be destroyed, the delicacy of the sex be violated, the dignity of halls of legislation destroyed, by an attempt to introduce them there. Such duties are inconsistent with those of a mother ; and then we have ludicrous pictures of ladies in hysterics at the polls, and senate chambers filled with cradles.

But if, in reply, we admit as truth that woman seems destined by nature rather to the inner circle, we must add that the arrangements of civilized life have not been as yet such as to secure it to her. Her circle, if the duller, is not the quieter. If kept from excitement, she is not from drudgery. Not only the Indian carries the burdens of the camp, but the favorites of Louis the Fourteenth accompany him in his journeys, and the washerwoman stands at her tub and carries home her work at all seasons, and in all states of health.

As to the use of the pen, there was quite as much opposition to woman's possessing herself of that help to free-agency as there is now to her seizing on the rostrum or the desk ; and she is likely to draw, from a permission to plead her cause that way, opposite inferences to what might be wished by those who now grant it.

As to the possibility of her filling, with grace and dignity,

any such position, we should think those who had seen the
great actresses, and heard the Quaker preachers of modern
times, would not doubt, that woman can express publicly
the fulness of thought and emotion, without losing any of
the peculiar beauty of her sex.

As to her home, she is not likely to leave it more than
she now does for balls, theatres, meetings for promoting
missions, revival meetings, and others to which she flies, in
hope of an animation for her existence, commensurate with
what she sees enjoyed by men. Governors of Ladies'
Fairs are no less engrossed by such a charge, than the
Governor of the State by his; presidents of Washingtonian
societies, no less away from home than presidents of conventions. If men look straitly to it, they will find that,
unless their own lives are domestic, those of the women
will not be. The female Greek, of our day, is as much in
the street as the male, to cry, What news? We doubt not
it was the same in Athens of old. The women, shut out
from the market-place, made up for it at the religious fes-
tivals. For human beings are not so constituted, that they
can live without expansion; and if they do not get it one
way, must another, or perish.

And, as to men's representing women fairly, at present,
while we hear from men who owe to their wives not only
all that is comfortable and graceful, but all that is wise in
the arrangement of their lives, the frequent remark, " You
cannot reason with a woman," when from those of delicacy, nobleness, and poetic culture, the contemptuous
phrase, " Women and children," and that in no light sally
of the hour, but in works intended to give a permanent
statement of the best experiences, when not one man in
the million, shall I say, no, not in the hundred million, can
rise above the view that woman was made *for man,* when
such traits as these are daily forced upon the attention, can
we feel that man will always do justice to the interests of
woman? Can we think that he takes a sufficiently discerning and religious view of her office and destiny, ever
to do her justice, except when prompted by sentiment;
accidentally or transiently, that is, for his sentiment will
vary according to the relations in which he is placed. The
lover, the poet, the artist, are likely to view her nobly. The
father and the philosopher have some chance of lib-

erality; the man of the world, the legislator for expediency, none.

Under these circumstances, without attaching importance in themselves to the changes demanded by the champions of woman, we hail them as signs of the times. We would have every arbitrary barrier thrown down. We would have every path laid open to woman as freely as to man. Were this done, and a slight temporary fermentation allowed to subside, we believe that the Divine would ascend into nature to a height unknown in the history of past ages, and nature, thus instructed, would regulate the spheres not only so as to avoid collision, but to bring forth ravishing harmony.

Yet then, and only then, will human beings be ripe for this, when inward and outward freedom for woman, as much as for man, shall be acknowledged as a right, not yielded as a concession. As the friend of the negro assumes that one man cannot, by right, hold another in bondage, so should the friend of woman assume that man cannot, by right, lay even well-meant restrictions on woman. If the negro be a soul, if the woman be a soul, apparelled in flesh, to one master only are they accountable. There is but one law for all souls, and, if there is to be an interpreter of it, he comes not as man, or son of man, but as Son of God.

Were thought and feeling once so far elevated that man should esteem himself the brother and friend, but nowise the lord and tutor of woman, were he really bound with her in equal worship, arrangements as to function and employment would be of no consequence. What woman needs is not as a woman to act or rúle, but as a nature to grow, as an intellect to discern, as a soul to live freely, and unimpeded to unfold such powers as were given her when we left our common home. If fewer talents were given her, yet, if allowed the free and full employment of these, so that she may render back to the giver his own with usury, she will not complain, nay, I dare to say she will bless and rejoice in her earthly birth-place, her earthly lot.

Let us consider what obstructions impede this good era, and what signs give reason to hope that it draws near.

I was talking on this subject with Miranda, a woman, who, if any in the world, might speak without heat or bit-

terness of the position of her sex. Her father was a man
who cherished no sentimental reverence for woman, but a
firm belief in the equality of the sexes. She was his eldest
child, and came to him at an age when he needed a companion. From the time she could speak and go alone, he
addressed her not as a plaything, but as a living mind.
Among the few verses he ever wrote were a copy addressed to this child, when the first locks were cut from her
head, and the reverence expressed on this occasion for that
cherished head he never belied. It was to him the temple
of immortal intellect. He respected his child, however, too
much to be an indulgent parent. He called on her for
clear judgment, for courage, for honor and fidelity, in short
for such virtues as he knew. In so far as he possessed the
keys to the wonders of this universe, he allowed free use
of them to her, and by the incentive of a high expectation
he forbade, as far as possible, that she should let the privilege lie idle.

   Thus this child was early led to feel herself a child of
the spirit. She took her place easily, not only in the
world of organized being, but in the world of mind. A
dignified sense of self-dependence was given as all her portion, and she found it a sure anchor. Herself securely an-
chored, her relations with others were established with
equal security. She was fortunate, in a total absence of
those charms which might have drawn to her bewildering
flatteries, and of a strong electric nature, which repelled
those who did not belong to her, and attracted those who
did. With men and women her relations were noble ; affectionate without passion, intellectual without coldness.
The world was free to her, and she lived freely in it.
Outward adversity came, and inward conflict, but that faith
and self-respect had early been awakened, which must always lead at last to an outward serenity, and an inward
peace.

   Of Miranda I had always thought as an example, that
the restraints upon the sex were insuperable only to those
who think them so, or who noisily strive to break them.
She had taken a course of her own, and no man stood in
her way. Many of her acts had been unusual, but excited
no uproar. Few helped, but none checked her ; and the
many men, who knew her mind and her life, showed to her

confidence as to a brother, gentleness as to a sister. And not only refined, but very coarse men approved one in whom they saw resolution and clearness of design. Her mind was often the leading one, always effective.

When I talked with her upon these matters, and had said very much what I have written, she smilingly replied, And yet we must admit that I have been fortunate, and this should not be. My good father's early trust gave the first bias, and the rest followed of course. It is true that I have had less outward aid, in after years, than most women, but that is of little consequence. Religion was early awakened in my soul, a sense that what the soul is capable to ask it must attain, and that, though I might be aided by others, I must depend on myself as the only constant friend. This self-dependence, which was honored in me, is deprecated as a fault in most women. They are taught to learn their rule from without, not to unfold it from within.

This is the fault of man, who is still vain, and wishes to be more important to woman than by right he should be.

Men have not shown this disposition towards you, I said.

No, because the position I early was enabled to take, was one of self-reliance. And were all women as sure of their wants as I was, the result would be the same. The difficulty is to get them to the point where they shall naturally develop relf-respect, the question how it is to be done.

Once I thought that men would help on this state of things more than I do now. I saw so many of them wretched in the connections they had formed in weakness and vanity. They seemed so glad to esteem women whenever they could !

But early I perceived that men never, in any extreme of despair, wished to be women. Where they admired any woman they were inclined to speak of her as above her sex. Silently I observed this, and feared it argued a rooted skepticism, which for ages had been fastening on the heart, and which only an age of miracles could eradicate.

Ever I have been treated with great sincerity; and I look upon it as a most signal instance of this, that an intimate friend of the other sex said in a fervent moment, that I deserved in some star to be a man. Another used as highest praise, in speaking of a character in literature, the words "a manly woman."

It is well known that of every strong woman they say she has a masculine mind.

This by no means argues a willing want of generosity towards woman.   Man is as generous towards her, as he knows how to be.

Wherever she has herself arisen in national or private history, and nobly shone forth in any ideal of excellence, men have received her, not only willingly, but with triumph. Their encomiums indeed are always in some sense mortifying, they show too much surprise.

In every-day life the feelings of the many are stained with vanity.   Each wishes to be lord in a little world, to be superior at least over one; and he does not feel strong enough to retain a life-long ascendant over a strong nature. Only a Brutus would rejoice in a Portia.   Only Theseus could conquer before he wed the Amazonian Queen.   Hercules wished rather to rest from his labors with Dejanira, and received the poisoned robe, as a fit guerdon.   The tale should be interpreted to all those who seek repose with the weak.

But not only is man vain and fond of power, but the same want of development, which thus affects him morally in the intellect, prevents his discerning the destiny of woman.   The boy wants no woman, but only a girl to play ball with him, and mark his pocket handkerchief.

Thus in Schiller's Dignity of Woman, beautiful as the poem is, there is no "grave and perfect man," but only a great boy to be softened and restrained by the influence of girls.   Poets, the elder brothers of their race, have usually seen further; but what can you expect of every-day men, if Schiller was not more prophetic as to what women must be?   Even with Richter one foremost thought about a wife was that she would "cook him something good."

The sexes should not only correspond to and appreciate one another, but prophesy to one another.   In individual instances this happens.   Two persons love in one another the future good which they aid one another to unfold. This is very imperfectly done as yet in the general life. Man has gone but little way, now he is waiting to see whether woman can keep step with him, but instead of

calling out like a good brother; You can do it if you only
think so, or impersonally ; Any one can do what he tries to
do, he often discourages with school-boy brag ; Girls cant do
that, girls cant play ball. But let any one defy their taunts,
break through, and be brave and secure, they rend the air
with shouts.

No ! man is not willingly ungenerous. He wants faith
and love, because he is not yet himself an elevated
being. He cries with sneering skepticism ; Give us a sign.
But if the sign appears, his eyes glisten, and he offers not
merely approval, but homage.

The severe nation which taught that the happiness of
the race was forfeited through the fault of a woman, and
showed its thought of what sort of regard man owed her,
by making him accuse her on the first question to his God,
who gave her to the patriarch as a handmaid, and, by the
Mosaical law, bound her to allegiance like a serf, even they
greeted, with solemn rapture, all great and holy women as
heroines, prophetesses, nay judges in Israel ; and, if they
made Eve listen to the serpent, gave Mary to the Holy
Spirit.   In other nations it has been the same down to our
day.   To the woman, who could conquer, a triumph was
awarded.   And not only those whose strength was recommended to the heart by association with goodness and
beauty, but those who were bad, if they were steadfast and
strong, had their claims allowed. In any age a Semiramis,
an Elizabeth of England, a Catharine of Russia makes her
place good, whether in a large or small circle.

How has a little wit, a little genius, always been celebrated in a woman !   What an intellectual triumph was that
of the lonely Aspasia, and how heartily acknowledged !
She, indeed, met a Pericles.   But what annalist, the rudest
of men, the most plebeian of husbands, will spare from his
page one of the few anecdotes of Roman women? — Sap-
pho, Eloisa! The names are of thread-bare celebrity.
The man habitually most narrow towards women will be
flushed, as by the worst assault on Christianity, if you say
it has made no improvement in her condition.   Indeed,
those most opposed to new acts in her favor are jealous of
the reputation of those which have been done.

We will not speak of the enthusiasm excited by actresses, improvisatrici, female singers, for here mingles the
charm of beauty and grace, but female authors, even

learned women, if not insufferably ugly and slovenly, from the Italian professor's daughter, who taught behind the curtain, down to Mrs. Carter and Madame Dacier, are sure of an admiring audience, if they can once get a platform on which to stand.

But how to get this platform, or how to make it of reasonably easy access is the difficulty. Plants of great vigor will almost always struggle into blossom, despite impediments. But there should be encouragement, and a free, genial atmosphere for those of more timid sort, fair play for each in its own kind. Some are like the little, delicate flowers, which love to hide in the dripping mosses by the sides of mountain torrents, or in the shade of tall trees. But others require an open field, a rich and loosened soil, or they never show their proper hues.

It may be said man does not have his fair play either; his energies are repressed and distorted by the interposition of artificial obstacles. Aye, but he himself has put them there, they have grown out of his own imperfections. If there *is* a misfortune in woman's lot, it is in obstacles being interposed by men, which do *not* mark her state, and if they express her past ignorance, do not her present needs. As every man is of woman born, she has slow but sure means of redress, yet the sooner a general justness of thought makes smooth the path, the better.

Man is of woman born, and her face bends over him in infancy with an expression he can never quite forget. Eminent men have delighted to pay tribute to this image, and it is a hacknied observation, that most men of genius boast some remarkable development in the mother. The rudest tar brushes off a tear with his coat-sleeve at the hallowed name. The other day I met a decrepit old man of seventy, on a journey, who challenged the stage-company to guess where he was going. They guessed aright, "To see your mother." "Yes," said he, "she is ninety-two, but has good eye-sight still, they say. I've not seen her these forty years, and I thought I could not die in peace without." I should have liked his picture painted as a companion piece to that of a boisterous little boy, whom I saw attempt to declaim at a school exhibition.

"O that those lips had language! Life has passed
With me but roughly since I heard thee last."

He got but very little way before sudden tears shamed him from the stage.

Some gleams of the same expression which shone down upon his infancy, angelically pure and benign, visit man again with hopes of pure love, of a holy marriage. Or if not before, in the eyes of the mother of his child they again are seen, and dim fancies pass before his mind, that woman may not have been born for him alone, but have come from heaven, a commissioned soul, a messenger of truth and love.

In gleams, in dim fancies, this thought visits the mind of common men. It is soon obscured by the mists of sensuality, the dust of routine, and he thinks it was only some meteor or ignis fatuus that shone. But, as a Rosicrucian lamp, it burns unwearied, though condemned to the solitude of tombs. And, to its permanent life, as to every truth, each age has, in some form, borne witness. For the truths, which visit the minds of careless men only in fitful gleams, shine with radiant clearness into those of the poet, the priest, and the artist.

Whatever may have been the domestic manners of the ancient nations, the idea of woman was nobly manifested in their mythologies and poems, where she appeared as Sita in the Ramayana, a form of tender purity, in the Egyptian Isis, of divine wisdom never yet surpassed. In Egypt, too, the Sphynx, walking the earth with lion tread, looked out upon its marvels in the calm, inscrutable beauty of a virgin's face, and the Greek could only add wings to the great emblem. In Greece, Ceres and Proserpine, significantly termed "the great goddesses," were seen seated, side by side. They needed not to rise for any worshipper or any change ; they were prepared for all things, as those initiated to their mysteries knew. More obvious is the meaning of those three forms, the Diana, Minerva, and Vesta. Unlike in the expression of their beauty, but alike in this, — that each was self-sufficing. Other forms were only accessories and illustrations, none the complement to one like these. Another might indeed be the companion, and the Apollo and Diana set off one another's beauty. Of the Vesta, it is to be observed, that not only deep-eyed, deep-discerning Greece, but ruder Rome, who represents the only form of good man (the always busy warrior) that

could be indifferent to woman, confided the permanence
of its glory to a tutelary goddess, and her wisest legislator
spoke of Meditation as a nymph.

In Sparta, thought, in this respect as all others, was expressed in the characters of real life, and the women of
Sparta were as much Spartans as the men. The Citoyen,
Citoyenne, of France, was here actualized. Was not the
calm equality they enjoyed well worth the honors of chivalry? They intelligently shared the ideal life of their
nation.

Generally, we are told of these nations, that women occupied there a very subordinate position in actual life. It
is difficult to believe this, when we see such range and
dignity of thought on the subject in the mythologies, and
find the poets producing such ideals as Cassandra, Iphi-
genia, Antigone, Macaria, (though it is not unlike our own
day, that men should revere those heroines of their great
princely houses at theatres, from which their women were
excluded,) where Sibylline priestesses told the oracle of the
highest god, and he could not be content to reign with a
court of less than nine Muses. Even Victory wore a female form.

But whatever were the facts of daily life, I cannot complain of the age and nation, which represents its thought by
such a symbol as I see before me at this moment. It is a
zodiac of the busts of gods and goddesses, arranged in
pairs. The circle breathes the music of a heavenly order.
Male and female heads are distinct in expression, but equal
in beauty, strength, and calmness. Each male head is that
of a brother and a king, each female of a sister and a
queen. Could the thought, thus expressed, be lived out,
there would be nothing more to be desired. There would
be unison in variety, congeniality in difference.

Coming nearer our own time, we find religion and poetry
no less true in their revelations. The rude man, but just
disengaged from the sod, the Adam, accuses woman to his
God, and records her disgrace to their posterity. He is
not ashamed to write that he could be drawn from heaven
by one beneath him. But in the same nation, educated by
time, instructed by successive prophets, we find woman in
as high a position as she has ever occupied. And no figure,
that has ever arisen to greet our eyes, has been received

with more fervent reverence than that of the Madonna. Heine calls her the Dame du Comptoir of the Catholic Church, and this jeer well expresses a serious truth.

And not only this holy and significant image was worshipped by the pilgrim, and the favorite subject of the artist, but it exercised an immediate influence on the destiny of the sex. The empresses, who embraced the cross, converted sons and husbands. Whole calendars of female saints, heroic dames of chivalry, binding the emblem of faith on the heart of the best-beloved, and wasting the bloom of youth in separation and loneliness, for the sake of duties they thought it religion to assume, with innumerable forms of poesy, trace their lineage to this one. Nor, however imperfect may be the action, in our day, of the faith thus expressed, and though we can scarcely think it nearer this ideal than that of India or Greece was near their ideal, is it in vain that the truth has been recognised, that woman is not only a part of man, bone of his bone and flesh of his flesh, born that men might not be lonely, but in themselves possessors of and possessed by immortal souls. This truth undoubtedly received a greater outward stability from the belief of the church, that the earthly parent of the Saviour of souls was a woman.

The Assumption of the Virgin, as painted by sublime artists, Petrarch's Hymn to the Madonna, cannot have spoken to the world wholly without result, yet oftentimes those who had ears heard not.

Thus, the Idea of woman has not failed to be often and forcibly represented. So many instances throng on the mind, that we must stop here, lest the catalogue be swelled beyond the reader's patience.

Neither can she complain that she has not had her share of power. This, in all ranks of society, except the lowest, has been hers to the extent that vanity could crave, far beyond what wisdom would accept. In the very lowest, where man, pressed by poverty, sees in woman only the partner of toils and cares, and cannot hope, scarcely has an idea of a comfortable home, he maltreats her, often, and is less influenced by her. In all ranks, those who are amiable and uncomplaining, suffer much. They suffer long, and are kind; verily, they have their reward. But wherever man is sufficiently raised above extreme poverty, or

brutal stupidity, to care for the comforts of the fireside, or
the bloom and ornament of life, woman has always power
enough, if she choose to exert it, and is usually disposed to
do so in proportion to her ignorance and childish vanity.
Unacquainted with the importance of life and its purposes,
trained to a selfish coquetry and love of. petty power, she
does not look beyond the pleasure of making herself felt at
the moment, and governments are shaken and commerce
broken up to gratify the pique of a female favorite.   The
English shopkeeper's wife does not vote, but it is for her
interest that the politician canvasses by the coarsest flattery.
France suffers no woman on her throne, but her proud nobles kiss the dust at the feet of Pompadour and Dubarry,
for such flare in the lighted foreground where a Roland
would modestly aid in the closet.   Spain shuts up her
women in the care of duennas, and allows them no book
but the Breviary ; but the ruin follows only the more surely
from the worthless favorite of a worthless queen.

It is not the transient breath of poetic incense, that
women want ; each can receive that from a lover.   It is
not life-long sway ; it needs but to become a coquette, a
shrew, or a good cook, to be sure of that.   It is not money,
nor notoriety, nor the badges of authority, that men have
appropriated to themselves.   If demands made in their
behalf lay stress on any of these particulars, those who
make them have not searched deeply into the need. It is for
that which at once includes all these and precludes them ;
which would not be forbidden power, lest there be temptation to steal and misuse it ; which would not have the mind
perverted by flattery from a worthiness of esteem.   It is
for that which is the birthright of every being capable to
receive it, — the freedom, the religious, the intelligent freedom of the universe, to use its means, to learn its secret
as far as nature has enabled them, with God alone for their
guide and their judge.

Ye cannot believe it, men ; but the only reason why
women ever assume what is more appropriate to you, is
because you prevent them from finding out what is fit for
themselves.   Were they free, were they wise fully to develop the strength and beauty of woman, they would
never wish to be men, or manlike.   The well-instructed
moon flies not from her orbit to seize on the glories of her

partner. No; for she knows that one law rules, one heaven contains, one universe replies to them alike. It is with women as with the slave.

> "Vor dem Sklaven, wenn er die Kette bricht,
>   Vor dem freien Menschen erzittert nicht."

Tremble not before the free man, but before the slave who has chains to break.

In slavery, acknowledged slavery, women are on a par with men. Each is a work-tool, an article of property, — no more! In perfect freedom, such as is painted in Olympus, in Swedenborg's angelic state, in the heaven where there is no marrying nor giving in marriage, each is a purified intelligence, an enfranchised soul, — no less!

> Jene himmlische Gestalten
> Sie fragen nicht nach Mann und Weib,
>   Und keine Kleider, keine Falten
> Umgeben den verklärten Leib.

The child who sang this was a prophetic form, expressive of the longing for a state of perfect freedom, pure love. She could not remain here, but was transplanted to another air. And it may be that the air of this earth will never be so tempered, that such can bear it long. But, while they stay, they must bear testimony to the truth they are constituted to demand.

That an era approaches which shall approximate nearer to such a temper than any has yet done, there are many tokens, indeed so many that only a few of the most prominent can here be enumerated.

The reigns of Elizabeth of England and Isabella of Castile foreboded this era. They expressed the beginning of the new state, while they forwarded its progress. These were strong characters, and in harmony with the wants of their time. One showed that this strength did not unfit a woman for the duties of a wife and mother; the other, that it could enable her to live and die alone. Elizabeth is certainly no pleasing example. In rising above the weakness, she did not lay aside the weaknesses ascribed to her sex; but her strength must be respected now, as it was in her own time.

We may accept it as an omen for ourselves, that it was

Isabella who furnished Columbus with the means of coming hither. This land must pay back its debt to woman, without whose aid it would not have been brought into alliance with the civilized world.

The influence of Elizabeth on literature was real, though, by sympathy with its finer productions, she was no more entitled to give name to an era than Queen Anne. It was simply that the fact of having a female sovereign on the throne affected the course of a writer's thoughts. In this sense, the presence of a woman on the throne always makes its mark. Life is lived before the eyes of all men, and their imaginations are stimulated as to the possibilities of woman. "We will die for our King, Maria Theresa," cry the wild warriors, clashing their swords, and the sounds vibrate through the poems of that generation. The range of female character in Spenser alone might content us for one period. Britomart and Belphoebe have as much room in the canvass as Florimel; and where this is the case, the haughtiest Amazon will not murmur that Una should be felt to be the highest type.

Unlike as was the English Queen to a fairy queen, we may yet conceive that it was the image of *a* queen before the poet's mind, that called up this splendid court of women.

Shakspeare's range is also great, but he has left out the heroic characters, such as the Macaria of Greece, the Britomart of Spenser. Ford and Massinger have, in this respect, shown a higher flight of feeling than he. It was the holy and heroic woman they most loved, and if they could not paint an Imogen, a Desdemona, a Rosalind, yet in those of a stronger mould, they showed a higher ideal, though with so much less poetic power to represent it, than we see in Portia or Isabella. The simple truth of Cordelia, indeed, is of this sort. The beauty of Cordelia is neither male nor female; it is the beauty of virtue.

The ideal of love and marriage rose high in the mind of all the Christian nations who were capable of grave and deep feeling. We may take as examples of its English aspect, the lines,

> "I could not love thee, dear, so much,
> Loved I not honor more."

The address of the Commonwealth's man to his wife as
she looked out from the Tower window to see him for the
last time on his way to execution. "He stood up in the
cart, waved his hat, and cried, 'To Heaven, my love, to
Heaven! and leave you in the storm!'"

Such was the love of faith and honor, a love which
stopped, like Colonel Hutchinson's, "on this side idolatry,"
because it was religious. The meeting of two such souls
Donne describes as giving birth to an "abler soul."

Lord Herbert wrote to his love,

> "Were not our souls immortal made,
>   Our equal loves can make them such."

In Spain the same thought is arrayed in a sublimity,
which belongs to the sombre and passionate genius of the
nation. Calderon's Justina resists all the temptation of the
Demon, and raises her lover with her above the sweet lures
of mere temporal happiness. Their marriage is vowed at
the stake, their souls are liberated together by the martyr
flame into "a purer state of sensation and existence."

In Italy, the great poets wove into their lives an ideal
love which answered to the highest wants. It included
those of the intellect and the affections, for it was a love of
spirit for spirit. It was not ascetic and superhuman, but
interpreting all things, gave their proper beauty to details
of the common life, the common day; the poet spoke of
his love not as a flower to place in his bosom, or hold carelessly in his hand, but as a light towards which he must
find wings to fly, or "a stair to heaven." He delighted
to speak of her not only as the bride of his heart, but the
mother of his soul, for he saw that, in cases where the right
direction has been taken, the greater delicacy of her frame,
and stillness of her life, left her more open to spiritual in-
flux than man is. So he did not look upon her as betwixt
him and earth, to serve his temporal needs, but rather betwixt him and heaven, to purify his affections and lead him
to wisdom through her pure love. He sought in her not so
much the Eve as the Madonna.

In these minds the thought, which glitters in all the le-
gends of chivalry, shines in broad intellectual effulgence,
not to be misinterpreted. And their thought is reverenced
by the world, though it lies so far from them as yet, so far,
that it seems as though a gulf of Death lay between.

Even with such men the practice was often widely different from the mental faith. I say mental, for if the heart were thoroughly alive with it, the practice could not be dissonant. Lord Herbert's was a marriage of convention, made for him at fifteen; he was not discontented with it, but looked only to the advantages it brought of perpetuating his family on the basis of a great fortune. He paid, in act, what he considered a dutiful attention to the bond; his thoughts travelled elsewhere, and, while forming a high ideal of the companionship of minds in marriage, he seems never to have doubted that its realization must be postponed to some other stage of being. Dante, almost immediately after the death of Beatrice, married a lady chosen for him by his friends.

Centuries have passed since, but civilized Europe is still in a transition state about marriage, not only in practice, but in thought. A great majority of societies and individuals are still doubtful whether earthly marriage is to be a union of souls, or merely a contract of convenience and utility. Were woman established in the rights of an immortal being, this could not be. She would not in some countries be given away by her father, with scarcely more respect for her own feelings than is shown by the Indian chief, who sells his daughter for a horse, and beats her if she runs away from her new home. Nor, in societies where her choice is left free, would she be perverted, by the current of opinion that seizes her, into the belief that she must marry, if it be only to find a protector, and a home of her own.

Neither would man, if he thought that the connection was of permanent importance, enter upon it so lightly. He would not deem it a trifle, that he was to enter into the closest relations with another soul, which, if not eternal in themselves, must eternally affect his growth.

Neither, did he believe woman capable of friendship, would he, by rash haste, lose the chance of finding a friend in the person who might, probably, live half a century by his side. Did love to his mind partake of infinity, he would not miss his chance of its revelations, that he might the sooner rest from his weariness by a bright fireside, and have a sweet and graceful attendant, "devoted to him alone." Were he a step higher, he would not carelessly enter into a relation, where he might not be able to do the duty of a friend, as well as a protector from external ill, to the other party, and have a being in his power pining for sympathy, intelligence, and aid, that he could not give.

Where the thought of equality has become pervasive, it shows itself in four kinds.

The household partnership. In our country the woman looks for a "smart but kind" husband, the man for a "capable, sweet-tempered" wife.

The man furnishes the house, the woman regulates it. Their relation is one of mutual esteem, mutual dependence. Their talk is of business, their affection shows itself by practical kindness. They know that life goes more smoothly and cheerfully to each for the other's aid; they are grateful and content. The wife praises her husband as a "good provider," the husband in return compliments her as a "capital housekeeper." This relation is good as far as it goes.

Next comes a closer tie which takes the two forms, either of intellectual companionship, or mutual idolatry. The last, we suppose, is to no one a pleasing subject of contemplation. The parties weaken and narrow one another; they lock the gate against all the glories of the universe that they may live in a cell together. To themselves they seem the only wise, to all others steeped in infatuation, the gods smile as they look forward to the crisis of cure, to men the woman seems an unlovely syren, to women the man an effeminate boy.

The other form, of intellectual companionship, has become more and more frequent. Men engaged in public life, literary men, and artists have often found in their wives companions and confidants in thought no less than in feeling. And, as in the course of things the intellectual development of woman has spread wider and risen higher, they have, not unfrequently, shared the same employment. As in the case of Roland and his wife, who were friends in the household and the nation's councils, read together, regulated home affairs, or prepared public documents together indifferently.

It is very pleasant, in letters begun by Roland and finished by his wife, to see the harmony of mind and the difference of nature, one thought, but various ways of treating it.

This is one of the best instances of a marriage of friendship. It was only friendship, whose basis was esteem;
probably neither party knew love, except by name.

Roland was a good man, worthy to esteem and be esteemed, his wife as deserving of admiration as able to do
without it. Madame Roland is the fairest specimen we
have yet of her class, as clear to discern her aim, as val-
iant to pursue it, as Spenser's Britomart, austerely set
apart from all that did not belong to her, whether as woman or as mind. She is an antetype of a class to which
the coming time will afford a field, the Spartan matron,
brought by the culture of a book-furnishing age to intellectual consciousness and expansion.

Self-sufficing strength and clear-sightedness were in her
combined with a power of deep and calm affection. The
page of her life is one of unsullied dignity.

Her appeal to posterity is one against the injustice of
those who committed such crimes in the name of liberty.
She makes it in behalf of herself and her husband. I
would put beside it on the shelf a little volume, containing a similar appeal from the verdict of contemporaries
to that of mankind, that of Godwin in behalf of his wife,
the celebrated, the by most men detested Mary Wolstonecraft. In his view it was an appeal from the injustice of
those who did such wrong in the name of virtue.

Were this little book interesting for no other cause, it
would be so for the generous affection evinced under the
peculiar circumstances. This man had courage to love and
honor this woman in the face of the world's verdict, and of
all that was repulsive in her own past history. He believed
he saw of what soul she was, and that the thoughts she
had struggled to act out were noble. He loved her and
he defended her for the meaning and tendency of her inner
life. It was a good fact.

Mary Wolstonecraft, like Madame Dudevant (commonly
known as George Sand) in our day, was a woman whose existence better proved the need of some new interpretation of
woman's rights, than anything she wrote. Such women as
these, rich in genius, of most tender sympathies, and capable of high virtue and a chastened harmony, ought not to
find themselves by birth in a place so narrow, that in breaking bonds they become outlaws. Were there as much

room in the world for such, as in Spenser's poem for Britomart, they would not run their heads so wildly against its
laws.   They find their way at last to purer air, but the
world will not take off the brand it has set upon them.
The champion of the rights of woman found in Godwin
one who plead her own cause like a brother.   George
Sand smokes, wears male attire, wishes to be addressed as
Mon frère ; perhaps, if she found those who were as brothers
indeed, she would not care whether she were brother or
sister.

We rejoice to see that she, who expresses such a painful
contempt for men in most of her works, as shows she must
have known great wrong from them, in La Roche Mauprat,
depicting one raised, by the workings of love, from the
depths of savage sensualism to a moral and intellectual life.
It was love for a pure object, for a steadfast woman, one of
those who, the Italian said, could make the stair to heaven.

Women like Sand will speak now, and cannot be silenced ;
their characters and their eloquence alike foretell an era
when such as they shall easier learn to lead true lives
But though such forebode, not such shall be the parents of
it.   Those who would reform the world must show that
they do not speak in the heat of wild impulse ; their lives
must be unstained by passionate error ; they must be severe
lawgivers to themselves.   As to their transgressions and
opinions, it may be observed, that the resolve of Eloisa to
be only the mistress of Abelard, was that of one who saw
the contract of marriage a seal of degradation.   Wherever
abuses of this sort are seen, the timid will suffer, the bold
protest.   But society is in the right to outlaw them till she
has revised her law, and she must be taught to do so, by
one who speaks with authority, not in anger and haste.

If Godwin's choice of the calumniated authoress of the
"Rights of Woman," for his honored wife, be a sign of
a new era, no less so is an article of great learning and
eloquence, published several years since in an English review, where the writer, in doing full justice to Eloisa, shows
his bitter regret that she lives not now to love him, who
might have known better how to prize her love than did
the egotistical Abelard.

These marriages, these characters, with all their imperfections, express an onward tendency.   They speak of aspi-

ration of soul, of energy of mind, seeking clearness and
freedom.   Of a like promise are the tracts now publishing
by Goodwyn Barmby (the European Pariah as he calls himself) and his wife Catharine.   Whatever we may think of
their measures, we see in them wedlock, the two minds are
wed by the only contract that can permanently avail, of a
common faith, and a common purpose.

We might mention instances, nearer home, of minds,
partners in work and in life, sharing together, on equal
terms, public and private interests, and which have not on
any side that aspect of offence which characterizes the attitude of the last named ; persons who steer straight onward,
and in our freer life have not been obliged to run their
heads against any wall.   But the principles which guide
them might, under petrified or oppressive institutions, have
made them warlike, paradoxical, or, in some sense, Pariahs.
The phenomenon is different, the law the same, in all these
cases.   Men and women have been obliged to build their
house from the very foundation.   If they found stone ready
in the quarry, they took it peaceably, otherwise they alarmed
the country by pulling down old towers to get materials.

These are all instances of marriage as intellectual companionship.   The parties meet mind to mind, and a
mutual trust is excited which can buckler them against a
million.   They work together for a common purpose, and,
in all these instances, with the same implement, the pen.

A pleasing expression in this kind is afforded by the
union in the names of the Howitts.   William and Mary
Howitt we heard named together for years, supposing them
to be brother and sister ; the equality of labors and reputation, even so, was auspicious, more so, now we find them man
and wife.   In his late work on Germany, Howitt mentions
his wife with pride, as one among the constellation of distinguished English women, and in a graceful, simple manner.

In naming these instances we do not mean to imply that
community of employment is an essential to union of this
sort, more than to the union of friendship.   Harmony exists in difference no less than in likeness, if only the same
key-note govern both parts.   Woman the poem, man the
poet ; woman the heart, man the head ; such divisions are
only important when they are never to be transcended.   If

nature is never bound down, nor the voice of inspiration stifled, that is enough. We are pleased that women should write and speak, if they feel the need of it, from having something to tell; but silence for a hundred years would be as well, if that silence be from divine command, and not from man's tradition.

While Goetz von Berlichingen rides to battle, his wife is busy in the kitchen; but difference of occupation does not prevent that community of life, that perfect esteem, with which he says,

"Whom God loves, to him gives he such a wife!"

Manzoni thus dedicates his Adelchi.

"To his beloved and venerated wife, Enrichetta Luigia Blondel, who, with conjugal affections and maternal wisdom, has preserved a virgin mind, the author dedicates this Adelchi, grieving that he could not, by a more splendid and more durable monument, honor the dear name and the memory of so many virtues."

The relation could not be fairer, nor more equal, if she too had written poems. Yet the position of the parties might have been the reverse as well; the woman might have sung the deeds, given voice to the life of the man, and beauty would have been the result, as we see in pictures of Arcadia the nymph singing to the shepherds, or the shepherd with his pipe allures the nymphs, either makes a good picture. The sounding lyre requires not muscular strength, but energy of soul to animate the hand which can control it. Nature seems to delight in varying her arrangements, as if to show that she will be fettered by no rule, and we must admit the same varieties that she admits.

I have not spoken of the higher grade of marriage union, the religious, which may be expressed as pilgrimage towards a common shrine. This includes the others; home sympathies, and household wisdom, for these pilgrims must know how to assist one another to carry their burdens along the dusty way; intellectual communion, for how sad it would be on such a journey to have a companion to whom you could not communicate thoughts and aspirations, as they sprang to life, who would have no feeling for the more and more glorious prospects that open as we advance, who would never see the flowers that may be gathered by the most industrious traveller. It must include all these. Such a fellow pilgrim Count Zinzendorf seems to have found in his countess of whom he thus writes.

"Twenty-five years' experience has shown me that just the help-mate whom I have is the only one that could suit my vocation. Who else could have so carried through my family affairs? Who lived so spotlessly before the world? Who so wisely aided me in my rejection of a dry morality? Who so clearly set aside the Pharisaism which, as years passed, threatened to creep in among us? Who so deeply discerned as to the spirits of delusion which sought to bewilder us? Who would have governed my whole economy so wisely, richly, and hospitably when circumstances commanded? Who have taken indifferently the part of servant or mistress, without on the one side affecting an especial spirituality, on the other being sullied by any worldly pride? Who, in a community where all ranks are eager to be on a level, would, from wise and real causes, have known how to maintain inward and outward distinctions? Who, without a murmur, have seen her husband encounter such dangers by land and sea? Who undertaken with him and sustained such astonishing pilgrimages? Who amid such difficulties always held up her head, and supported me? Who found so many hundred thousands and acquitted them on her own credit? And, finally, who, of all human beings, would so well understand and interpret to others my inner and outer being as this one, of such nobleness in her way of thinking, such great intellectual capacity, and free from the theological perplexities that enveloped me?"

An observer* adds this testimony.

"We may in many marriages regard it as the best arrangement, if the man has so much advantage over his wife that she can, without much thought of her own, be, by him, led and directed, as by a father. But it was not so with the Count and his consort. She was not made to be a copy; she was an original; and, while she loved and honored him, she thought for herself on all subjects with so much intelligence, that he could and did look on her as sister and friend also."

Such a woman is the sister and friend of all beings, as the worthy man is their brother and helper.

Another sign of the time is furnished by the triumphs of female authorship. These have been great and constantly

---

* Spangenberg.

increasing. They have taken possession of so many prov-
inces for which men had pronounced them unfit, that
though these still declare there are some inaccessible to
them, it is difficult to say just *where* they must stop.

The shining names of famous women have cast light
upon the path of the sex, and many obstructions have been
removed. When a Montague could learn better than her
brother, and use her lore to such purpose afterwards as an
observer, it seemed amiss to hinder women from preparing
themselves to see, or from seeing all they could when prepared. Since Somerville has achieved so much, will any
young girl be prevented from attaining a knowledge of the
physical sciences, if she wishes it ? De Staël's name was
not so clear of offence ; she could not forget the woman in
the thought ; while she was instructing you as a mind, she
wished to be admired as a woman ; sentimental tears often
dimmed the eagle glance. Her intellect, too, with all its
splendor, trained in a drawing room, fed on flattery, was
tainted and flawed ; yet its beams make the obscurest school
house in New England warmer and lighter to the little
rugged girls, who are gathered together on its wooden
bench. They may never through life hear her name, but
she is not the less their benefactress.

This influence has been such that the aim certainly is,
how, in arranging school instruction for girls, to give them
as fair a field as boys. These arrangements are made as
yet with little judgment or intelligence, just as the tutors
of Jane Grey, and the other famous women of her time,
taught them Latin and Greek, because they knew nothing
else themselves, so now the improvement in the education
of girls is made by giving them gentlemen as teachers, who
only teach what has been taught themselves at college,
while methods and topics need revision for those new cases,
which could better be made by those who had experienced
the same wants. Women are often at the head of these
institutions, but they have as yet seldom been thinking
women, capable to organize a new whole for the wants of
the time, and choose persons to officiate in the departments.
And when some portion of education is got of a good sort
from the school, the tone of society, the much larger proportion received from the world, contradicts its purport.
Yet books have not been furnished, and a little elementary

instruction been given in vain. Women are better aware how large and rich the universe is, not so easily blinded by the narrowness and partial views of a home circle.

Whether much or little has or will be done, whether women will add to the talent of narration, the power of systematizing, whether they will carve marble as well as draw, is not important. But that it should be acknowledged that they have intellect which needs developing, that they should not be considered complete, if beings of affection and habit alone, is important.

Yet even this acknowledgment, rather obtained by woman than proffered by man, has been sullied by the usual selfishness. So much is said of women being better educated that they may be better companions and mothers *of men!* They should be fit for such companionship, and we have mentioned with satisfaction instances where it has been established. Earth knows no fairer, holier relation than that of a mother. But a being of infinite scope must not be treated with an exclusive view to any one relation. Give the soul free course, let the organization be freely developed, and the being will be fit for any and every relation to which it may be called. The intellect, no more than the sense of hearing, is to be cultivated, that she may be a more valuable companion to man, but because the Power who gave a power by its mere existence signifies that it must be brought out towards perfection.

In this regard, of self-dependence and a greater simplicity and fulness of being, we must hail as a preliminary the increase of the class contemptuously designated as old maids.

We cannot wonder at the aversion with which old bachelors and old maids have been regarded. Marriage is the natural means of forming a sphere, of taking root on the earth: it requires more strength to do this without such an opening, very many have failed of this, and their imperfections have been in every one's way. They have been more partial, more harsh, more officious and impertinent than others. Those, who have a complete experience of the human instincts, have a distrust as to whether they can be thoroughly human and humane, such as is hinted at in the saying, "Old maids' and bachelors' children are well cared for," which derides at once their ignorance and their presumption.

Yet the business of society has become so complex, that
it could now scarcely be carried on without the presence of
these despised auxiliaries, and detachments from the army
of aunts and uncles are wanted to stop gaps in every
hedge.   They rove about, mental and moral Ishmaelites,
pitching their tents amid the fixed and ornamented habita-
tions of men.

They thus gain a wider, if not so deep, experience. They
are not so intimate with others, but thrown more upon
themselves, and if they do not there find peace and incessant life, there is none to flatter them that they are not very
poor and very mean.

A position, which so constantly admonishes, may be of
inestimable benefit.   The person may gain, undistracted
by other relationships, a closer communion with the One.
Such a use is made of it by saints and sibyls.   Or she may
be one of the lay sisters of charity, or more humbly only
the useful drudge of all men, or the intellectual interpreter
of the varied life she sees.

Or she may combine all these.   Not "needing to
care that she may please a husband," a frail and limited
being, all her thoughts may turn to the centre, and by
steadfast contemplation enter into the secret of truth and
love, use it for the use of all men, instead of a chosen few,
and interpret through it all the forms of life.

Saints and geniuses have often chosen a lonely position,
in the faith that, if undisturbed by the pressure of near ties
they could give themselves up to the inspiring spirit, it
would enable them to understand and reproduce life better
than actual experience could.

How many old maids take this high stand, we cannot
say ; it is an unhappy fact that too many of those who
come before the eye are gossips rather, and not always
good-natured gossips.   But, if these abuse, and none make
the best of their vocation, yet, it has not failed to produce
some good fruit.   It has been seen by others, if not by
themselves, that beings likely to be left alone need to be
fortified and furnished within themselves, and education
and thought have tended more and more to regard beings
as related to absolute Being, as well as to other men.   It
has been seen that as the loss of no bond ought to destroy
a human being, so ought the missing of none to hinder

him from growing. And thus a circumstance of the time
has helped to put woman on the true platform. Perhaps
the next generation will look deeper into this matter, and
find that contempt is put on old maids, or old women at all,
merely because they do not use the elixir which will keep
the soul always young. No one thinks of Michael Ange-
lo's Persican Sibyl, or St. Theresa, or Tasso's Leonora, or
the Greek Electra as an old maid, though all had reached
the period in life's course appointed to take that degree.

Even among the North American Indians, a race of men
as completely engaged in mere instinctive life as almost any
in the world, and where each chief, keeping many wives as
useful servants, of course looks with no kind eye on celibacy in woman, it was excused in the following instance
mentioned by Mrs. Jameson. A woman dreamt in youth
that she was betrothed to the sun. She built her a wig-
wam apart, filled it with emblems of her alliance and means
of an independent life. There she passed her days, sustained by her own exertions, and true to her supposed engagement.

In any tribe, we believe, a woman, who lived as if she
was betrothed to the sun, would be tolerated, and the rays
which made her youth blossom sweetly would crown her
with a halo in age.

There is on this subject a nobler view than heretofore, if
not the noblest, and we greet improvement here, as much
as on the subject of marriage. Both are fertile themes,
but time permits not here to explore them.

If larger intellectual resources begin to be deemed necessary to woman, still more is a spiritual dignity in her, or
even the mere assumption of it listened to with respect.
Joanna Southcote, and Mother Anne Lee are sure of a
band of disciples; Ecstatica, Dolorosa, of enraptured believers who will visit them in their lowly huts, and wait for
hours to revere them in their trances. The foreign noble
traverses land and sea to hear a few words from the lips of
the lowly peasant girl, whom he believes especially visited
by the Most High. Very beautiful in this way was the
influence of the invalid of St. Petersburg, as described by
De Maistre.

To this region, however misunderstood, and ill-develop-
ed, belong the phenomena of Magnetism, or Mesmerism,

as it is now often called, where the trance of the Ecstatica purports to be produced by the agency of one human being on another, instead of, as in her case, direct from the spirit.

The worldling has his sneer here as about the services of religion. "The churches can always be filled with women." "Show me a man in one of your magnetic states, and I will believe."

Women are indeed the easy victims of priestcraft, or self-delusion, but this might not be, if the intellect was developed in proportion to the other powers. They would then have a regulator and be in better equipoise, yet must retain the same nervous susceptibility, while their physical structure is such as it is.

It is with just that hope, that we welcome everything that tends to strengthen the fibre and develop the nature on more sides. When the intellect and affections are in harmony, when intellectual consciousness is calm and deep, inspiration will not be confounded with fancy.

The electrical, the magnetic element in woman has not been fairly developed at any period. Everything might be expected from it; she has far more of it than man. This is commonly expressed by saying, that her intuitions are more rapid and more correct.

But I cannot enlarge upon this here, except to say that on this side is highest promise. Should I speak of it fully, my title should be Cassandra, my topic the Seeress of Prevorst, the first, or the best observed subject of magnetism in our times, and who, like her ancestresses at Delphos, was roused to ecstasy or phrenzy by the touch of the laurel.

In such cases worldlings sneer, but reverent men learn wondrous news, either from the person observed, or by the thoughts caused in themselves by the observation. Fenelon learns from Guyon, Kerner from his Seeress what we fain would know. But to appreciate such disclosures one must be a child, and here the phrase, "women and children," may perhaps be interpreted aright, that only little children shall enter into the kingdom of heaven.

All these motions of the time, tides that betoken a waxing moon, overflow upon our own land. The world at large is readier to let woman learn and manifest the capacities of her nature than it ever was before, and here is a less encumbered field, and freer air than anywhere else.

And it ought to be so; we ought to pay for Isabella's jewels.

The names of nations are feminine. Religion, Virtue, and Victory are feminine. To those who have a superstition as to outward signs, it is not without significance that the name of the Queen of our mother-land should at this crisis be Victoria. Victoria the First. Perhaps to us it may be given to disclose the era there outwardly presaged.

Women here are much better situated than men. Good books are allowed with more time to read them. They are not so early forced into the bustle of life, nor so weighed down by demands for outward success. The perpetual changes, incident to our society, make the blood circulate freely through the body politic, and, if not favorable at present to the grace and bloom of life, they are so to activity, resource, and would be to reflection but for a low materialist tendency, from which the women are generally exempt.

They have time to think, and no traditions chain them, and few conventionalities compared with what must be met in other nations. There is no reason why the fact of a constant revelation should be hid from them, and when the mind once is awakened by that, it will not be restrained by the past, but fly to seek the seeds of a heavenly future.

Their employments are more favorable to the inward life than those of the men.

Woman is not addressed religiously here, more than elsewhere. She is told to be worthy to be the mother of a Washington, or the companion of some good man. But in many, many instances, she has already learnt that all bribes have the same flaw; that truth and good are to be sought for themselves alone. And already an ideal sweetness floats over many forms, shines in many eyes.

Already deep questions are put by young girls on the great theme, What shall I do to inherit eternal life?

Men are very courteous to them. They praise them often, check them seldom. There is some chivalry in the feeling towards "the ladies," which gives them the best seats in the stage-coach, frequent admission not only to lectures of all sorts, but to courts of justice, halls of legislature, reform conventions. The newspaper editor " would be better pleased that the Lady's Book were filled up ex-

clusively by ladies. It would then, indeed, be a true gem,
worthy to be presented by young men to the mistresses of
their affections." Can gallantry go farther?

In this country is venerated, wherever seen, the character which Goethe spoke of as an Ideal. "The excellent
woman is she, who, if the husband dies, can be a father to
the children." And this, if rightly read, tells a great deal.

Women who speak in public, if they have a moral power, such as has been felt from Angelina Grimke and Abby
Kelly, that is, if they speak for conscience' sake, to serve a
cause which they hold sacred, invariably subdue the prejudices of their hearers, and excite an interest proportion-
ate to the aversion with which it had been the purpose to
regard them.

A passage in a private letter so happily illustrates this,
that I take the liberty to make use of it, though there is
not opportunity to ask leave either of the writer or owner
of the letter. I think they will pardon me when they see
it in print; it is so good, that as many as possible should
have the benefit of it.

Abby Kelly in the Town-House of ———

"The scene was not unheroic, — to see that woman, true to
humanity and her own nature, a centre of rude eyes and tongues,
even gentlemen feeling licensed to make part of a species of
mob around a female out of her sphere. As she took her seat
in the desk amid the great noise, and in the throng full, like a
wave, of something to ensue, I saw her humanity in a gentleness and unpretension, tenderly open to the sphere around her,
and, had she not been supported by the power of the will of
genuineness and principle, she would have failed. It led her
to prayer, which, in woman especially, is childlike; sensibility
and will going to the side of God and looking up to him; and
humanity was poured out in aspiration.

"She acted like a gentle hero, with her mild decision and
womanly calmness. All heroism is mild and quiet and gentle,
for it is life and possession, and combativeness and firmness
show a want of actualness. She is as earnest, fresh, and simple as when she first entered the crusade. I think she did much
good, more than the men in her place could do, for woman feels
more as being and reproducing; this brings the subject more
into home relations. Men speak through and mostly from intellect, and this addresses itself in others, which creates and is
combative."

Not easily shall we find elsewhere, or before this time, any written observations on the same subject, so delicate and profound.

The late Dr. Channing, whose enlarged and tender and religious nature shared every onward impulse of his time, though his thoughts followed his wishes with a deliberative caution, which belonged to his habits and temperament, was greatly interested in these expectations for women. His own treatment of them was absolutely and thoroughly religious. He regarded them as souls, each of which had a destiny of its own, incalculable to other minds, and whose leading it must follow, guided by the light of a private conscience. He had sentiment, delicacy, kindness, taste, but they were all pervaded and ruled by this one thought, that all beings had souls, and must vindicate their own inheritance. Thus all beings were treated by him with an equal, and sweet, though solemn courtesy. The young and unknown, the woman and the child, all felt themselves regarded with an infinite expectation, from which there was no reaction to vulgar prejudice. He demanded of all he met, to use his favorite phrase, "great truths."

His memory, every way dear and reverend, is by many especially cherished for this intercourse of unbroken respect.

At one time when the progress of Harriet Martineau through this country, Angelina Grimke's appearance in public, and the visit of Mrs. Jameson had turned his thoughts to this subject, he expressed high hopes as to what the coming era would bring to woman. He had been much pleased with the dignified courage of Mrs. Jameson in taking up the defence of her sex, in a way from which women usually shrink, because, if they express themselves on such subjects with sufficient force and clearness to do any good, they are exposed to assaults whose vulgarity makes them painful. In intercourse with such a woman, he had shared her indignation at the base injustice, in many respects, and in many regions done to the sex ; and been led to think of it far more than ever before. He seemed to think that he might some time write upon the subject. That his aid is withdrawn from the cause is a subject of great regret, for on this question, as on others, he would have known how to sum up the evidence and take, in the

noblest spirit, middle ground. He always furnished a platform on which opposing parties could stand, and look at
one another under the influence of his mildness and enlightened candor.

Two younger thinkers, men both, have uttered noble
prophecies, auspicious for woman. Kinmont, all whose
thoughts tended towards the establishment of the reign of
love and peace, thought that the inevitable means of this
would be an increased predominance given to the idea of
woman. Had he lived longer to see the growth of the
peace party, the reforms in life and medical practice which
seek to substitute water for wine and drugs, pulse for animal food, he would have been confirmed in his view
of the way in which the desired changes are to be effected.

In this connection I must mention Shelley, who, like all
men of genius, shared the feminine development, and, unlike many, knew it. His life was one of the first pulse-
beats in the present reform-growth. He, too, abhorred
blood and heat, and, by his system and his song, tended to
reinstate a plant-like gentleness in the development of energy. In harmony with this his ideas of marriage were
lofty, and of course no less so of woman, her nature, and
destiny.

For woman, if by a sympathy as to outward condition,
she is led to aid the enfranchisement of the slave, must no
less so, by inward tendency, to favor measures which
promise to bring the world more thoroughly and deeply
into harmony with her nature. When the lamb takes
place of the lion as the emblem of nations, both women
and men will be as children of one spirit, perpetual learn-
ers of the word and doers thereof, not hearers only.

A writer in a late number of the New York Pathfinder,
in two articles headed " Femality," has uttered a still more
pregnant word than any we have named. He views woman
truly from the soul, and not from society, and the depth
and leading of his thoughts is proportionably remarkable.
He views the feminine nature as a harmonizer of the vehe-
ment elements, and this has often been hinted elsewhere ;
but what he expresses most forcibly is the lyrical, the inspiring and inspired apprehensiveness of her being.

Had I room to dwell upon this topic, I could not say

anything so precise, so near the heart of the matter, as may be found in that article ; but, as it is, I can only indicate, not declare, my view.

There are two aspects of woman's nature, expressed by the ancients as Muse and Minerva. It is the former to which the writer in the Pathfinder looks. It is the latter which Wordsworth has in mind, when he says,

> "With a placid brow,
> Which woman ne'er should forfeit, keep thy vow."

The especial genius of woman I believe to be electrical in movement, intuitive in function, spiritual in tendency. She is great not so easily in classification, or re-creation, as in an instinctive seizure of causes, and a simple breathing out of what she receives that has the singleness of life, rather than the selecting or energizing of art.

More native to her is it to be the living model of the artist, than to set apart from herself any one form in objective reality ; more native to inspire and receive the poem than to create it. In so far as soul is in her completely developed, all soul is the same ; but as far as it is modified in her as woman, it flows, it breathes, it sings, rather than deposits soil, or finishes work, and that which is especially feminine flushes in blossom the face of earth, and pervades like air and water all this seeming solid globe, daily renewing and purifying its life. Such may be the especially feminine element, spoken of as Femality. But it is no more the order of nature that it should be incarnated pure in any form, than that the masculine energy should exist unmingled with it in any form.

Male and female represent the two sides of the great radical dualism. But, in fact, they are perpetually passing into one another. Fluid hardens to solid, solid rushes to fluid. There is no wholly masculine man, no purely feminine woman.

History jeers at the attempts of physiologists to bind great original laws by the forms which flow from them. They make a rule ; they say from observation, what can and cannot be. In vain ! Nature provides exceptions to every rule. She sends women to battle, and sets Hercules spinning ; she enables women to bear immense burdens, cold, and frost ; she enables the man, who feels maternal love, to nourish his infant like a mother. Of late she plays still

gayer pranks. Not only she deprives organizations, but
organs, of a necessary end. She enables people to read
with the top of the head, and see with the pit of the
stomach. Presently she will make a female Newton, and
a male Syren.

Man partakes of the feminine in the Apollo, woman of
the masculine as Minerva.

Let us be wise and not impede the soul. Let her work as
she will. Let us have one creative energy, one incessant
revelation. Let it take what form it will, and let us not
bind it by the past to man or woman, black or white. Jove
sprang from Rhea, Pallas from Jove. So let it be.

If it has been the tendency of the past remarks to call
woman rather to the Minerva side, — if I, unlike the more
generous writer, have spoken from society no less than the
soul, — let it be pardoned. It is love that has caused this,
love for many incarcerated souls, that might be freed could
the idea of religious self-dependence be established in them,
could the weakening habit of dependence on others be
broken up.

Every relation, every gradation of nature, is incalculably
precious, but only to the soul which is poised upon itself,
and to whom no loss, no change, can bring dull discord, for
it is in harmony with the central soul.

If any individual live too much in relations, so that he
becomes a stranger to the resources of his own nature, he
falls after a while into a distraction, or imbecility, from
which he can only be cured by a time of isolation, which
gives the renovating fountains time to rise up. With a society it is the same. Many minds, deprived of the tra-
ditionary or instinctive means of passing a cheerful existence, must find help in self-impulse or perish. It is therefore
that while any elevation, in the view of union, is to be hailed
with joy, we shall not decline celibacy as the great fact of
the time. It is one from which no vow, no arrangement,
can at present save a thinking mind. For now the rowers
are pausing on their oars, they wait a change before they
can pull together. All tends to illustrate the thought of a
wise contemporary. Union is only possible to those who
are units. To be fit for relations in time, souls, whether of
man or woman, must be able to do without them in the
spirit.

It is therefore that I would have woman lay aside all thought, such as she habitually cherishes, of being taught and led by men. I would have her, like the Indian girl, dedicate herself to the Sun, the Sun of Truth, and go no where if his beams did not make clear the path. I would have her free from compromise, from complaisance, from helplessness, because I would have her good enough and strong enough to love one and all beings, from the fulness, not the poverty of being.

Men, as at present instructed, will not help this work, because they also are under the slavery of habit. I have seen with delight their poetic impulses. A sister is the fairest ideal, and how nobly Wordsworth, and even Byron, have written of a sister.

There is no sweeter sight than to see a father with his little daughter. Very vulgar men become refined to the eye when leading a little girl by the hand. At that moment the right relation between the sexes seems established, and you feel as if the man would aid in the noblest purpose, if you ask him in behalf of his little daughter. Once two fine figures stood before me, thus. The father of very intellectual aspect, his falcon eye softened by affection as he looked down on his fair child, she the image of himself, only more graceful and brilliant in expression. I was reminded of Southey's Kehama, when lo, the dream was rudely broken. They were talking of education, and he said,

" I shall not have Maria brought too forward. If she knows too much, she will never find a husband ; superior women hardly ever can."

" Surely," said his wife, with a blush, " you wish Maria to be as good and wise as she can, whether it will help her to marriage or not."

" No," he persisted, " I want her to have a sphere and a home, and some one to protect her when I am gone."

It was a trifling incident, but made a deep impression. I felt that the holiest relations fail to instruct the unprepared and perverted mind. If this man, indeed, would have looked at it on the other side, he was the last that would have been willing to have been taken himself for the home and protection he could give, but would have been much more likely to repeat the tale of Alcibiades with his phials.

But men do *not* look at both sides, and women must leave off asking them and being influenced by them, but retire within themselves, and explore the groundwork of being till they find their peculiar secret. Then when they come forth again, renovated and baptized, they will know how to turn all dross to gold, and will be rich and free though they live in a hut, tranquil, if in a crowd. Then their sweet singing shall not be from passionate impulse, but the lyrical overflow of a divine rapture, and a new music shall be elucidated from this many-chorded world.

Grant her then for a while the armor and the javelin. Let her put from her the press of other minds and meditate in virgin loneliness. The same idea shall reappear in due time as Muse, or Ceres, the all-kindly, patient Earth-Spirit.

I tire every one with my Goethean illustrations. But it cannot be helped.

Goethe, the great mind which gave itself absolutely to the leadings of truth, and let rise through him the waves which are still advancing through the century, was its intellectual prophet. Those who know him, see, daily, his thought fulfilled more and more, and they must speak of it, till his name weary and even nauseate, as all great names have in their time. And I cannot spare the reader, if such there be, his wonderful sight as to the prospects and wants of women.

As his Wilhelm grows in life and advances in wisdom, he becomes acquainted with women of more and more character, rising from Mariana to Macaria.

Macaria, bound with the heavenly bodies in fixed revolutions, the centre of all relations, herself unrelated, expresses the Minerva side.

Mignon, the electrical, inspired lyrical nature.

All these women, though we see them in relations, we can think of as unrelated. They all are very individual, yet seem nowhere restrained. They satisfy for the present, yet arouse an infinite expectation.

The economist Theresa, the benevolent Natalia, the fair Saint, have chosen a path, but their thoughts are not narrowed to it. The functions of life to them are not ends, but suggestions.

Thus to them all things are important, because none is

necessary. Their different characters have fair play, and
each is beautiful in its minute indications, for nothing is
enforced or conventional, but everything, however slight,
grows from the essential life of the being.

Mignon and Theresa wear male attire when they like,
and it is graceful for them to do so, while Macaria is confined to her arm chair behind the green curtain, and the
Fair Saint could not bear a speck of dust on her robe.

All things are in their places in this little world because
all is natural and free, just as "there is room for everything out of doors." Yet all is rounded in by natural harmony which will always arise where Truth and Love are
sought in the light of freedom.

Goethe's book bodes an era of freedom like its own, of
"extraordinary generous seeking," and new revelations.
New individualities shall be developed in the actual
world, which shall advance upon it as gently as the figures
come out upon his canvass.

A profound thinker has said "no married woman can
represent the female world, for she belongs to her husband.
The idea of woman must be represented by a virgin."

But that is the very fault of marriage, and of the present
relation between the sexes, that the woman does belong to
the man, instead of forming a whole with him. Were it
otherwise there would be no such limitation to the thought.

Woman, self-centred, would never be absorbed by any
relation; it would be only an experience to her as to man.
It is a vulgar error that love, *a* love to woman is her whole
existence; she also is born for Truth and Love in their
universal energy. Would she but assume her inheritance,
Mary would not be the only Virgin Mother. Not Manzoni
alone would celebrate in his wife the virgin mind with the
maternal wisdom and conjugal affections. The soul is ever
young, ever virgin.

And will not she soon appear? The woman who shall
vindicate their birthright for all women; who shall teach
them what to claim, and how to use what they obtain?
Shall not her name be for her era Victoria, for her country
and her life Virginia? Yet predictions are rash; she herself
must teach us to give her the fitting name.

UNCIVIL LIBERTY

E[zra] H. Heywood

UNCIVIL LIBERTY.

AN ESSAY

TO SHOW

THE INJUSTICE AND IMPOLICY OF RULING

WOMAN

WITHOUT HER CONSENT.

BY E. H. HEYWOOD,

AUTHOR OF "HARD CASH," "YOURS OR MINE," "THE LABOR PARTY," "CLOSET AND STREET," "THE GOOD OF EVIL," "WAR METHODS OF PEACE," "INNER LIFE," "THE CHURCH," "SOCIAL JUSTICE," AND OTHER ADDRESSES.

———o———

EIGHTIETH THOUSAND.

———o———

PRINCETON, MASS.:
CO-OPERATIVE PUBLISHING CO.
1877.

UNCIVIL LIBERTY.

THE independence of British American Colonies, asserted in 1776, was an emphatic declaration of the right of peoples to manage their own affairs; an appeal from governments to justice, from men to man. Till then nations were subject to enthroned power, whose will was superior to popular dissent. Singularly enough, the managers of that revolution, after affirming life and liberty to be inalienable rights, proceeded to destroy life by wholesale in battle, and were so insincere as to deny liberty to a weaker race. The same hands which slew tyrants on Bunker Hill spread the shield of Federal law over chattel bondage at the South, and the Union of '89 became "a herd of States hunting slaves." Retributive justice has emancipated and enfranchised black men, but the insincerity of the fathers reappears in the dogma of exclusive male sovereignty, which rules one-half our adult citizens—the women—against their consent. This rude resistance to the logic of events affronts the essential principles of liberty, which inspired what self-government is yet thought safe in private affairs, and were designed to secure, at least, good manners in rulers.

Human government originated in force; in the heaviest fist, or with those able to control the mere animal strength of the hour; the exponent of concrete opinion, of what certain men think best to be done, with a large infusion of fraud and violence, it now appears as emperor, president, or pound keeper, set over prone multitudes, until they get on two feet and acknowledge the dominion of principles. Through John Baptist or Herod, Brutus or Cæsar, Cromwell or Stuart, Lincoln or Buchanan, the moral sense, often stifled or perverted, but never conquered, here and there gets into creed, deed, or positive law, and makes the epoch memorable. One evolves a truth and is reviled, starved, or murdered outright for it; the truth survives, overrules law and custom, and men grow famous in eulogizing what they killed the discoverer for announcing. The king's arm being too short to reach the circumference of his realm, he delegates his will to subordinate executors, on whom, in turn, he is somewhat dependent. Thus all governments, in their way, are representative, and rest on consent; though they differ in the width of the circle in the number of nobles taken into royal confidence. But despotism makes the will of monarchy its ultimate appeal, while liberty, accepting as final nothing this side of natural right, defers to popular reason, and is served or cheated, by that democratic king, the average man, the majority. In that marvel to monarchs, a State without a king, all citizens are nobles in so far as they incarnate equity. Hence our fathers, according to their luck, derived just powers of government from consent of the governed; and, to be as good as they, we must be enough better to apply the democratic idea impartially.

SOURCES OF CIVIL LAW.

In determining essential right we settle woman's rights, for the greater includes the less ; every political or reformatory convention is the re-appearance of government, through imperfect mediums, the people, from its primary source, natural equity. The subtle law which regulates movements of sovereign particles of the body politic, the cardinal principle of civil liberty allows every one to do what she or he will, provided they invade not the equal right of every other one to do the same. Out of this come freedom of thought, expression and movement ; the right of association, habeas corpus, trial by jury, all the safeguards which experience has thrown up around dissent, to withstand invasion, and enable right to give law to intrusive fact. Parties, majorities, state, church—all institutions are despotisms when in conflict with incarnate truth. Legitimate civil authority may be traced to one of two origins : 1st, Enlightened reason, natural equity. 2d, Positive legislation. Since the latter is void unless it enact the former, valid law can have but one source, abstract right, essential truth. Hence government, not less than liberty, must justify its existence, and opponents of impartial suffrage should be classed as tyrants until proved innocent. That this is a correct view some competent exponents of thought, in different ages, may be cited to witness. Socrates: "Whatever inconvenience ensue, nothing is to be preferred before justice." New Testament : "Whether it be right to hearken unto you, more than unto God, judge ye ;........the law is fulfilled in one word, love thy neighbor as thyself." Cicero : "If nature does not ratify law all virtues lose their sway." Bacon : "There are in nature certain fountains of justice, whence all civil laws are derived but as streams." Shakspeare : "In love the heavens themselves do guide the state." Hampden : "What is unjust is not law, and what is not law ought not to be obeyed." Blackstone : "No human laws are of any validity if contrary to the law of nature ; and such of them as are valid derive all their force and authority from this original." Kant : "Act so that the immediate motive of your will may become a universal rule for all intelligent beings." Hallam : "God forbid that we should submit our liberties to a jury of antiquaries." Carlyle : "One strong thing I find here below, the just thing, the true thing; if the thing is unjust, thou hast not succeeded." Spooner : "No one can know what the written law is until he knows what it ought to be." Emerson : "Law is only a memorandum ; absolute right is the first governor." Lieber : "The forbearing use of power is a sure attribute of a gentleman." The right to rule first claimed by brute force, then by good will, charity, finally rests in liberty, delegated trust, consent. If principal or representative goes wrong, integrity dissents, bides its time and wins, though the true king be in a dungeon, and a culprit on the throne. The world will settle down into a community of peoples when abstract right is obeyed as supreme interpersonal, interstate, international law, and the clearest self-interest.

From this cursory glance at the principles which authorize legitimate government, much now obeyed as law appears destitute of moral justification. An old play represents Adam crossing the stage going to be created ; democracy is yet so much in embryo that its reputed statesmen think national unity is promoted by centralized dictation, and extol as "a republican form of government" that which forces the allegiance of dissenting men, and dooms to political servitude all women. But civil law being merely the creature of man, and binding only as it enacts right, those who presume to legislate for citizens—permanent residents of ma ture age and sound mind, who contribute to the material or moral welfare of society—of either sex or any race without power of attorney, or other definite commission, are guilty of fraudulent usurpation, and their acts morally void. "Taxation without representation is tyranny," was a potent rallying cry in the struggle for a male independence, which compels women to pay for the support of governments they had no voice in creating.* It is a recognized principle of democracy that persons indicted for crime are entitled t > be tried by their peers ; yet women are arrested, imprisoned and judicially murdered, by their self-constituted masters. By constitutional decree and custom, a majority of votes cast decide the election ; in Massachusetts, according to the census of 1865, there are 63,011 more females than males ; and, by the majority rule, the women may rightfully expel Legislature and Governor from thé State House, as usurpers. Yet these are the fellows who set themselves up as gods, to be petitioned and prayed to, instead of coming down on penitent knees for their transgressions! The validity of the national war debt, the binding force of marriage laws, chartered powers of corporations, title deeds to property, public and private contracts are vitiated by the all-pervading usurpation. Under existing laws only a " prostitute " can claim her child ; any married father, whether of age or not, by will or deed may dispose of his child, "born or to be born," and its mother is liable to fines and imprisonment for presuming to dispute his marital " rights." A Boston woman of wealth, culture and talent, allowed a servant to conduct her two little girls, one two and the other five years old, to see their father, then living in another house belonging to her ; he immediately took them aboard an Atlantic steamer, carried them to Paris, and she did not see them again for ten years! He acted on legal advice, and the statute which permitted the outrage is still law in most, if not all, of the States. Recently a prominent member of the medical profession compelled his wife to die under his own treatment, rather than be cured, or even prescribed for by the physician of her own choice ; and government permits husbands to exercise this murderous power. One unfit to have authority over a fly is made absolute master of his wife ; and while he could be arrested for cruelty to a horse in the street, he may enter his house—a castle to him, a prison to her—and whip the mother of his children at pleasure. A just man blushes to look into the statute book, so often does he find himself judged and sentenced by the acts of his sex.

The legal subjection of women is thought to be justified by an assumed natural dependence on man. The old claim of tyranny, "The king can do no wrong," is reasserted by that many-headed monster, the majority, which widens the circle of despot-   MALE
ism, but retains the fact. As people were to the king,   SUPREMACY.
so woman is now an appendage of man, who claims to be her "head," though nature seems not to have limited heads to the exclusive possession of either sex. That there is no natural feeling of dependence, on one hand, or of superiority on the other, is evident to the most casual observer of spontaneous dealings of the sexes. In practical sense and force a girl of fourteen is often ten years older than a boy of the same age ; tells him how to act and protects him from the big boys at school. A widow lady who maintains herself and daughter and lays up money by keeping a half-dozen families in clean clothes,

*An attempt has been made in this State to ascertain the number of females in their respective municipalities who are taxed directly, and also the number of such who have property standing in other people's names. According to these imperfect returns there are 3,341 females in Massachusetts who pay a tax of $1,427,655 11 on a total valuation of $161,683,346 28.—*Boston Daily Journal.*

rejoices that she has no man on her hands to support. Her next door neighbor, who sold, one day, forty cents' worth of her husband's service for two pounds of beef, said, that for another piece as large she would part with him entirely. At a court ball in Berlin, Bismarck, much pleased with the wife of a foreign diplomat present, with characteristic audacity, reached out to pluck a flower from the bouquet she carried; rapping his knuckles with her fan she said: "Pardon, Mr. Count, but that flower is not a German State; you must ask for it." Man instinctively defers to woman until poverty, marriage or ungentle-manly arrogance subjects her to his dictation. Popular reverence for her person forbids public laying on of hands to correct her, and private insolence dares not until she is under his legal thumb. She is a stronger body guard to man in a mob than a battalion of soldiers, and the sanctity of her person is the only barrier the savage atrocities of war never quite overleap. A body, ears, eyes, nose, taste, touch, sensitive to beauty of thought, color, sound; all requisites to admit men to the realm of sense, and a knowledge of material things, woman has; while, in intuition, the income of spiritual wealth, she is admitted to excel man. By what authority, then, is she required to look up to him for guidance, while he looks to Infinite Truth as the source of right and duty? The ruling class rarely yield a privilege until whipped out of it; so man now legislates with his fist rather than his conscience, robs his "better half" of all the ballot, simply because he is physically the strongest. To compel her to obey father before marriage, husband afterward, then her eldest son, may be consistent with Mormonism, which aspires to build an empire on Isaiah's prophecy that in the last days seven women shall cling to one man, and honors as "the wisest man" a patriarch who had seven hundred wives and three hundred concubines; it may be suited to a theology which makes man lord of creation and woman an afterthought, designates boys as the "sons of God" and girls as the "daughters of men," and paves hell, not in good intentions even, but with "infants' skulls not a span long;" it may be agreeable to her position in a Turkish harem, a Chinese palace, on a blazing funeral pile of a Hindoo husband, or in the hotter fires of a Boston brothel, but it is quite repulsive to the free ideas which transformed the dark realms of the American Indian into a constellation of powerful States.

The protesting indignation of some women who had the honor to be, at least, rebellious slaves, widespread and increasing unrest broke out in the first formal declaration of independence, issued in 1848, from Seneca Falls, N. Y., by Elizabeth Cady Stanton, Lucretia Mott, and others. It enumerated grievances equal in number and seriousness to those set down in the famous manifesto of '76, and is destined to work a more extended and beneficent revolution. Current objections to woman's enfranchisement can hardly be accounted for, except on the supposition that the sexes, even husbands and wives, are not yet personally acquainted with each other or truth. Justice unites persons widely remote; injustice separates infinitely those standing side by side. Men reputed to know something of the nature of liberty, so-called radicals who have ceased to represent the moral sense, or even the intelligence of the hour, talk flippantly of "universal suffrage" while shutting out one-half of human-kind. A wit believed in universal salvation, provided he could pick the men; so perhaps these recreant "radicals" will conquer their prejudices against impartial suffrage, when assured

WOMAN INSURGENT.

that new comers will vote their party ticket. The right of man to political freedom appears in the fact that he is a sentient being, capable of reason and choice, looking before and after. To rule adult citizens against their will is tyranny; women are adult citizens, hence those who deny them the ballot are tyrants. A dozen years ago or more, the writer, with other specimens of sophomoric assurance, one morning at breakfast, questioned the propriety of Lucy Stone's refusal to pay taxes, allowing her furniture to be sold in preference; the combined, college-learned, male wisdom thinking it a great ado about a small matter. A lady opposite, who first called his attention practically to peace and anti-slavery reform, flung over the table, "No taxation without representation. Did you ever hear of Sam. Adams and John Hampden?" It was the first and last argument he ever attempted to make against woman's suffrage. To justify himself, her oppressor must class her psychologically with brutes, deny her a soul, prove either that she has no functions equal with man, or that she is incapable of exercising them — neither of which can be done. Boys who toss their empty heads at this reform, use freely that epithet which reveals so much contempt for the human understanding — "strong-minded." Men are thought to personate reason, and women sentiment; but generally male objectors to this claim are noted for nothing more than their plentiful lack of logic and superabundance of mulish prejudice. Notwithstanding these disparaging exceptions, men yield to reason; and, at no distant day, physical strength will rally under the banner of moral beauty.

Whether suffrage is a right or privilege, natural or conventional, its denial to woman is equally indefensible. Minors become of age, slaves are emancipated, lunatics regain reason, idiots are endowed with intelligence, criminals are pardoned, traitors amnestied, disfranchised males of every class shed their disabilities and are restored to liberty; but the fact of sex — the crime of womanhood — dooms one to perpetual vassalage! Not the ability to drink, chew, smoke, lie, steal and swear, votes — though election day too often indicates these vices to be important conditions of membership in the male body politic — but intellect, conscience, character, are supposed to vote; and the boy proudly becoming "a man before his mother," is crowned a sovereign at twenty-one, because in thought and discretion he ceases to crawl as an animal, and stands an upright intelligence. Is she who endowed him with these royal qualities less capable of exercising them? If the admission fee to franchise is not age, but property, why are poor men received and rich women excluded? If the door swings open to integrity and courage, why are these turned away in women while their absence is welcomed in men? Simply because this booted, spurred and whiskered thing called government is a usurpation, and men choose to have it so. Since, then, custom not reason, fraud not justice, prejudice not good sense, object, this is a question not for argument, but for affirmation. Those who acknowledge the validity of existing government, by increasing its numerical power, not merely drop a stitch in their logic, but surrender the flag of impartial suffrage to its enemies. The negro certainly has quite as good a right to vote as his late masters. If ignorant, they made it a penal offence to teach him to read; if poor, they robbed him of his earnings by law. But who are negro men and Chinese that we should confer irresponsible power on them? To admit any man, be he black, red, yellow, or a minor — our curled, white darling just come of age — to the franchise, who is not pledged to share it with women, is treason to liberty, a desertion of the logical duty of the hour.

A cruel kindness, thought to be friendly regard, assumes to "protect" those who, by divine right of rational being, are en
VICARIOUS titled, at least, to be let alone. We are not among wild
PROTECTION. beasts; from whom, then, does woman need protection?
From her protectors. While making marriage almost
her only possible means of permanent subsistence, and working for a
living unpopular, custom forbids her to "propose," to seek a husband;
hence this vicarious theory of government owes her, what Socrates
claimed for himself, a support at the public expense. If, in the old law
phrase, "the husband and wife are one person, and he that one;" if,
married or unmarried, her personality is buried in his, man should also
embody her responsibility — be taxed for her food, clothing, leisure,
pleasure, and punished for her sins. But, in practice, he does not recognize this obliging doctrine; for, while reserving the hottest corner
of his future hell for her, in this life his responsibility ends with the
gratification of his personal desires, and she is "abandoned" — thrown
upon the tender mercies of public censure and charity. If there is
hanging to be done, it is her head which goes through the noose; if
imprisonment is decreed, her body is locked up; if starvation ensues,
she perishes, while he lives on fat, and free to protect new victims of
this loving kindness. If she is to be restrained, can one inferior in rectitude and continence be her keeper? It is said that beauty leans on
strength; that Venus rides on a lion, now as in the old fable; but evidently the protector will despoil, unless she is armed with self-supporting and self-defending weapons.

We form societies to prevent cruelty to dumb animals, but horses and
dogs are better fed and lodged, in our cities, than thousands of working women. Instead of the scythe, in the primer, we should now have
the skeleton figure of Death sewing shirts. The following cases, taken
at random from numberless facts reported and unreported by the press,
sadly illustrate the inevitable result of denying woman direct access to
the sources of life and liberty:

Last evening a girl, apparently about seventeen or eighteen years of age, committed suicide by leaping into the North river from the ferry-boat James Watt. She wore a plain silk dress, with a plaid shawl and hood For some time after the boat left the Hoboken side, she walked to and fro in the cabin, deeply agitated. Finally she sat down beside a lady, and said the cabin was very close; to another she made a similar remark, and said she had been to Hoboken to mail a letter to her friends in Germany. Greatly excited, when the boat reached the middle of the river, she rushed out, leaped over the chains, and disappeared in the water. Her body was not recovered.—*N. Y. Evening Post.*

The other day an interesting child, for she was really no more, went into the Workingwomen's Home, Franklin street, when the following dialogue occurred between her and one of the superintendents: "What is your name?" "Mary Thompson." How old are you?" "Nearly sixteen." "Where do you live?" "With my mother, in Eldridge street." "What can we do for you?" "Get me some work, please." "Where have you been working?" (Hesitatingly). "In a concert saloon." "Where?" "Corner of Chatham street and Bowery." "That's it eh? Why did you leave it?" "Well, you see, I got into a row there. Two men came in one night, and I heard them say they were going to rob a young man who was kind to me, when I told them I wouldn't let them in spite, they said I stole money from them. I was taken to the Toombs, and the judge after discharging me, sent me here for work." "Where were you before g ing to the saloon?" "In a factory." "Why did you leave it?" "Because I only got $3 a week; my sister got the same, but it wasn't enough to support us, and we could make a great deal more as waiter girls." "How much were you paid at the saloon?" "Three dollars a week, and what we could make." "What do you mean by 'what you can make'?" "Well you see, ma'am, we are allowed five cents on every drink, and then the young men treat us, and when they give us a dollar, if they are spunky and decent. they will not take back the change; besides, we get lots of jewelry, brooches, ear-rings, &c." "How much did you make a week?" "From $15 to $18, according to trade; if it was good we'd go up to $20, then down to $10." "But isn't it wicked?" (Hanging down her head). "I suppose so, ma'am; but it is hard to be hungry." "Would you like to leave the saloon?" "Yes, if I can make a living and help my poor mother." She was sent to work where she could make from $3 to $4 a week. Nothing has been heard of her since. Poor Mary! she is a good subject for some of the city and philanthropy now going round loose in John Allen's quarters.—*New York Sun.*

One result of the religious meetings held in the dance-halls of that
famous locality, was the awakening of wayward ones by the exhortations and prayers of the warm-hearted missionary. As the penitent
girls stood around him in tears, ready to earn their living by better

means, if permitted, he did not know what to do with his converts, who though fit for Heaven were thought unfit for society in this world, and he was obliged to confess that the religion he represented had no salvation for them here; that the boasted Christianity of the great metropolis had not heart, wit or money enough to open a way of escape from their fearful surroundings. When the women of Lyons took to suicide in great numbers, and "from no apparent cause," it was checked, as a similar mania before by the Roman Senate, by an order that the bodies of all who drowned themselves should be publicly exposed in the market place, naked. Thus was even the right to die denied by rude legislators, who thought to cure the evil, not by making life more attractive, but death more repulsive. The Welsh girl, Hester Vaughn, comes to our country in quest of relatives and work. Betrayed by a trusted protector she seeks shelter in the solitude of the great city of brotherly love. In a lone garret in mid winter, without fire, food or friend, she gives birth to the man's child, which is found dead when she revives from the terror and agony of nearly three days' labor. Government comes not to relieve and amend, but to damn its victim to darker infamy. Execrated or ignored by self-righteous public opinion, she is arrested — tried — her last dollar taken by a lawyer for defence not made — and sentenced to be hanged. After many months' imprisonment she is pardoned by the Governor of Pennsylvania, only on condition that she will leave the country! Her "protector" is at large and votes for that Governor's re-election. In a city, known as the "heart" of the Commonwealth of Massachusetts, a young woman of intelligence, beauty, refinement, with a father, husband, brothers, uncles, able to provide material support, but unable to perceive that unliberated and unemployed energies are self-destructive, brought back to a life she loathed, and endeavored to destroy once by laudanum, walks out to the railway depot, flings herself under the wheels of a moving freight-train and is killed instantly. Like the slaveholder's jury of inquest over the body of a murdered negro, who concluded he "died of the will of God or some other disease," the coroner's verdict in this case was that she came to her death by "temporary mental aberration." Well may women assail the constituted order which assumes to restrain, rule, judge and condemn her without a hearing; for while this vicarious guardianship, with man, is conveniently impossible, to her it is a disastrous cheat. For her the prison, the scaffold, the brothel and the street; but not for her the emoluments of office, the golden prizes of business, or even a chance for an honest existence.

The drift of our social relations is from status to contract, from accepting life at second-hand to an original acquaintance with its sources. While the slave becomes a SELF GOVERNMENT citizen, and the hireling an owner, it is a poor commentary on man's gallantry and good sense that she, whom he loves beyond all other beings incarnate, should be the last instead of the first object of this ameliorating law. The most significant spectacle of modern civilization is the trial of institutions in the court of reason, the liberation of intellect, from much which has been "bowed down to as the intention of nature and the ordinance of God." Personality, the origin and mainspring of reform, the point where renewing life enters decaying fact, is the germ of that wilderness of pronoun I's we call society, which was made for man, not man for it. When viewed from elevated points, the prominent outlooks of history, the human race, in all ages and nations, will be seen to have steadily obeyed an onward beat of things. Growth brings diversity, thinking isms, which are to be welcomed rather than deplored, when exposed to criticism, to that prophet and law-giver of the world, free inquiry. No sensible tree rests its reputation on last year's foliage, but greets each spring with new life. That power, behind which the party of rest so often encamp—custom—favors growth, not sterility; for the tendency to advance, the law of progress, is the perennial and overruling force of human society. Nothing is so revolutionary and convulsive, as the strain to keep things where they are, in opposition to expanding tendencies. The established government is a criticism, an amendment of a former, itself again to be revised or displaced by a larger thought. The form is less than what informs it, the temple than the deity enshrined. A violet or a cedar of Lebanon, serf, sovereign, individual being everywhere has its declaration of independence, its claim to life and scope. The all-animating impulse now bids woman "mix with action lest she wither by despair." More willing to incur responsibilities than to fulfill them, too much of man's self-government has been an effort to govern everybody except himself. The case of Sickles and Key, of Cole and Hiscox, of McFarland and Richardson, all such outbreaking evidence of the latent tragedy of domestic life, is justified on the theory of woman's incompetency to decide for herself. The husband as hereditary ruler, allowing no interference with his divine right to "protect," is self-constituted judge, jury and executioner to inflict death on any one disposed to befriend her. Marriage is not a free civil contract, cognizant of mutually grave moral responsibilities as it should be, but a consolidated union, of which man as proposer and disposer, is supreme law. Boys are "bound out" till twenty-one, girls are bound in for life. The negro was just whose cuffy he happened to be; the wife is just whose birdie or drudge she happens to be. As masters quoted law and gospel over their slaves, so husbands emphasize their claim to wedded chattels. There is not one word in all these objections to woman's suffrage but would justify slavery or imperialism. We must therefore grant her claim, or turn our portraits of Washington and Adams to the wall, level Bunker Hill monument into the harbor, haul down the democratic republican flag and go back under king and pope. In punishing her we admit she has a moral sense to be convinced or coerced; but while conceding her the right to be hanged, we yet hold that men, eligible to the State prison and the gallows, are also eligible to Congress. Not the family, but the citizen is the social unit; for both politics and religion make individual moral being a law unto itself. Because woman is a citizen, not by the courtesy of man, but by the will of God, the fact of existence, all offensive institutions and personalities are now on trial before this fair judge.

Having shown the injustice of ruling woman without her consent, its impolicy is apparent; for what is morally wrong cannot EQUALITY be practically right, or innocently approved. If she has a THE BEST soul, if she is a party to be consulted, her legal self-re-POLICY. sponsible equality cannot be denied, for there is no middle ground between chatteldom and freedom. The change proposed, the recognition of one half the race, hitherto ignored, is indeed momentous, though dreadful only to those who fear to do right, and trust the consequences—but forget its disastrous alternative. "The worst thing that can befall one guilty of sin, is not to be punished for it ;" mindful of this fact, nature ordains her laws, more honored in the breach than the observance, to be self-executing; every evil from a civil war to a bruised finger warns us not to do so again. Enforced bondage of blacks at the South sent death to Northern homes, and those who mobbed abolitionists, by the unseen omnipotence of an idea, were hurled in embattled legions against slaveholders in the tune of "glory hallelujah." In the aberration of moral as of physical laws we get a clue to the true normal course. The festive growth of crime in those savage wilds called cities; the tragic life of women, and deadly collision of man with man; the widespread harvest of disease, deformity, insanity, degeneracy; the increasing prevalence of sexual evils before which statesmanship is baffled, religion powerless, and science dumb — these retributive results are the kindest answer nature can give to a practice which disowns divinity in its fairest human form. In the prevailing ignorance of what true affectional intercourse is, and the studied avoidance of domestic ethics both by scholars and moralists, suffrage is, of course, but the initiative, the beginning of wisdom. Women should not be too solicitous about men's sins, for they have plenty of their own to answer for. The angels we hear so much about, like men, eat, drink and catch cold, and like men, in an emergency, will lie and steal. Appealing from women to woman we aim to establish a principle, not especially to vindicate persons, and merely assert her right to opportunity and fair dealing; angel or fiend, she is entitled to work out her own salvation, to be and to do as well as to suffer.

Present practice defeats the policy it is intended to serve. To those who think women should be perpetually watched and taken care of we commend the following specimen fruit of their oriental theory fresh from China, and described in the *San Francisco Bulletin:* —

A remarkable spectacle was the landing of the women and girls, of whom there were two hundred and forty on board. It was like landing a drove of sheep or cows. At all points of the compass were men to drive them, and they came off the boat in squads of fifteen or twenty each. The policemen and Chinese " bosses " kept each squad together and drove the entire crowd into a corner under a shed, where they stood watched as closely as ever was guarded a gang of slaves in the South. If a Chinawoman, resident here, approached too near, she was seized and pushed away; and if any of the new comers left the crowd, she was driven back, or seized by the back of the neck and shoved to her place again. Most of those who come are young girls, many not over twelve or fifteen years of age, and nine-tenths, at least, for purposes of prostitution. Into seven or eight cars, reserved to transport them to the Chinese quarters, these creatures were driven in squads and hauled to a point on Jackson street. The women then ran the gauntlet again. The alley, which is one of the narrowest and filthiest in the city, was lined with Chinamen and women, as the strangers were driven through it, up some old rickety steps into the Dupont street theatre, and in the pit of that wretched place were again herded. Here they were assorted, marked over, and sent to the " six companies " to which they were consigned.

Men have had chief control of the world thus far, and of the results they have not much reason to be proud. For those who decline, or are denied monogamous marriage, politics, theology, science, literature, philosophy, public opinion, all the social intelligence of which history brings us an account, has evolved but three methods of solving the woman question — chattel and capital bondage, polygamy, and prostitution. Men are so much better than their laws, free instincts so often interpose to relieve victims of the "assembled wisdom," which, from State House and Congress, imposes its authoritative ignorance upon us, that many escape these sad results. But, judged by the law, and life which come out of this man-the-head-of-woman theory, it were a compliment to the male managers thereof to think society has yet no head at all. Milton being asked why a king is sometimes allowed to take his place on a throne at fourteen but not to marry until he is eighteen, replied: "Because it is easier to govern a kingdom than a woman." The poor figure men make, under the present *regime*, is the result not so much of incapacity as of attempting the impossible.

The imposing deference which, while it affects to regard woman as the pride and ornament of creation, degrades her to a toy, a cipher, fears natural order will not keep its footing, if she is allowed to go at large without keepers. But will the skeptic behind that objection please explain to us the nature of the tie which now joins, or may join him to the woman called wife? If it is force, who gave him authority to wield it! If it is fraud, the officers of justice should lay hands on him. If it is poverty, by what process did this once fascinating being, capable of infinite endeavor, become a menial in his service, dependent at his board? Is it not rather the memory of equality, of the hour when he, a glad suppliant, courted her, a free intelligence, able to accept or reject his proposals? Surrendering virgin liberty she entered his legal cage; the blooming maiden, "quickly scorned when not adored,", is now the worn and faded wife, in the back-yard of his affections; and real respect for her has declined, just in proportion as she has lost the power of choice, and the control of her person. There may be men who, seeking a parlor ornament, or a subservient mistress, prefer languid helplessness to original strength in a wife; but the case of him who married the one he did, because she was the only girl in town he was not sure of before proposing, well indicates how much continent deference of the husband on the one hand, and free existence of the wife on the other, depend on her power to decline or even defy his advances. As one would rather be called a knave than a fool, so men respect woman's wickedness more than her weakness; the thorn and the bramble more than dependent vines wedded to masculine oaks. The pope said, "If we allow the right of private judgment, Protestantism may win, but Christendom will be split into sects;" Luther took the risk, and co-extensive with the prevalence of this dissolving progress of thought, the right to differ, has the believer become a law unto himself, more religious than the church. The most impressive admonition which comes to us from Jesus is, "Why even of yourselves judge ye not what is right?" The elements of order are: 1st, justice; 2d, liberty; 3d, union to repel invasion of these in any person, and which especially pledges the whole force of society to defend woman's right to decline male advances. There can be no union except between units; without keeping wedded ones always on their good behavior, as during courtship. Constantly acknowledged twoness is indispensable to coincident oneness. In urging the political question, woman brings not mere avoirdupois weight, but living mind, to be admitted to citizenship. Her enfranchisement will prove the advent of reason and conscience to politics, obedience to "law whose throne is in the bosom of God, and whose voice is the harmony of the world." The prejudice against her fulfilling any function which makes her an independent, thoughtful, self-sustaining being is excited by narrow and despotic selfishness. We have created antagonism by establishing a privileged male class.

Painful results of this effort to make two lives serve one erring will, may be seen in family quarrels, which are nature's protest against enforced coincidence. Instead of agreement, mutual deference and concord in the home, "the heart's country," we too often find hatred, conflict and chronic anarchy. These are thought to be the fault of one or both of the parties concerned, as indeed they often are, though they generally spring from deeper causes—from coerced allegiance, ill-defined rights and duties. A Frenchman, though married, was accustomed to spend his evenings

Marginal notes: ELEMENTS OF ORDER. FAMILY FEUDS.

with a certain maiden lady; when his wife died, being asked why he did not marry the other, he replied that "if he did, he should not have anywhere to spend his evenings." It was remarked of another "he loved her so that one never would have thought she was his wife." An American woman brought into court, charged with pouring a pail of boiling water over a man, defended herself on the ground that she supposed it was her husband. An English wife paints her once loved lord, the courtly Bulwer, with "the head of a goat and the body of a grasshopper." Such eccentric instances are not entirely untruthful satire of the alienation which "wedded bliss" promotes when parties thereto are not free and equal factors. Approaching her before marriage with requests, afterward with commands, the lover, kneeling to an adored maid, will swear himself incapable of one of the thousand hurts he may not hesitate to inflict on her as wife. As we do not find two hills without a hollow between them, so two intelligent beings, however loving, cannot abide together in healthful peace unless the separate, intact liberty of each is perpetually held inviolate. To commit one's self beyond recall to a finite being, for any purpose whatever, makes unitary concord impossible and undesirable. A clear-headed business man says: "The chief cause of matrimonial inharmony is in the fatal error that parties recognized in law as capable of making a contract are not also thought capable of dissolving that contract." Forced consent annihilates existing love and makes its revival impossible. Those who think liberty so dangerous an element in love would do well to, at least, imagine how the simplest affairs could proceed on the grab game their frenzied conservatism adheres to. The methods of chance, fraud and deceit, which now determine the most sacred and eventful experiences of life, would be deemed evidence of insanity if proposed as the basis of business partnership. Science, which respects aspiring insects, traverses infinite space, makes pilgrimages to the Arctic, the Amazon, the Alps and Adirondacks, studies breed in birds and herds, will ere long find it worth while to wait on women and men, and explore those dark places of the world — the kitchen, the bed-chamber, and the nursery. Matrimonial bureaus and newspaper personals, used for purposes shameful enough; the great relief a careful father feels when a daughter is well married off his hands; the scientific matchmaking; the deep-laid plans of those skillful love-brokers, mothers and maiden aunts—these indicate that business, not affection, is at the bottom of much of this romance, and make it all the more imperative on legislators to see to it that woman, in going inside the castle of law, is not disarmed and bound.

It is thought that politics will unsex her, that she will "lose her tender little ways and bashful modesties, and the bloom be rubbed off every enjoyment." This is but the revival of an old cry of tyrants, now masquerading as republicans and democrats, that the people are incapable of self-government. As an exhausted receiver defines the sphere of a rabbit suffocated under it, so imprisoning conditions within which the ages have bound woman limit her natural right to life. While men's functions and opportunities are of their own choice, women's are forced on them by circumstances. Man's duties and avocations send the soul outward; woman must always stay at home with her heart. What right has one adult citizen to forcibly determine the *status* of another? The sphere of a slave is the circle described by his driver's lash; the sphere of woman free is the realm her heart fills, the range

CONCERNING
SPHERES.

and height of her faculty. The ability of one marks the present sphere of that one, but leaves all space this side of God to enlarge upon. It is said that woman cannot engage in politics, or other business, because she must marry; but she is compelled to unpaid toil of many kinds, beside child-bearing, if married. Will it require more effort to go to the town hall twice than it does to attend church fifty-two times a year. Politics are merely a matter of business, the ways and means to certain ends. Principle is the what, policy is the how of affairs. The Queen of England is conceded to be, in the gentler traits, a model to her sex, though she rules an empire which encircles the globe; will our queen of hearts be less a woman when dropping a piece of paper into a box? Women in Congress, at salaries of $5,000 a year, could hardly be more damaged or damaging than as waiter girls or mistresses of those august legislators. If politics are vicious, it is high time they were cured, for "sound policy always coincides with substantial justice." The plea that women will be rudely treated by men at the polls, so far as it has any weight, only proves that male ruffians should be disfranchised; but this "chivalry objection comes about two centuries too late, for· the cour- tesy of men has increased as the freedom of woman has been accorded." If men are so bad they cannot be trusted to vote with women ought they to vote for women? Those accustomed to govern in schools, able to teach more than males can learn, will not consent to be life-long vas- sals of boys they educate. The mother of nine children, successfully raised and started in life, why prefer a whiff of cigar smoke to her for President? Government is a bloody, barbarous thing, chiefly because it ignores ethics of which woman is the clearer and most steadfast ex- ponent.

> "For contemplation he and valor formed;
> For softness she and sweet attractive grace.
> He for God only; she for God and him"—

was a poet's idea, which Paul put in this presuming way: "Neither was the man created for the woman, but the woman for the man." It is because we have thus stepped between conscience and God, severed the moral law of gravitation which binds finite sovereignties to the creative centre, that our social astronomy is so sadly distracted. If the heavenly bodies are viewed as revolving around the earth, their movements appear chaotic and inexplicable; but when you reckon from the sun as centre, the watch in your pocket may be timed and regulated by their exact and wondrous whirl through space. Whoso makes woman a satellite of himself is behind Copernicus in practical science; if he quote Bibles, let him listen to Jesus, who applauded a woman for *not* attending to housekeeping. If his dinner is uncooked, and his home deserted, it may be a divine voice which beckons her forth, and sordid avarice which bids her stay and grind in the prison- house of his selfism. By whose decree is one immortal being insphered within, and made a martyr to the private interest of another? We have no fears that, dowered with liberty, she will be less feminine, for nothing unwomanly can prevail among women. More respected in a shop or counting-room than in the kitchen, a girl acquires character and self-control in proportion as her sphere enlarges. The magnetic, thrilling touch, graceful form and movement, this animated beauty and use has laws, tendencies, and a career of its own. Superstitious bats may denounce the rising sun as a "reform against nature," for night is their day; but rose and violet welcome light and are adorned in its redeeming presence. Woman, "as God made her," we wait to see, having already too much of the man made woman. Her artificial, superinduced, enervated nature may disappear, but nature's nature will revive and prevail.

A gentle bachelor fears conscriptions of war may invade his peace if women vote, and that our fair rulers may draft for husbands. Fatally married, the wife controls one-third his property, MEN'S while he loses claim to any share in hers. He can deed RIGHTS. nothing away without her signature, and has no use of her credit at the store, while she can buy heavily on his account, and law compels him to pay the uttermost. Withdrawing from his lordship's imperial nothingness she may levy perpetual alimony on him for a living, while he must delve to earn it, and count himself lucky to be rid of her at that. A gay creature, blushing behind her fan, outwits an elegant fop in lavender kids, who thinks all the girls dying to marry him, ensnares him in an engagement, provokes him to break it, and, in damages for breach of promise, carries off the bulk of his fortune. If this be his fate now, who can protect him when the "suppressed sex" are free, and he is obliged to risk his charms in an open market? Armed with jealousy and cunning, in the absence of better weapons of defence, ignorant, frivolous, exacting, woman now often drags man down; her subjected condition being fruitful in vices of artifice and power, of unnatural dependence, and imperious self-assertion, the aggressor, as usual, suffers most. Imbruted mind is the reflex result of the exercise of arbitrary power, and those who trample on the weak are the first to cringe to the strong. None but base natures assume to rule equals, or domineer over inferiors. We must count it, therefore, the first and chief of man's rights to undo, without asking, this injustice to woman; for in so far as he deprives her of vigor and scope does he maim himself. Alas! that any man can wish women perishing in luxurious inactivity, wedded to vice or imbecility, impaled on a needle, or starving in a garret, to be contented! Doubtless many superiors to Elizabeth Browning, Margaret Fuller, Charlotte Bronte, and George Sand are buried under our household, sewing shop, fashionable and factory life. England has one Stuart Mill, America one Emerson, but it were unlucky to have two; for why should nature be so given out as to repeat herself? In requiring woman to be the shadow, or echo of man, we mar creative intention, and rob society of the better service which intuitive sense waits to render. The value of self-supporting independence doubtless suggested the remark of a wit—"A wife is a fortune—when she is poor." As the adjective is said to be the greatest enemy of the noun, though agreeing with it in gender, number and person, so woman as an adjective, an appendage of man, is useless or worse to him, and a mockery to herself, having an inalienable right to be a noun, a person accountable to infinite intelligence. Since in correcting wrong we enact right, men's actual influence will not only not be lessened, but vastly increased, by abolishing the despotic and irresponsible power they now wield. If authority is natural and beneficent, the votes of a world united cannot overthrow it; if it is usurped, the quicker it falls the better.

Fascinating weakness, "sweet irresponsibility," becomes a nullity, or hostile, when allegiance is forced, and suggests truth in an old maxim, "As many slaves, so many enemies." Since we AS YOU offer a premium to adverse influence, practical sense and per- LIKE IT. suasive eloquence are turned against us; "measures which statesmen have meditated a whole year may be overturned by women in a day," and often have they conquered a nation by simply making up faces. The victims of false deference on one hand and tyrannical subjection on the other, they win through diplomatic artifice, or by sacrifices inconsistent with personal sanctity and social well-being. Impulses, which rightly directed would outflow in tenderness and rectitude, invigorate, adorn and bless mankind, now take the sexes to houses of assignation, and the very materials with which perfect society will be constructed, when the builder arrives, are added fuel to flaming heats our ignorance kindles. The "social evil," which despairing philanthropy says "no law can restrain and no power suppress," is a vast business system of supply and demand, whose natural causes and retributive results point outcasts and outcasters to the ways of healthful sanity. Not to quote Solomon and Samson, the reputed wisest and strongest of men, both of whom were conquered by women, why in Europe and America to-day are men of genius, writers, statesmen and reformers, involved in family feuds, tenants of desolate homes, wanderers from what should be domestic quiet, or indulging in practices they dare not defend as right ? These things cannot be dismissed with a sneer, or religiously attributed to the Prince of Evil ; for the devil is only unexplained adversity, and may yet turn out to be Deity in disguise. The old theory of natural depravity and vicarious atonement will no longer serve to darken counsel with words ; for the instincts and attractions God made are not essentially unclean. Conjugal law, which in all ages and nations has " confined woman to one man, has never confined man to one woman." Virtuous Congressmen, who urge war on Mormon polygamists, should first face domestic problems at home. whose solution will require clearer heads and braver hearts than have yet appeared. In Utah husbands are responsible for their wives, required by law, at least, to provide them bread. In Boston and New York men are quite as much married, though in a clandestine and unscrupulous way. Spectacled bookworms may explore traditions of the past, grave divines declaim against laxity of morals, conceited stoics affect to be superior to fascination, but the fact remains that woman, incarnating love, has ruled and will rule man, for better for worse, just in proportion as she is assured or denied a right to herself. Not responsible to law, because unrecognized by it, she is now driven to secure recognition of her existence by depravity or rebellion. If frivolous or perverse, it is the result of false conditions ; for nature has a seriously honest intent in creating a woman as in creating a man. If he makes badness a necessity and bribes to silence her moral sense, designed tocall him to order, why may not the "weaker vessel" plot to upset the stronger?

Inspired by intuitive reason, this reform is also guided to its object by the light of experience. History, which is at once A POLITICAL "a record of the past, interpretation of the present, WASHING DAY. and prophecy of the future," brings inductive evidence of what we have deduced from essential truth ; that since woman is more intuitive and moral than man, her entrance into politics is guarantee of increased order and cleanliness. A few generations back literature was so obscene that an old book can hardly be trusted, without expurgation, in the hands of youth. The advent of woman as a writer swept the realm of letters clean of that infection, and made decency the first requisite of authorship. It is thought Shakespeare's elevated conception of feminine character was sensibly influenced by the fact that he wrote when Elizabeth sat upon the

English throne. Be that as it may, Portia, Desdemona and Imogen heralded the sovereignty of woman on the stage, which has made the theatre a powerful auxiliary to reform. Twenty years ago many good Americans thought novel reading sinful; the appearance of "Uncle Tom's Cabin" consecrated it a pleasurable duty, set clergymen to writing stories and quickened courts and senates to memorable acts of justice. The country store, with its nightly gathering of local orators, was a scene of vulgar filth until woman stood behind the counter. The ladies' room at railroad depots, how different from the gentlemen's room, where one would suppose cattle congregate, though cattle do not need spittoons. Statistics of temperance societies show many male drunkards to one female, and the records of courts a fearful superabundance of manhood depravity. Telegraph operators stole money and profaned the wires with vile messages; when girls were put in, the receipts of cash increased and obscenity ceased. Celibate priesthoods, monkeries and nunneries have been the scandal of the church in all ages.

The precious geniuses, the beardless barbarians of colleges, "out of whom they make ministers to guide and govern us," tread under foot law, and repeal all the commandments, until girls enter to compete for the laurels of scholarship, and tame these "savage sons of God." Western colleges, to most of which both sexes are admitted, are clearly superior in moral discipline to their celibate elders of the East. Said Horace Mann of the one his name has made illustrious, "We have the most orderly, sober, diligent, exemplary institution in the country. We passed through last term, and are more than half through the present, without my having to make a single entry of any misdemeanor in our record book; not a case of any serious discipline. There is no rowdyism in the village, no nocturnal rampages making night hideous. All is quiet and peaceful; and the women of our village feel the presence of our students, when met in the streets in the evening, to be a protection rather than an exposure." Commenting on these and other facts a writer says: "Male students were first called gentlemen at Antioch." It is needless to adduce further evidence to show the right way to be the safe way. Woman's enfranchisement will renovate public affairs quite as soon as men are ready for it; and much private dirty linen is to be overhauled in the great political washing-day near at hand. With an ideal object and courage to work towards it, her arrival in literature, theatres, churches, schools or business brings reformation. As a bevy of girls were playing under my window, and one slip of womanhood put her saucy foot on a mutual right, the others scattered screaming "I'll tell mother, I'll tell mother." It seemed childish, but there was deep wisdom in the method of reconciliation, for "an ounce of mother is worth a pound of clergy," and tons of statesmen. Natural equity, whose lawgiver is love, has foreordained that the same free and equal meeting of the sexes which inspires private order and ineffable enjoyment will insure public rectitude in political action.

The recognition of woman's personality, though not regarded by any one as a cure for all evils, will be a renovating tendency, an entrance into new fields of ethics and experience yet unexplored. Statesmen and even ministers of religion now frankly confess that they dare not voice their deepest convictions in public, but have two sets of morals, one for the closet and one for the street. Government helps reform chiefly by getting out of its way, does right from "necessity," wrong from choice; deity seems about the most impotent being known,

BREAD AND THE BALLOT.

3

while the devil has full swing, and wins, except here and there, when he builds his badness "up so high it topples down to the other side," and makes a sort of goodness. Judged by the records of legislation thus far, men are made of the "queerest dregs chaos ever churned up" into sentient form. The fact that for centuries they have had representative rulers of some kind, proves that mere voting will not enact order. But the hand which denies women the ballot shuts the college and filches her earnings. Since a disfranchised class have less power of redress on account of that disability, the Labor Reform League puts her right to vote side by side with the claim of service to its reward. We thereby do not solve the labor question, but impanel a more impartial jury to try it. Not good will or votes regulate wages, but supply and demand, now generally overruled by the inequitable custom which allows one to take from another the largest possible value for the least possible return, provided he keeps out of jail. Since employers have preferred to speculate on their suffering necessities rather than concede their natural right to self-supporting independence, to equal pay for equal work with men, the few trades women have entered and mastered are so crowded that they must submit to the terms offered or surrender their places to more destitute applicants knocking at the door. We do not agree with the prevalent infidelity to right which affirms this dependence natural, and poverty of workers a "necessary evil," but summon a new judge into court—Equity. For seventy years one-eightieth part of the American people ruled our States with the iron rod of property in man; that form of political robbery is now broken, but, through subtler methods, slaveholders survive, and North and South get the earnings of labor more successfully than ever; working women, because physically the weakest, being their most deeply defrauded and helpless victims. Since one can justly take from another only what he renders an equivalent for in labor cost, the right to hold property he has not earned or received as the free bequest of others' service is purely imaginary. Interest on money, rent and profit, or dividends, are therefore inadmissible, except for work done or risk incurred; and speculative gain, in all these forms, we arraign as inherently sinful, and enforce the consequent duty of its immediate abolition. In fixing the rate of interest, Wall street, which bribes or browbeats government to do its will, fixes what proportion of earnings shall go to capital and what to labor; fixes the price of a house or calico dress, of a farm or a bunch of matches, of the largest and minutest commodity, in the remotest village of the Union. It is apparent, therefore, that the beneficent law of supply and demand has not free play, but is perverted from natural courses, and made to bring grist to the speculator's mill. A few financiers in New York and London, Paris and Berlin, controlling money, the representative of property, control the material destinies of mankind, and hold the laboring classes of all nations in wretched vassalage. The parent fraud of this gigantic system is the piratical principle that one may take from another what he does not render an equivalent for, incarnate in the government monopoly, the political usurpation which, determining by force the nature and amount of currency, makes free money a penal offence. This is the first great wrong the labor movement has risen to overthrow, and, with woman's heart and vote on the right side of the battle, we are sure to win. If servant girls, plow boys and gravel tossers are with us in a moral issue, Wall street and Washington must come round. The election asks. what think ye of government? The ballot is a reply to that question,

the symbol at once of opinion and power, capable of immense service
to labor, peace, marriage and other reforms, though now controlled by
parties who have stolen the livery of progress to serve retrogression in.
Since to rule woman without her consent is tyranny, and every concession may be recalled unless the ballot forbids, we assert her right to this
weapon of defence, and would inscribe on the flag of authority the
noble motto of St. Simon : "To each according to capacity, to all
according to their work."

"But," says a gentle wife to this feminine rebellion breaking into
her luxurious home, "I have all the rights I want, why
come here to disturb our peace?" And the robust, ten-   AGAINST
der husband, after they have spent years to construct a   THE TIDE.
temple of mutual rights, thinks it a pity that like "the
house which Jack built," the whole thing should tumble now. Notwithstanding the tyrannic advantage man now holds, to the honor of
human nature, there are homes where he scorns to use it, where love
is law, reason rules, "none command and none obey." Yet comparatively few are so fortunate in their partners as this contented wife, while
vast and increasing numbers are not married, and, under existing laws,
can never be. From Maine, New Hampshire, and other States ; from
the Canadas and beyond the seas, girls disgusted with or starved out
of household service, go to factories; thence to the clothing marts of
cities; thence — the path thither strewn with the diseased, the dying
and the dead, such is the reluctance of nature — they crowd the swiftly
descending ways of prostitution ! And though the average length of
life there is but four years, statistics show that the "social evil" is less
destructive to woman's physical beauty and vitality than the labor system as now organized. The drift of girls (and most of these are Americans), from household and factory life to these whirlpools of vice, shows,
at least, a hope of bettering their condition in that direction ; and many
are known to write back to their friends that they rather die there than
return to what they fled from. The average life of slaves on cotton
plantations was seven years, in rice fields five years ; the recital of these
facts roused Northern indignation and created a great political party
to put down the bad thing. But our laws and customs to-day actually
destroy more girls and women than slave codes murdered negroes then !
How long must American girls be crucified, on the fiery cross of self-
destruction, to save this people? Does not the heart of this contented
wife yearn to help us right the wrongs? Her own dear girl, left pen-
niless and an orphan, may have to enter the struggle for life alone ;
will she not arm her for the conflict? Will she not save her darling
boy from the savage custom of presuming to rule the one being whom
he should respect as an equal?

Besides, women can afford to be indifferent to nothing which degrades women ; the sad fact that "the contentment of slaves renders
objection to liberty possible," makes it a more imperative duty to bestir
ourselves to see justice done. Living in a world of petty details engen-
ders narrow habits of mind, and the bounding aspirations of youth are
killed out in the dull round of restricted life. "It might have been"
is written over the tomb of many buried hopes. To think slavery liberty and dependence an honor ; to be satisfied "with what we have rather
than with what we want," that is the calamity. Speculative thought
has ranged from asserting the absolute non-existence of mind, save as
a form or function of matter, to a belief in the merely phenomenal existence of matter dependent on a sentient immaterial entity, mind, which,

wresting from philosophy a recognition of its distinct independent being here, now comes back from the other side of death to say it lives there also. So woman from the dead level of oriental materialism, quickened by Judean religion, Grecian thought, Roman justice, German insight, and Saxon common sense, has risen to assert an original right to life. He who denies or ignores her claim must be something less than a man ; while she who goes forth to proclaim it, is backed by the finest impulses of civilization, and gives new evidence of an ever-living and redeeming spiritual presence.

Our male objector who thinks it bad husbandry to harrow up wedded contentment with these exciting themes, that a strong-minded woman is an intellectual tower of Pisa, under the shadow of which it were unsafe to live, forgets that domestic, like political order, rests on consent, not coercion. A large and increasing majority of applicants for divorce are women ;* intelligent, sensitive natures decline proposals or accept them as a dreadful necessity to secure bread and a home ; marriage is on the decline, partly for its being too expensive, but chiefly because it hinders free enterprise, and is repulsive to personal sanctity ; from this one slave state emancipation did not reach there are more fugitives than ever fled from chattel bondage ; men sound an alarm that the institution is imperilled, while women are in open revolt, or silently, patiently biding their time—such phenomena indicate deep-seated disease, whose infection spreads to every member of the body politic. Those who would send the fugitives back, tighten the laws and double the guards, are little aware of what a moral earthquake they are reading the riot act to. The old notion that slavery was the corner-stone of the republic was not more absurd and monstrous than the idea that woman's legal suppression is the corner-stone of the family. The question is not whether reform will disturb existing relations, but whether any system should continue if that system invades essential right and public interest. The simple fact that she was not consulted in framing the marriage contract, to which from the origin of society she has been forced to submit, alone justifies the woman's rights agitation ; for all admit that contracts are morally binding only when parties thereto have a free voice in determining their conditions. This institution, for whose safety male keepers are so alarmed, now stands on usurped irresponsible power, and until reconstructed on the basis of equality and justice, rebellion against it is a duty. Brigham Young, who assumes woman's natural servility as a justification of his concubinal system, is consistent—giving her the ballot there is only a trick to divert attention from the settled policy to crush out all dissent by orthodox violence—but monogamist objectors seem unaware that she must go back to polygamy, or forward to liberty. One cannot always remain suspended between something and nothing. To say the wife "belongs" to the husband, or the husband to the wife, implies ownership and calls for the deed of purchase. In denying her equality he herds her with brutes ; claims himself to be a freeman, but insists that she shall live under rude codes of the dark ages. He lives in the nineteenth century, she in the ninth, and he puts a thousand years between himself and his lady-love in disfranchising her. We do not make love by statute and cannot unmake it

BAD HUS-
BANDRY.

*In Vermont, out of 581 divorces granted, 315 were applied for by women ; in Massachusetts, out of 1,234, 860 ; in Connecticut, out of 810, 549 ; two-thirds of the libellants, were women. In the list of divorces granted during five years published by order of the Legislature of Massachusetts, by the side of one hundred and nineteen divorces, or separation granted for cruelty of the husband, there appear three for cruelty of the wife.— *Woolsey's Divorce and Divorce Legislation, pp. 205, 251.*

that way. The law of cohesion between souls is as natural and inevitable as between atoms and globes. The fascinating intelligence at whose feet, in his truest moment, the male lover lays all; the qualities of devotion, fortitude, self-sacrifice all bow to, in the gravest epochs of life—at the altar, the cradle and the tomb—will assert a regulating control if allowed free play. The true nuptial knot is in the heart, not on the house top. In drawing-room or convention, nursery or senate, sewing circle or market-place, it matters little where thought ranges if light spreads and souls are born again.

What is apparent in the outer, material phases of life man inhabits, is so much more deeply true of its inner, spiritual realms, native to woman, that her emancipation will prove, not a ADVENT OF source of discord, but the beginning of agreement. Had AGREEMENT. the wits of sham conservatives aimed at extreme badness, they could not have invented a scheme more fruitful, in conflict and immorality, than the present *regime*. The grave apprehensions of stately editors and divines, who think it unsafe to break every yoke, and obey good rather than evil, like the anxiety of slave masters for the results of negro liberty, would be more noteworthy if they had the merit of disinterested intelligence. So far are we from ignoring the potential force of the sexual passions, or undervaluing the claims of maternity and offspring, that the originators of the woman's rights re1 m were the first to give those themes serious and intelligent consideration. Since this question touches the quick of life, goes to the foundations of order and being; precisely because its subject is woman, not a weak man, because the tragedy of motherhood is fraught with momentous interests to herself and the race, must she have free right to live and move independent of finite dictation. The maternal instinct is impaired by the very method now frantically clung to. Statistics prove that fœticide is not generally induced by pressure on the means of subsistence, but rather originates in causes attendant on dainty caretaking and luxury. Domestic animals often kill and devour their young; petted hens while sitting chip and eat their eggs. Child-murder is comparatively rare in poor countries like Ireland and among laboring people of all nations; while in Paris and New York, by the "upper" classes, it is increasingly practiced; mothers often provoking abortion to preserve their physical beauty, and escape from the "home sphere" into the delirious whirl of fashionable life. Dr. Storer shows[*] that the practice of abortion, by the American women of Massachusetts and New York, is so limiting the increase of population that it is maintained chiefly by foreign immigration. The number and success of abortionists is notorious; hardly a newspaper that does not contain their open and printed advertisements, or a drug store whose shelves are not crowded with nostrums publicly and unblushingly displayed. The feminine instinct of these "womanly" women—not strong-minded, and never seen in suffrage conventions—is so perverted that they seem unconscious of the crime to themselves and society they are guilty of; and in selfish egotism rival even those of the most luxurious cities of Europe and Asia, who, subsisting on fugitive attachments, find in marriage a convenient screen behind which to shelter their indiscretions. Our critics must cease this wise nonsense which says to woman "Be Good," and makes man the sample piece of what

[*] "Why Not?" and "Criminal Abortion in America." See also in M. Huc's "Journey Through the Chinese Empire" vol. II., page 327, the shocking prevalence of infanticide where the subjection of women is reduced to a system.

she is to copy from. It is high time that the one most deeply interested in marriage and reproduction should be consulted as a responsible partner; that the maker of men should have free choice of materials, methods and conditions wherewith to perfect her wondrous work.

Educating her for service, not for show, pleasure or sacrifice merely, we must first aim to make a woman, of whom the wife and mother will be, more important, complete and attractive attributes than hitherto. But education, which should develop strength, not cripple it, has been to her, thus far, mainly perversion. As man is trained to get money she is trained to get married, adorned or distorted to suit the whims of a destined master. If nature rebels she is damned to living burial as an " abandoned woman," an " old maid;" if devoted, " constant," she has the honor to expire in flames of lust on the funeral pile of a husband morally dead though physically living. Nothing can exceed the presumption, the devilish criminality, of such wretches as Sickles and Mc-Farland who, because they "love her," deliberately murder a wife's friend on the ground that to give her aid and comfort is an "overt act" of treason to marriage? Her natural right to be a mother or anything else, unless she first gets herself a legal dictator, is yet to be conceded. But neither the tyranny of law nor the merciless grasp of marital "rights" will prevail against the steady advance of woman to equality and fair play. " He that sitteth in the heavens shall laugh, the Lord shall have them in derision;" governments, nations, races perish, but liberty and love are immortal. The affection of the sexes for each other, of parents for children, new every morning, fresh every evening, and repeated every moment, overrules all other human forces, defies all intrusive impertinence, and will outlive all legislative dictation. The spiritual life which overflows and interfuses these tenements of clay, now and forever, waits to ennoble the most forlorn outcast if she will but believe and strive. Woman is woman because tenderness, reason, love, intuition, beauty, the truly feminine qualities, flow direct from infinite sources, and are not reservoired exclusively in any male protector. Pecuniary not less than political justice must be granted, for men cannot share the privileges of free, honorable love until they cease to steal. Marriage, not the subject under discussion, is foreign to the purpose of this essay; it will come up in due time, but sufficient unto the day is the good thereof. It is desired now only to affirm woman's natural, inalienable claim to that principle of common law, everywhere conceded to man, which holds all persons innocent until proved guilty; to share in the serviceable government which lifts up the oppressed, in pulling down oppressors, and finds its chief guarantee in popular freedom, and the imperishable sense of right. Who says democracy will not justify itself in her as in him? If the Goddess of Liberty is worthy of the imperial honor of a statue on the dome of the Federal Capitol, she may enter ward rooms and town halls as a voter. When the mailed hand of force is withdrawn, leaving woman free like man to do wrong even at her own cost, to stand or fall on her own merits, she will do well—in making love or laws, a leaf of bread or an immortal being—just in proportion as responsibility is recognized, intelligence enlarged and liberty inviolate. All hail, Equality! Then indeed will moral regeneration begin, and social concord be possible, when the sexes, meeting as intelligent beings, mutually accountable to each other and to destiny, engaged irretrievably to nothing but right, reason together on the issues of life, and welcome its yet untried privileges.

The male

> " Has no more subtle master under Heaven
> Than is the maiden passion for a maid;
> Not only to keep down the base in him,
> But teach high thought and amiable words,
> And courtliness and the desire of fame,
> And love of truth and all that makes a man."

Woman has no better friends incarnate than men whom she can freely love, respect and trust; and no worse enemy than him who, for any purpose whatever, would subordinate her being to his. Liberated, self-loyal womanhood is to be the connecting link between isolation and society, the "guardian angel of our associated destiny." Both sexes need to be profoundly converted to truth and honor; for liberty is not the goddess we read of, but male, incontinent, libertine when not over-ruled by an intelligent moral sense. Rights obtained should impel to corresponding duties; and free, intelligent inter dependence make love relations less formal and promiscuous, but more select, intimate and re-fining. Each belongs to self and others, one being only half man with-out woman, and the other only half woman without man. The family retains its place, in the hope of unity and honesty, at least in a narrow circle; enlightened liberty will eliminate its defects and universalize its merits. As the old spinning-wheel and power loom have given place to great factories; so the single tenement, with its cooking drudgery, washtubs and neglected children, will disappear in reorganized house-keeping, the scientific classification of woman's industrial and maternal functions. Be just and fear not; what love has joined, can be put asunder only by destroying the conditions out of which love springs and flourishes. Whether marriage is induced by affinity of likes or un-likes, the subtle attraction of essential worth and beauty, the fascina-tion of form and touch, the base allurement of money, tyranny of cir-circumstances, or carnal coalition from mere proximity; whether socie-ty rests on a combination of opposing or concurrent forces, everything good is to be gained, and nothing but bad lost, in the new departure involved in woman's enfranchisement.

That it will bring revolutionary and startling changes is evident; but, knowing in whom and what they have believed, new seas of agitation, however tempestuous, have no perils THE COMING to those who sail by the compass of right. In the con- WOMAN. flict of thought with idolatry, feudalism, priestcraft, po-litical and chattel slaveholders, the hearts of strong men often failed them for fear; yet, impelled by the inward might of faith, through ig-norance, superstition, avarice, infidelity and cowardice, the moral sense steadily gropes its way toward order, system, empire. The same law which holds ocean in its bed and planets in their courses will inspire these two mysterious sovereignties we call man and woman to transact their gayest and gravest affairs, with no jar or hurt, but mutual assist-ance to each other, and the general welfare. That widely looked-for personage, yet to rise from this agitation, like Venus from surf of the Grecian sea, the coming woman, no feminine man or masculine oppo-site, with greater physical vigor of finer fibre, will bring impressive beauty, melting tenderness, ethereal grace, mental force, moral recti-tude, such as the exhaustless sources of being yearn to incarnate. That passion now thought incapable of analysis, uncertain in its origin, acci-dental in its course, inspiring alike the darkest and brightest experi-ences, replete with ecstasy and tragedy, love, inherently pure, ineffably beneficent, is destined to make inclination one with duty, liberty the bride of order, and justice the security of citizens and the life of states.

CUPID'S YOKES

E[zra] H. Heywood

CUPID'S YOKES:

OR,

The Binding Forces of Conjugal Life.

An Essay to Consider some Moral and Physiological
Phases of

LOVE AND MARRIAGE,

Wherein is
Asserted the Natural Right and Necessity of

SEXUAL SELF-GOVERNMENT;

The Book which the United States Government and Local
Presumption have repeatedly sought to suppress,
but which Still Lives, Challenging Attention.

BY

E. H. HEYWOOD.

AUTHOR OF "HARD CASH," UNCIVIL LIBERTY," "YOURS OR MINE,"
"THE LABOR PARTY," "THE GOOD OF EVIL,"" WAR METHODS OF
PEACE," AND OTHER ADDRESSES.

FIFTIETH THOUSAND.

PRINCETON, MASS.
CO-OPERATIVE PUBLISHING CO.

FEW HAPPY MATCHES.

By Isaac Watts, D. D. August, 1701.

Say, mighty Love, and teach my song,
To whom my sweetest joys belong,
  And who the happy pairs
Whose yielding hearts, and joining hands,
Find blessings twisted with their bands,
  To soften all their cares.

Not the wild herd of nymphs and swains
That thoughtless fly into the chains,
  As custom leads the way ;
If there be bliss without design,
Ivies and oaks may grow and twine,
  And be as blest as they.

Not sordid souls of earthly mould
Who drawn by kindred charms of gold
  To dull embraces move ;
So two rich mountains of Peru
May rush to wealthy marriage too,
  And make a world of Love.

Not the mad tribe that hell inspires
With wanton flames, those raging fires
  The purer bliss destroy :
On Ætna's top let furies wed,
And sheets of lightning dress the bed
  T' improve the burning joy.

Nor the dull pairs whose marble forms
None of the melting passions warm,
  Can mingle hearts and hands ;
Logs of green wood that quench the coals
Are married just like stoic souls,
  With osiers for their bands.

Not minds of melancholy strain,
Still silent, or that still complain,
  Can the dear bondage bless ;
As well may heavenly concerts spring
From two old lutes with ne'er a string,
  Or none beside the bass.

Nor can the soft enchantments hold
Two jarring souls of angry mould,
  The rugged and the keen ;
Sampson's young foxes might as well
In bands of cheerful wedlock dwell,
  With firebrands tied between.

Nor let the cruel fetters bind
A gentle to a savage mind,
  For Love abhors the sight ;
Loose the fierce tiger from the deer,
For native rage and native fear
  Rise and forbid delight.

Two kindred souls alone must meet,
'Tis friendship makes the bondage sweet,
  And feeds their mutual loves ;
Bright Venus on her rolling throne
Is drawn by gentlest birds alone,
  And Cupids yoke* the doves.

---

*Since some " cultured " critics think Cupid's Yokes are " salacious " words, the Springfield Republican saying that I ought to be imprisoned for giving such a title to my book, it is interesting to note that the venerated Orthodox hymnist, Dr. Watts, used these very words nearly two centuries ago voicing in the above poem the same sentiments which the United States Courts have adjudged " obscene !" The passages on which I was convicted will be found, in Parker Pillsbury's Letter to me, entitled " Cupid's Yokes and the Holy Scriptures Contrasted," advertised on another page.—E. H. H.

CUPID'S YOKES.

LOVE in its dual manifestations, implies agreement, he who loves and she who reciprocates the inspiration therein are quickened, neither to hurt the other, nor evade any moral or pecuniary obligation which the incarnate fruits of their passion may present. When a man says of a woman, " She suits me "—that is, she would be to him a serviceable mate, — he does not often as seriously ask if *he* is likely to suit *her* ; still less, if this proposed union may not become an ugly domestic knot which the best interests of both will require to be untied. Whether the number outside of marriage, who would like to get in, be greater or less than the number inside who want to get out, this mingled sense of esteem, benevolence, and passional attraction called Love, is so generally diffused that most people know life to be incomplete until the calls of affection are met in a healthful, happy and prosperous association of persons of opposite sex. That this blending of personalities may not be compulsive, hurtful, or irrevocable ; but, rather, the result of mutual discretion — a free compact, dissolvable at will — there is needed, not only a purpose in Lovers to hold their bodies subject to reason ; but also radical change of the opinions, laws, customs, and institutions which now repress and inebriate natural expressions of Love. Since ill-directed animal heat promotes distortion rather than growth ; as persons who meet in convulsive embraces may separate in deadly feuds, — sexual desire here carrying invigorating peace, there desolating havoc, into domestic life, — intelligent students of sociology will not think the marriage institution a finality, but, rather, a device to be amended, or abolished, as enlightened moral sense may require.

When the number of opinions for and against a given measure are equal, it is called " a tie vote," and is without force and void, unless the speaker of the assembly throws his " casting vote," thereby giving to his side a majority of one, and enabling the measure to become a " law," binding, not only on those who favored, but also on those who opposed it! Not to note the manifest injustice and absurdity of such " an act," in the popular connubial assembly of bride and groom both vote one way, — that is, to "have" each other, — while the binding, or casting, vote is given by a " speaker," called priest or magistrate, who is supposed to represent society so far as it is a Civil act, and God so far as it is a sacrament* or religious matter. But, since neither society nor deity has ever " materialized " at weddings in a manner definite enough to become responsible for what Lovers may do or suffer in their untried future, we have no further use for a " speaker" in our nuptial congress, and must search elsewhere for the moral obligations which Lovers, by their tie vote to be " one," incur. In its desire to

MORAL
TIES.

---

* A sacrament is any ceremony producing an obligation, sacredly binding.— *Worcester*. An invisible hand from heaven mingles hearts and souls by strange, secret, and unaccountable conjunctions.— *South*. The mind is God's book, and its healthy attractions are his laws.— *Austin Kent*.

"confirm this amity by nuptial knot," society forgets that Lovers are Lovers by mutual attraction which does not ask leave to be, or to cease to be, of any *third* party; that its effort to "confirm" Love by visible bonds tends to destroy Magnetic Forces which induce unity; and that Lovers are responsible only for what they, themselves, do, and the fruits thereof. Since the words "right" and "duty" derive their ethical qualities from our relations to what is essentially reasonable and just, — to the nature of things,* — legislative "acts" neither create nor annul moral ties. As "alone we are born, alone we die, and alone we go up to judgment," so no one can escape from himself; but each must administer the Personal and Collective interests which he or she embodies. Being the authors and umpires of their rights and duties, the sexes weave moral ties by free and conscientious intimacy, and constantly give bonds for their mutual good behaviour. Cause and effect are as inseparable in human actions as in the general movements of Nature; choose as you please, the results of the choice you are the responsible author of. Relieving one from outer restraint does not lessen, but increases this Personal Accountability: for, by making him *Free*, we devolve on him the necessity of self-government; and he must respect the rights of others, or suffer the consequences of being an invader. In claiming freedom for myself, I thereby am forbidden to encroach.† When man seeks to enjoy woman's person *at her cost*, not a Lover, he is *a libertine*, and she a martyr. How dare woman say she loves man, when seeking her own good at his expense? Perfect Love "casts out fear," and also sin; if derived from the Greek *sinein*, to injure, the word sin implies invasion, injury; thus gratification of sexual desire in a way that *injures* another is *not* Love, but sin. Though they have a right to enjoy themselves at their own cost, yet, if their passion is hurtful, a sense of duty to themselves and others should teach Lovers continence.

VIRTUE, CHASTITY.

Having its root in the Latin *vir*, a man, the radical import of the word virtue is manly strength: usage invests it with intelligence to know and power to resist wrong.‡ One cannot choose without comparing the objects of choice; without judging for himself what is right, and personally placing himself at the disposal of Reason; hence, Virtue consists in ability to reason correctly, and force of will to obey Thought. But, since one cannot choose or act, when mental and physical movement is suppressed, Liberty, occasion, is the primary and indispensable condition of Virtue; while vice originates in stagnant ignorance, which the policy of repression enforces. The conscience, feeling, or impres-

* Everything is right which is conformable to the supreme rule of human action; but that only is *a right* which, being conformable to this supreme rule, is realized in society, and vested in a particular person. What is our duty to do we must do because it is right, not because any one can demand it of us.— *Whewell.* Duty is a moral obligation imposed from within; obligation a duty imposed from without.— *Worcester.* Duty is the relation or obliging force of that which is morally right.— *Webster.* There are no rights without corresponding duties.— *Coleridge.* Men have no right to do what is not reasonable.— *Burke.*

† True self-love and social are the same.— *Pope.* Love worketh no ill to his neighbor; therefore love is the fulfilling of the law.— *St. Paul.*

‡ Virtue implies opposition to passion or wrong.— *Fleming.* That course of action, by which a man fulfills or tends to fulfill the purposes of his being, is virtuous.— *Worcester.* Virtue is nothing but voluntary obedience to truth.— *Dwight* The four cardinal virtues are prudence, fortitude, temperance, and justice.— *Paley* The virtuous freely choose to live in accordance with the right reason of Nature.— *Philo.*

sions which precede and inspire thought announce the presence of ethical intelligence, and indicate how largely human actions are influenced by spiritual impulse. While, therefore, Liberty is the father, Conscience is the mother of Virtue. Chastity is power to choose between æsthetic health and disease, a power born of the same mental scope and activity which promote Virtue.* Sexual passion is not so much in fault as reason ; flesh is willing, but spirit is weak; the mind is unable to tell the body what to do. When the true relation of the sexes is known, ideas rule and bodies obey brain; purity of motive —just and ennobling action—follow the lead of free inquiry. The popular idea of sexual purity, (freedom from fornication or adultery, abstinence from sexual intercourse before marriage, and fidelity to its exclusive vows afterwards), rests on intrusive laws, made and sustained by men, either ignorant of what *is* essentially virtuous, or whose better judgment bows to Custom that stifles the cries of affection and ignores the reeking licentiousness of marriage beds. Is coition pure only when sanctioned by priest or magistrate? Are scandal-begetting clergymen and bribe-taking statesmen the sources of virtue? The lascivious deliriums prevalent among men, the destructive courses imposed on women, and the frightful inroads of secret vice on the vitality of youth of both sexes, all show the sexual nature to be, comparatively, in a savage state ; and that even public teachers have *not begun* to reason originally on questions of Love, virtue, continence or reproduction.

While Passion impels movement in one person towards another, and tends to overleap *unnatural* barriers, its proposals are, nevertheless subject to rejection ; created and nourished by   PASSION, the object of attraction, it is toned by Love which gener-   REASON. ates, but never annuls moral obligations. If intrusive, passion is hurtful; but, the person assailed, has a natural right of resistance ; and, if a woman or girl, her effort in self-defence will be reinforced by disinterested strength around her. If men do not rally to protect a woman thus imperiled, it is because their sense of right is distorted by an idea that women belong to men, and that the person of this particular woman is, somehow, the property of the man who can overpower her. Our applause of an example of Love measures the contempt which right-minded people feel for a man who imposes himself, or the unwelcome fruit of his passions, on woman. She is "safe" among men, not through laws which deny Liberty, but by prevailing knowledge of the fact that Nature vests *in herself* the right to control and dispose of her own person. If Lovers err, it is due not to Liberty,† but to ignorance, and the demoralizing effect of the marriage system If free to go wrong, disciplined by ideas, they will work out their own salvation in the school of experience. The Free Love faith proclaims the fact that persons recognized in law as capable of making a sexual contract are, when wiser by experience, morally able to dissolve that contract; and that Passion is not so depraved as to be incapable of redemption and self-government.

---

* Chastity is the regulated and strictly temperate satisfaction, without injury to others, of those desires which are natural to all healthy, adult beings.—*Benjamin Franklin.* Prostitution, sexual intercourse *without* affection ; Chastity, sexual intercourse *with* affection.—*Robert Owen.*

† Freedom is the only cure for the evils which freshly acquired freedom produces. —*Macauley.* When appetite draws one way, it may be opposed, not by any appetite or passion, but by some cool principle of action, which has authority without any impulsive force.—*Reid.* They only are free who are divinely bound.—*John Orvis.*

The essential principle of Nature; Love, is a law unto itself; but, resisted by custom, its natural intent and scope are not generally understood. We were all trained in the school of repression or inebriacy; and taught that, to express ourselves otherwise than by established rules, is sinful.*

FORCE OF CUSTOM.

To get out of one's body to think, to destroy all his old opinions, is almost necessary, to enable him to approach and investigate a new subject impartially. The grave tendencies of the Love question, its imperative force in human destiny, its momentous relations to government, religion, life, and property, demand revolution in social doctrines, and institutes, more beneficently severe than is yet fully conceived of. But, since nothing is fixed but natural right, the most radical method of treatment is the most truly conservative. Evils like libertinism and prostitution, which have baffled the wisest human endeavor, will yield only to increasing intelligence, and the irresistible forces of Conscience. I beg my readers, therefore, to bring to this subject honest intent to know truth and obey it. That the grand Principle of Love is potent with greater good than is realized in human affairs, is certain; that this noblest element of human being does not logically lead to the marital and social ills around us, is equally evident. The way out of domestic infelicity, then, must lie through larger knowledge of the nature of Love and of the rights and duties involved in its evolution.

Since the sexual union, (for life or until legally divorced), of one woman with several men — Polyandry; or that of one man with several women — Polygamy; or that of one man with one woman — Monogamy, is a conventional agreement between two or more individual contractors and a collective third, society, marriage, in either of its three historical forms, is a human device to tame, utilize, and control the sexual passion, which is supposed to be naturally ferocious and ungovernable. What Nature "hath joined," man need not attempt to "put asunder;" but, since the legalized marital relation† is so chaotic and mischievous, (clergymen and legislators themselves often being the first to violate what they profanely assume to be a divine ordinance); and since Deity has never yet come forward to own that he is "the author and finisher" of marriage laws, it is better to attribute them to the erring men who enacted them, than to accuse Divine Wisdom of so much folly. Marriage, then, being the creature of *men's* laws, we have the same right to alter or abolish it that we have respecting any other human institution. The principles of Nature derived from a careful study of essential liberty and equity, are a safer guide than crude social codes which come to us from the ignorant and despotic past. Woman,

MARRIAGE, A HUMAN DEVICE.

---

* The rules of etiquette, the provisions of the statute book, and the commands of the decalogue have grown from the same root, Custom. *** The right of private judgment, which our fathers wrung from the Church, remains to be claimed from Fashion, the dictator of our habits.—*Herbert Spencer.* The Orinoco-Indian woman, who would not hesitate to leave her hut without a fragment of clothing on, dare not commit such a breach of decorum as to go out unpainted.—*Humboldt.* Habit is the deepest law of human nature.—*Carlyle.* We gain a residence in the senses by birthright, but are born late into ideas, the country of the mind.—*Alcott.*

† I have observed so few happy matches, and so many unfortunate ones, and have so rarely seen men love their wives at the rate they did whilst they were their mistresses, that I wonder not that legislators thought it necessary to make marriages indissoluble to make them lasting. I cannot fitlier compare marriage than to a lottery: for in both he that ventures may succeed and may miss; if he draws a prize he hath a rich return for his venture: but in both lotteries there is a pretty store of blanks for every prize.—*Hon. Robert Boyle,* 1665.

who, being up first in the morning hours of history, played a winning hand in this marriage game,* is again coming to the front ; and, in the parliament of Reason, where the thought, impulse, attraction, and conscience of both sexes have free play, better methods of social intercourse and reproduction will be matured than exclusive *male* wisdom has yet invented.   It is for the Free Love School to develope an order of sexual unity worthy to be called a sacrament, and which sensible people need not blush to share.

" Will you have me ? " is the prayer by which man seeks partnership in the being of woman ; and she also has persuasive ways and means to pray to, and " capture," him. This would   MARRIAGE, be well, were it not a compulsory choice of evils, and COMPULSIVE. were they able to determine, in advance, the grave interests of offspring, industry, business, health, temperaments, and attractions, which mutually concern them, and on the adjustment of which depends their future weal or woe.   Girls become pubescent† at about 12, and boys at 14, though girls, then, are much older, sexually, than boys : from these ages young people are capable of all the pleasures and miseries of passional experience.   But, since sexual union for life is extremely hazardous for both parties, — it being impossible to correct the fatal mistake of marriage without the commission of crime by one or the other, — they are usually left to illicit intercourse, or to exhaust their vitality in secret vices.   Even when married, — coming into this new relation without knowledge of its uses or of self-control, — they prey on each other, and a few years of wedded life and child-bearing may leave the wife an emaciated wreck of her former self, and the husband

---

* The evolution of human society commenced in the institution of complex marriage. But we are informed by authentic historical documents, that, in the very early times, public opinion becoming more and more enlightened in certain favored communities, the women of these communities — sustained by that public opinion and shocked and scandalized by the social condition in which they found t' e.n-selves — were enabled to successfully revolt against complex marriage, and to overthrow it. Strange as it may seem, the old-world women established a new social organization for the more advanced communities, and a new marriage system, based on the ground of absolute female supremacy. (How the women managed to do it the writer shows, but I have not space to quote.—E. II. II.) In the new order of things the husband became the subject of the wife ; the woman was absolute owner of the homestead ; property descended, and relationships were counted, exclusively in the female line ; and the women seized and retained the principal share of political power.***The companions of Romulus (the founder of Rome) were men who ran away, took to the woods, to escape from the rigors of female government. These runaways establis ed themselves in easily-defended fastnesses, distributed the land surrounding them among themselves as " real estate," following out the lesson which the women had taught them.   It was in this way that the title to " real estate " began to vest in men, to the exclusion of women, and to descend in the male, instead of the female line. The heads of the groups in this new society were males, and members of the groups were also males. It was necessary, therefore, in order that the new society should become complete, that each male should steal a wife for himself from some neighboring tribe, and bring her to the mountain fastness. The men did not fail to perform the special duty that devolved upon them. The case of Rome was not an isolated one. All over Europe, and all over Asia, men rose against the women, transferred the titles to land, from the women to themselves by actual force, dethroned the sovereign witch-women by whom they had been so long governed, and supplied themselves with " CAPTIVE WIVES." This new institution of the " captive wife " gave occasion, in Europe, to the establishment of monogamy ; in Asia, to that of polygamy.— *Wm. B. Greene in " Socialistic, Communistic, Mutualistic, and Financial Fragments," pp.*188–208.

† Puberty is the time of life at which a person is capable of procreation or of bearing young, which, according to the civil law, is at 12 years of age for females, and 14 for males.—*Bacon.* This is the English view, but puberty varies with cli-

very much less, a man, than Nature designed him to be. Though *bewildered* moralists advise early marriage, they well know how often puny offspring rebuke the alliance,* teaching indiscreet parents that coition should have stopped short of reproduction. Those who think the evil is not in the essential immorality of the marriage system, but in its abuses, denounce with just severity the legalized slavery of women therein.† The absurdity to which Mr. Greene refers, below, consists in an effort to make the wife legally "equal" to the husband inside of nuptial bonds; it is an effort to make her an equal victim an an equal oppressor with him. Since marriage involves the loss of liberty, many of our best people, especially women, never marry, preferring to endure the ills of celibacy rather than fly to what may prove irretrievable ruin. Slavery is voluntary or involuntary; voluntary when one sells or yields his or her own person to the irresponsible will of another; involuntary when placed under the absolute power of another without one's own consent. The compulsive features of marital law are incidental and secondary to the marriage relation itself, which is unnatural and forced. Pen cannot record, nor lips express, the enervating, debauching effect of celibate life upon young men and women. Who supposes that, if allowed to freely consult their natural wits and good sense, they would tie themselves up in the social snarl of matrimony? Yet they are now compelled to choose between suicidal evils of abstinence and the legalized prostitution of marriage. Some, by clandestine intimacies, live below marriage; others, by personal defiance, and at the expense of social ostracism, attempt to live above it; but both are on the "ragged edge" of peril, as were "free negroes" who tried to live above or below the old slave system. The fierce blood-hounds put upon the track of fugitive slaves, were forerunners of the "dogs of war" which marriage now trains to hunt down its victims. A system so prolific of hypocrites and martyrs is compulsive in the most mischievous sense of that word, and will be abolished when free and virtuous people resolutely confront it.

Since marriage does not provide for the education of sexual desire or of its expression, but gives legal "right" and power to sin, every priest or magistrate, who "solemnizes" the rite, sells indulgences of a far more disastrous nature than those which scandalized the Romish Church. On account of her political, social, and pecuniary vassalage, woman is the chief martyr to the relentless license granted man; but cases are on record where the husband was effectually subdued by the tigress, with whom he went into the nuptial "paradise."‡ Founded on the supposition that man's love is naturally ferocious, marriage attempts, by legal means, to furnish food for his savage nature; and we have but to lift

TYRANNY
OF LUST.

---

mates; in temperate New England it is often delayed till 15 and 17, while in torrid regions it comes at 10 and 11, and earlier. It is said that one of Mahomet's wives bore him a son when she was but 10 years of age! What kind of a life does such a fact indicate that this especial "Prophet of God" led among young girls?

* In the entire animal kingdom, the fruits of the first signal of reproductive instinct are constantly imperfect.—*Aristotle* Marriages soon after puberty produce a diseased, puny, and miserable population.—*Montesquieu.* Give a boy a wife, and a girl a bird, and death will soon knock at the door.—*German Proverb.*

† Marriage is the only actual bondage known to our law. There remain no legal slaves, except the mistress of every house.—*J. S. Mill.* The definition of the wife's condition, as given in the English law-books, contain all the elements of a definition of domestic slavery. But the definition of the husband's status, as given in the same law-books, is that of a lord, not that of a slave. *** American legislation is more absurd than that of England.—*Greene's "Fragments,"* pp. 212-13.

‡ It is said of Valeria Messalina, wife of Claudius Cæsar, that "her husband's

the roofs of "respectable " houses to find the skeleton's of its femenine victims* It is because the marriage theory is unnatural and barbarous that it works out such shocking results. In the phrase "tyranny of lust," I have brought a good word into bad company, and must apologize for its misuse; for lust properly means desire, prayer, exuberant strength. So, likewise, the popular view of Love gives a devilish intent and drift to the divinest of words. Advocates of marriage cling to the exploded doctrine of natural depravity, and Freethinkers, Spiritualists and Atheists, who scout theological perdition, think social hells of permanent necessity in human life. Nowhere does the human intellect so disgrace itself as in its cowardly half-ashamed, and hypocritical attitude in the presence of Free Love. When woman's thought comes forward in the discussion, we hope for better things. In the early struggle of history which led to the establishment of polyandry (as in later domestic conflicts), the ruling impulse of the women was not sexual desire, but, rather, spiritual superiority, intuitional strategy, by virtue of which they were masters of men in the realm of religious mysticism. On the contrary, the repulsive evidence of sexual depravity, in men, referred to in the notes below, indicate the savage use, now made of animal force, which is capable of beneficent expenditure. When man loves woman intelligently, what is now consuming passional heat, will make him a genial, civil, and serviceable being. The unreserved devotion, with which a lover gives himself and his fortune to his bride, discloses the possible divine life on earth. But when impulsive, self-forgetting love, overflowing the narrow limits of family enclosures, gives one's heart and purse to deserving girls and women, the now, seemingly, savage suitor becomes Providence incarnate. Charles Sumner, in his will, gave money to the daughters of the poet Longfellow, of Dr. S. G. Howe, and of the Rev. Dr. Wm. H Furness, " in consideration of his profound regard for their estimable parents;" but cases have occurred, and will multiply, as civilization prevails, where men of no blood relation, and without a hint of sexual intimacy, give money, and even estates, to girls and women, worthy of love and distinction, irrespective of their parents, ennobling themselves and human kind in so doing.

---

chief officers became her adulterers, and were allied with her in all her abominations. She cast an eye of lust on the principal men in Rome, and whom she could not seduce to gratify her propensities she would contrive to destroy. She was so excessive in her sensuality, that she often required the services of the strongest and most vigorous men to satisfy her lusts."—*History and Philosophy of Marriage, pp.* 107-108,

* Victoria C. Woodhull speaks of a New York clergyman who married a beautiful woman, and, sometimes demanding indulgence, six or eight times a day, actually killed her by his lecherous excesses.—*Scarecrows of Sexual Freedom, p.* 23. M. Lallemand, in his work on spermatorrhœa, speaks of a Greek who for years indulged on an average fourteen times a day.—*Elements of Social Science, p.*84. I know a physician, who, the first year, and while his wife was pregnant with twins, indulged seven hundred and thirty times. * * * The woman is now broken down and barren.—*Quintus in Social Revolutionist, June,* 1875, *p.* 187. Here are my mother's words :—"Oh! your father's death is such a relief, he was so amative ; I could never talk to him on any subject, or lie one moment in the morning, without his becoming excited. I submitted to it all, because I thought I was married, and ought. I thought it a woman's duty to submit to what I conceived to be man's right. When I think of my suffering during child-bearing and nursing, when I look on a life of force and violation, I must say your father's death was a relief." My mother sleeps in the grave.—*Cora Corning in Social Revolutionist, July,* 1857.

Though man may "propose," and woman "accept," a notion inhabits the average *male* head that the irresistibly attractive **"who is** force of woman's nature makes *her* responsible for any **she?"** mutual wrong-doing. Thinking woman at the bottom of all mischief, when a male culprit is brought into court, the French ask "Who is she?" If he said that Mrs. Elizabeth R. Tilton "thrust her love on him unsought,"[*] the Rev. Henry Ward Beecher thereby indicated how much there is in him of the "old Adam," who remarked to the "Lord God," interviewing him after he had indulged in the "forbidden fruit," "The woman whom thou gavest to be with me, she gave me of the tree, and I did eat." The insanity plea put forward in courts of law by aggrieved "husbands" who, as in the Sickles and McFarland case, murder men that are attracted to their "wives," also affirms, in a round-about way, the supposed inability of a man to control himself when under the spell of woman's enchantment. Contrary to the old law which regarded the husband and wife as one, and the husband that one, when the twain sin, *she* is held responsible, and he is excused on the ground that he was over-persuaded, and too weak to withstand her wishes. From the Garden of Eden to Plymouth Church, skulking has been the pet method of man to escape from the consequences of sexual indiscretion. Beecher's confessions and "letters of contrition," with his later denials, sadly illustrate the pathetic penitence, the sniveling cowardice, and brazen-faced falsity with which "great men" endeavor to appease, cajole, and defy equivocal public opinion.[†] The harsh judgments pronounced on women which abound in the literature[‡] of all ages, are equalled only by the evidences of ludicrous puerility which men display when confronted with their sexual "deeds done in the body." The tragic anarchy which now distracts social life originates first in the "legal" denial of the right of people to manage their own sexual affairs; and secondly in the supposed exemption from moral responsibility of either man or woman in Love.

The facts of married and single life, one would suppose, are sufficiently startling to convince all serious-minded people of **national** the imperative need of investigation; especially of the **gag-law.** duty of young men and women to give religiously serious attention to the momentous issues of Sexual Science. But, on the threshold of good intent, they are met by established ignorance forbidding them to inquire. It is even thought dangerous to discuss the subject at all. § In families, schools, sermons, lectures, and newspapers its candid consideration is so studiously suppressed that children

---

[*] Mr. Beecher says he never made such a statement. [†] My allusions to Mr. B. are not intended to indorse the "exposure" view, for his alleged relations to Mrs. Tilton are none of *my* business; but I is words and acts as a public teacher of morals, and his false attitude, as an official "solemnizer" of the social crime of marriage, make him a legitimate subject of criticism. While his natural right to commit adultery is unquestionable, his right to lie about it is not so clear.

[‡] Better a thousand women should perish than that one man cease to see the light. —*Euripides.* Frailty! thy name is Woman!—*Shakespeare.* Unhappy sex! whose beauty is your snare!—*Dryden.* A state's anger should not take knowledge either of fools or women.—*Ben Jonson.* I will greatly multiply thy sorrow and conception; in sorrow thou shalt bring forth children; and thy desire shall be to thy husband and he shall rule over thee.—*Gen. iii.* 15. Her house is the way to hell, going down to the chambers of death. Who can find a virtuous woman?—*Solomon,* who kept 700 wives and 300 concubines, or "fast" women!

§ The woman that deliberates is lost, *Addison.* The man who reflects is a depraved animal,—*Rosseau.* Regarding physicians who do not follow the beaten

and adults know nothing of it, except what they learn from their own. diseased lives and imaginations, and in the filthy by-ways of society. Many noble girls and boys, whom a little knowledge from their natural guardians, *parents and teachers*, would have saved, are now, physically and morally, utter wrecks. Where saving truth should have been planted, error has found an unoccupied field, which it has busily sown, and gathers therefrom a prolific harvest. The alleged increase of "obscene" prints and pictures caused both Houses of the U. S. Congress, March 1, 1873, to pass a bill, (or, rather an amendment of the Post Office Act of June, 1872), which was immediately signed by the President, said to be "For the suppression of Obscene Literature," and from which I make the following extract :—

§ 148.—That no obscene, lewd, or lascivious book, pamphlet, picture, paper, print, or other publication of an indecent character, nor any article or thing designed or intended for the prevention or conception or procuring of abortion, nor any article or thing intended or adapted for any indecent or immoral use or nature, nor any written or printed card, circular, book, pamphlet, advertisement, or notice of any kind giving information, directly, or indirectly, where, or how, or of whom, or by what means either of the things before mentioned, may be obtained or made, nor any letter upon the envelope of which, or postal card upon which indecent or scurrilous epithets may be written, or printed, shall be carried in the mail ; and any person who shall knowingly deposit, or cause to be deposited, for mailing or delivery, any of the hereinbefore-mentioned articles or things, or any notice, or paper containing any advertisement relating to the aforesaid articles or things, and any person who, in pursuance of any plan or scheme for disposing of any of the hereinbefore-mentioned articles or things, shall take or cause to be taken, from the mail any such letter or package, shall be deemed guilty of a misdemeanor, and, on conviction thereof, shall, for every offence, BE FINED NOT LESS THAN ONE HUNDRED DOLLARS NOR MORE THAN FIVE THOUSAND DOLLARS, OR IMPRISONMENT AT HARD LABOR NOT LESS THAN ONE YEAR NOR MORE THAN TEN YEARS, OR BOTH, IN THE DISCRETION OF THE JUDGE.

I credit Congress and President Grant with good intentions in framing this "law;" for, ignorant of the cause of the evils they proposed to correct, they were probably unaware of the unwarrantable stretch of despotism embodied in their measure, and of the abuse which would be made of it. A humane man, Dr. Lewis has not the savage disposition which the extracts I have quoted, below, from his book, indicate ; the influence of "obscene literature" may be as depraving as he affirms; but his measures of repression are a clear invasion of natural right, and will serve only to hasten the downfall of marriage, which he writes to uphold. "Prohibition a Failure" is the title of a book, in which Dr. Lewis, by irrefutable logic, shows that the policy which he brings to the social question is indefensible and self-defeating when applied to the liquor traffic. When the Doctor as intelligently studies Social reform as he has temperance, he will blush to remember the heated words that have fallen from his pen. Regarding Anthony Comstock, representative of the Young Mens' Christian Association and the real author of the "law" quoted above, I regret to be unable to entertain so favorable an opinion. In a letter addressed to Hon. C. L. Merriam, M. C., dated Brooklyn, N. Y., Jan. 18, 1873, he says : "There were four publishers on the 2nd of last March ; *to-day three of these are in their graves, and it is charged by their friends that I* WORRIED THEM TO DEATH. BE THAT AS IT MAY, I AM SURE THAT THE WORLD IS BETTER OFF WITHOUT THEM." This is clearly the spirit that lighted the fires of the Inqusition. Appointed

path of custom in prescribing for sexual disease, Dr. Dio Lewis asks, "Is there no law by which such miscreants may be suppressed? * * * It seems hard that decent men are not allowed to shoot them on sight as they would shoot a mad dog —*Chastity*, pp. 23–205.

special supervisor of the U. S. Mails (by what authority I am unable
to learn); and, by religio-sectarian intolerance, constituted censor of
the of the opinions of the people in their most important channel of
inter-communication, he is chiefly known through his efforts to suppress
newspapers and imprison editors disposed to discuss the Social Question.
In Nov., B. L. 1, he procured the arrest and imprisonment of Victoria
C. Woodhull and her editorial associates for publishing a preliminary
ventilation of the "Brooklyn Scandal," which afterwards filled American
newspapers. Subsequently, he caused the incarceration, during seven
months, of George F. Train for publishing in his newspaper (The Train
Ligue) certain quotations from the Christian Bible, touching the same
"scandal" which the implicated churches employ Mr. Comstock to hush
up. As I write this (Jan. 1, Y. L. 4), a note from another subject of his
vengeance, John A. Lant, editor and publisher of the N. Y. Toledo Sun,
dated Ludlow St. Jail, New York, Dec. 30, 1875, says : "Judge Bene-
dict to-day sentenced me to imprisonment in Albany Penitentiary one
year and six months. I will endeavor to send you a copy of the sentence. It is worth to us all it costs me." Mr. Lant's crime is sending
through the mails his newspaper, containing criticisms of the "scandal,"
and of Rev. H. W. Beecher! Mr. Comstock's relation to Mr. Lant, as
heretofore to Mrs. Woodhull and Mr. Train, is that of *a religious mono-
maniac*, whom the mistaken will of Congress and the lascivious fanaticism
of the Young Mens' Christian Association have empowered to use the
Federal Courts to suppress free inquiry. The better sense of the American people moves to repeal the National Gag-Law which he now
administers, and every interest of public and private morality demands
thorough discussion of the issue which sectarian pride and intolerance
now endeavor to postpone.

"Beauty is a joy forever," and for all ; the quality of beauty being
to awaken admiration and esteem in observers to the
LOVE, NOT   extent of their ability to appreciate it. To be suscepti-
EXCLUSIVE.   ble of beauty in one thing does not unfit, but rather
prepares us to appreciate it in others. Love of the
beautiful in person, or of character, is not less involuntary and non-
exclusive than in things. A man cannot love even one woman truly
unless he is free to love what is lovable in all other women. The fact
that sexual love is passional, as well as æsthetic, does not make it
exclusive. The philosophic Irishman who liked to be alone, especially
"when his swate-heart was with him," expressed the natural privacy
of Love, and also indicated the scientific fact that the affectional union of
two creates a collective third personality, superior, in some respects, to
either constituent factor. If from this mystical confluence of two beings
there springs a child, even this Evolution of Love does not make either
one of the three persons less accountable to self and truth, or less per-
meable by material and spiritual, human and divine influences which
either may encounter. Monogamists hold that Love is possible only
between one man and one woman, the word monogamy meaning *to marry
to one only.** Yet, *so called* monogamists constantly violate that principle ; for, if divorced by death, crime, or the courts, scarcely a man or
woman hesitates to marry the second, third, or fifth time. Are they any

---

* To have one wife only and not to marry a second ; to disallow second marriage.
—*Webster.* Monogamy is the marriage of one wife only, as distinguished from
bigamy or polygamy.—*Blount.* It is the condition of not marrying a second wife
after the death of the first.—*Chambers.*

the less "pure" in doing so? Certainly not; second, third, or subsequent marriages may be more healthful and harmonious than the first, for the good reason that at least one of the parties has had the benefits of experience. It is admitted that, if the previous partners in her bed are divorced by death or other cause, a woman may truly love and wisely marry the second or fifth man; but the purity of her love for the fifth man is not determined by the previous four being dead or divorced; were they all living and her personal friends, she can love the last man as truly as she loved the first. Consistent with the teachings of the Bible, which sanctions polygamy,* Christians support missionaries in foreign lands, who welcome to church membership and the communion table, men who have a plurality of wives. David, the "man after God's own heart," compassed the death of Uriah to get possession of his wife, Bathsheba † and "took more wives and concubines out of Jerusalem after he was come from Hebron," for God "gave him the house of Saul and the wives of Saul into his bosom." Though Solomon was very "promiscuously" married, Sunday-School children are yet taught to revere him as "the wisest man." The monogamic or o, e-love theory is both theoretically and practically rejected by modern Christians, (as likewise by "Infidels") and, if they will honestly follow Jesus, — who, while he did not directly condemn polygamy, was yet, theoretically, a woman's emancipationist — he will take them into his Free Love Kingdom of Heaven, where he says, "they neither marry nor are given in marriage."

Though the Jehovah-God of the Bible, disliking irresponsible divorce, "hateth putting away," he is a thorough polygamist; its Jesus-God as plainly favors the entire abolition of mar- THE ONEIDA riage. Out of the modern Christian Church have come VIEW. three phases of sexual morality, — Shakerism, or the utter proscription of sexual intercourse; Mormonism, or sanctified polygamy; and Oneida-Perfection with its "free" love and omnigamy While the question of marriage and property are to be settled on the basis of Reason, the Bible and other records of the past thought being only incidental evidence, the Oneida Community ‡ are nearer sound on these two points than any other Christian sect. I give, therefore, a brief abstract of their Love doctrine, mainly in the words of their Seer and pastor, Rev. J. H. Noyes. The kingdom of heaven supplants all human governments; in it the institution of marriage, which assigns the possession of one woman to one man, does not exist, the intimate union of Love extending to the whole body of believers.§ The pentecostal spirit abolishes exclusiveness in regard to women and children, as respecting property. The new commandment is that we love each

* Polygamy existed legally, and was not put down by the moral sense of the Jewish nation.— *Woolsey's Divorce and Divorce Legislation*, p. 12. The Sacred Scriptures represent the wisest and best men that ever lived as practising polygamy with the divine blessing and approval.—*History and Philosophy of Marriage, p.* 63.

† God did not approve of his method of procedure, for he said to David, "I will take thy wives and give them to thy neighbor * * * And, of Bathsheba's child by him, he said it "shall surely die." David "wept and fasted" to atone for the "scandal," the Prophet Nathan being the *exposer* in this case, who, as Mrs. Woodhull to Beecher, said, *Thou art the man.* God let him have Bathsheba, who became the mother of Solomon.

‡ "Bible argument defining the relations of the sexes in the Kingdom of Heaven," being part of the First Report of the Oneida Association.

§ Those interested to consult texts are referred to Matt. vi. 10; xxii. 30. Eph. i. x. John xvii. 10-21. Acts ii. 44, 45; iv. 32. 1 Cor. vii. 29-31. Rom. iv. 15. 1 Cor. vi. 12. See "History of American Socialisms," pp. 621-9,

other fervently, not in pairs, but *en masse;* as religious excitements
act on amativeness, this is an indication of the natural tendency of
religion to Love. The union of hearts expresses and ultimates itself in
union of bodies. Love is attraction; seeking unity, it is desire; in
unity, happiness. In unobstructed Love, or the free play of the affini-
ties, sexual union is its natural expression. Experience teaches that
sexual love is not restricted to pairs; second marriages annul 'the
one-love theory and are often the happiest. Love is not burnt out in
one honeymoon, or satisfied by one lover; the secret history of the
human heart proves that it is capable of loving any number of times
and persons, and that the more it loves the more it can love. This is
the law of Nature, thrust out of sight and condemned by common
consent, yet secretly known to all. Variety is as beautiful and useful
in love as in eating and drinking. The one-love theory, based on
jealousy, comes not from loving hearts, but from the greedy claimant.
The law of marriage "worketh wrath;" provokes jealousy; unites
unmatched natures and sunders matched ones; and making no provision for sexual appetite, causes disease, masturbation, prostitution, and
general licentiousness. Unless the sexes come together *naturally,*
desire dammed up breaks out irregularly and destructively. The
irregularities and excesses of amativeness are explosions incident to
unnatural separations of male and female elements, as in the explosion
of electric forces. Mingling of the sexes favors purity; isolation, as
in colleges, seminaries, monasteries, &c., breeds salacity and obscenity.
A system of complex marriage, supplying want, both as to time and
variety, will open the prison doors both to the victims of marriage and
celibacy; to those in married life who are starved, and to those who
are oppressed by lust; to those who are tied to uncongenial natures,
and to those who are separated from their natural mates; and to those
in the unmarried state who are withered by neglect, diseased by unnatural abstinence, or ploughed into prostitution and self-pollution by
desires which have no natural channel. Carrying religion into life,
pledging the earnings of each for the support of the whole, the Oneidans seek "not the union of two but the harmony of all souls."

Whether the Oneida scheme succeeds or fails,* as an experiment it
is doing great service to civilization; and New York
State has the thanks of all intelligent reformers for per-
mitting Perfectionism to illustrate its ideas of sexuality
in its own way. But their conceited and self-righteous
contempt for Socialists who "have no religion," and
their belief that Liberty tends to demoralization, — "leads to hell," —
show the Oneidans to be ignorant of the source of the spirit of tolera-
tion and progress, which presided at their birth and has compelled
marriage bigots to leave them unmolested.† Making better use of
religion than any other Christian sect, the Oneidans yet fail to learn the
deepest lesson which Jesus taught, are mistaken in supposing that Free
Love and Free Labor are possible only within their iron-clad scheme of

CHOICE,
NOT
COERCION.

* The Oneida Community, coerced by religio-superstitious threats of Christians,
formally abandoned their complex-marriage system in November. Y. L. 7.
‡ If Christians had their way, their outraged sense of "virtue" would impel
them to assail and scatter the Oneida Community. The Presbyterians of Central
New York recently implored the State authorities to abate this "moral nuisance,"
as they call it. Always opposed to reform as a body, "Professing Christians"
are "conscientiously" hostile to efforts to free, legal and illicit "prostitutes,"
from their marriage masters.

Socialism, and that the first lesson of progress is to have one's Individuality broken on their religio-communistic wheel. Impelled with Paul to prove all things and hold fast to that which is good; inspired by the good old doctrine of Jesus, that each soul must *judge for itself what is right*, and be saved or "lost" on its own individual responsibility; declining to join the "bread-and-butter brigades" of Communism, Lovers will find their salvation in *Liberty* to choose,—to live on their own merits. The persistent growth of the "social evil" in defiance of all efforts to abate it, shows an irresistible tendency of people to associate even against law and custom; when they obey the higher law of Liberty, which makes social *choice sacred*, and Individual Integrity a duty, domestic life will gravitate towards unity, and Love become the potentially redeeming force which Nature intended it to be.*

But since human nature is imperfect, and passional heats often precede cool reason, young people cannot too early learn that they may choose wrongly; and that, if not guided   " HONEY-
by the rudder of thought, they must learn wisdom by   MOONS."
collision with the rocks of experience. It is better, however, to do wrong and suffer the consequences, than to be "saved" by mediatorial agencies which *act for us*, thereby overriding our necessity and power to reason, and divorcing us from an original relation to truth; better go to hell by choice than to heaven by compulsion. Those who hold, with Victor Hugo, that "the foolishness of Lovers is the wisdom of God," must have a large share of idiocy in *their* idea of Supreme Truth. The crude propensity of youth to unserviceable devotion to attractive maidens, when "life is half moonshine and half Mary Jane," is matched by the voluptuous freaks of Gray-Beard, who wants to be "better accommodated than with a wife." The amorous usurpation and delirious sentimentalism, which are the legitimate stock-in-trade of modern novelists, (in whose books Lovers are chiefly heroic in fornication, and, when married, cease to be interesting until "soiled" with adultery), are the main prop of the marriage system. The affinity-seekers,† whose insipidities mar even the best of poetry, and who expect "perpetual honey-moons" when they find "their mates," but who find "mates" only to soon loathe and discard them, are at once logical exponents and ludicrous examples of "wedded bliss." The philosophy which supposes another imperfect, or reprehensible, because she, or he, does not, and cannot suit me or you, is an insane philosophy. To waste under burdens of "inner life unshared," or vainly expect happiness in the union of blighted personalities, is our destiny, until we

---

* Adultery is an offence committed against a vicious social order among men, an imperfect social State, and is engendered by it exclusively; so that, when society comes or is acknowledged as the normal state of man, adultery will disappear as the fog of a marsh disappears before the morning sun. * * * Our existing conjugality, accordingly, is not marriage except in name, because it disallows an inward, free, or spontaneous tenure, and admits only a legally enforced or outward one. It is simply a legalized concubinage of the sexes.—*Henry James.*

† Marriage originated otherwise than in contracts by which one man bound himself to one woman exclusively, and, reciprocally, one woman to one man. It has been almost always based in modern times and in Christian countries on the "affinity theory," that is, on mutual consent grounded in natural attraction and the recognized natural interadaptation of the parties to each other, each being the affectional complement and counterpart of the other; such mutual consent following upon a necessary prelude of courting and love making, in which the fact of the "affinity" is authentically tested in respect to its genuineness.—*Greene's "Fragments," pp.* 201, 202.

learn that the human heart can find its home only in social concord which does not invade the sanctity of Individual Liberty.* The sexes naturally "expect each other," love to live and work together, love to find rest, and be lost in each other. Bating all the antagonism and heart-break which marriage causes, how much, even now, of rational joy, healthful association, and redeeming ecstacy there is in conjugal life! Greater than justice, stronger than reason, wiser than philosophy, is this widely diffused, and to be all-controlling Sentiment of Love.

In Experiencing the Ecstacy of Love, we accept the sway of Reason, and the inevitable sequences of cause and effect. What MYSTERY we sow, thereof we reap; Fate is unexplored fact. Wise OF SEX. heads have thought coition a mysterious lottery; but it is mystified by ignorance and superstition.† Whether it shall produce a child is a matter of choice; and the sex and character of the child are predetermined by its makers, the parents. "Queen bees lay female eggs first; afterwards, male eggs; so, with hens, the first-laid eggs give female, the last, male products. Mares shown the stallion late in their periods, drop horse-colts rather than fillies, If stock raisers wish to produce females, they should give the male at the first signs of heat; if males, at the end of the heat." With the human female, conception in the first half of the time between menstrual periods will probably produce girls; in the last half, boys. If coition occurs within six days from the cessation of the menses, girls are usually the result; if from nine to twelve after cessation, boys.‡ Regarding the physical, intellectual, and moral character of children it is surprising that parents who are careful to secure the best parentage for their canary birds and chickens, are utterly heedless in reproducing their own species. What graver act than to give life to a human being? What clearer right has a child than to be well-born? More impressive than the theological "Judgment-day" will be the tribunal

---

* The Shakers, who try to suppress sexual love, and the Oneidans, who would redeem and glorify it, are now the two leading exponents of Communism, in the States: amid the ruins of New Harmony Robt. Owen prophecied that individual property and marriage must go down together; while the old Brook-Farm Association died of too much love of marriage, usury, and "cultured" sentimentalism. There is some truth in Mr. Noyes' idea that a religious basis is necessary to successful association; but the "religion" must consist in obedience to Justice, Truth, and Liberty—not to a theological Christ merely. The Shakers and Oneidans have only taken women and children into the old property conspiracy, and, according to the popular idea of "co-operation," they divide the profits, or spoils, among a larger number of thieves. But, by abolishing interest, rent, and profits, we shall establish property on the basis of Equity: and Love and Liberty, in the absence of marriage, will promote associative unity.

† For this cause shall a man leave his father and mother, and be joined unto his wife, and they two shall be one flesh. This is a great mystery.—*St. Paul.* I should love to have such children as I can imagine, but I have no great desire to put into the great lottery of paternity.—*DeTocqueville.* I cannot doubt that the structure of animals is governed by principles of similar uniformity with that of the rest of the universe.—*Newton.* Little improvement can be expected in morality until the producing of large families is regarded with the same feeling as drunkenness, or any other physical excess.—*J. S. Mill.* Man scans with scrupulous care the character and pedigree of his horses, cattle, and dogs, before he matches them; but when he comes to his own marriage, he rarely, or ever, takes any such care.—*Darwin's "Descent of Man."*

‡ The above statements respecting human offspring are based on facts within my own knowledge. Other theories for predetermining sex are afloat, but this is the most reliable one I have met. Those wishing to pursue the interesting subject further are referred to Naphey's "Physical Life of Woman," pp. 129, 32; Trall's "Sexual Physiology," pp. 149, 200; and Noyes' "Scientific Propagation."

before which diseased and crime-cursed children summon guilty parents to answer for the sin-begetting use of their reproductive powers. People are little aware to what extent it is incumbent on them to forecordain what their children shall be. Better that every marriage bond in Christendom be severed than that one child be given life "legally," when it can have a superior parentage by coition above statute law. No woman or man should have a second child by his or her marital partner, when there is another person potently worthy of the selection by whom he or she can have a better child.* It was an ignorant and tyrannical prejudice which *forbade* Plato, Jesus, Paul, Newton, Humboldt, and other bachelors of the past, to give to the world that grandest achievement in art, — a Child. Many of the noblest Women now live as maligned "old maids," and will go down to their graves childless, because the natural right of maternity is denied them. "Good people" will think me rash in making such statements; but I appeal from them to the wiser future, which will *demand* that the reproductive instinct be inspired by intelligence and placed under the dominion of the will.†

That sexual intercourse is yet an Ethiopia, an unexplored tract of human experience, is due to a prevailing impression, among religious people, that it is "unclean," ‡ and, SEXUAL among Freethinkers, that it is uncontrollable; both HEALTH. views tend to remove it from the jurisdiction of Reason and Moral Obligation. But, "to the pure all things are pure," and, while "religion never was designed to make our pleasures less," Science brings disciples of God and Fate to answer for their misdeeds before the tribunal of Human Intelligence. Neither superstitious Supernaturalism with its theatrical terrors, nor learned Infidelity, "full of wise saws and modern instances," should deter the sexes from thought and experiment as to the best uses of themselves. That woman expects man, or man woman, is as natural and proper as desire for food or clothing. Since the mind cannot rule the body until it becomes acquainted with it, Lovers, — who are "servants of Providence, not slaves of Fate," — are divinely called to be *students in the laboratories of their own bodies*. The eye, the arm, or leg perishes by non-use; so without natural vent, exuberant sexual vitality wastes and destroys. Not to mention the fearful loss of vigor through involuntary emissions,

---

* Lycurgus laughed at those who revenge with war and bloodshed the communication of a married woman's favors; and allowed that if a man in years should have a young wife, he might introduce to her some handsome and honest young man, whom he most approved of, and when she had a child of this generous race, bring it up as his own. On the other hand, he allowed, that if a man of character should entertain a passion for a married woman on account of her modesty and the beauty of her children, he might treat with her husband for admission to her company, that so planting in a beauty-bearing soil, he might produce excellent children, the congenial offspring of excellent parents.—*Plutarch's Lives, p.* 36.

† Each generation has enormous power over the natural gifts of those that follow, and it is a duty we owe to humanity to investigate the range of that power, and to exercise it in a way that, without being unwise towards ourselves, will be most advantageous to future inhabitants of the earth. * * * All life is single in its essence, but various, ever-varying, and inter-active in its manifestations; men, and all other animals, are active workers and sharers in a vastly more extended system of cosmic action than any of ourselves, much less of them, can possibly comprehend.—*Galton's* "*Hereditary Genius,*" *pp.* 1, 376.

‡Thinking woman impure, the ancients called her monthly flowing *purgation.* Hence the command of Moses that men should not approach her at certain periods. But what theology calls "purgation," science proves to be "the sacred wound of love in which mothers conceive."

celibate abstinence and solitary vice probably engender more disease and death than all other causes combined.* Though he well knows the cause and cure of these ills, what physician dare prescribe the natural remedy? Accursed is the "civilization" which thus immolates its best life on the altars of superstitious ignorance! Retribution comes in wide-spread venereal diseases, syphilis so generally permeating male blood that it is unsafe for a lady to kiss a man lest she be infected fatally. Though probably less injurious than the fatal drain of involuntary emissions and self-abuse, yet, because illicit intercourse is usually undisciplined and excessive, it is often extremely hurtful. Since intense passion is never expressed in obscene terms, the sources of Love are pure; so vice does not consist in the judicious gratification of sexual desire, but in *repression* and disordered *excess*. Health, Temperance, Self-Control, and native graces are developed by intimate exchange of Heat and Magnetism, while both sexes are thereby fitted for Parentage.† The progress of civilization is marked by the degree of freedom and intimacy between the sexes. In the East, women appear in public veiled, it being thought sinful for them to allow their faces to be seen by any men not their husbands; here they walk, ride, dance, pray with, or kiss men, *strong in the dignity of a naturally beneficent mutualism.* We now forbid the sexes, unless married, to sleep together; but this restriction is a relic of Oriental customs, which will vanish as intelligence increases. In schools, churches, theatres, shops, factories, counting rooms, each sex is benefitted by the presence of the other. The same exchange of impulse, thought, emotion, magnetism, and grace, which develops and refines both sexes in industrial and social meeting publicly, will be still more improving in the most intimate

* Of those unfortunates who jump from bridges, take arsenic, hang themselves, or otherwise seek death, nearly *two-thirds* are unmarried, and in some years nearly *three-fourths*. In France, Bavaria, Prussia, and Hanover, four out of every five crazy women are unmarried, and throughout the civilized world there are three or four single to one married woman in the establishments for the insane.—*Naphey's* "*Physical Life of Woman*," *p.* 41. Sydenham says "Hysteric affections constitute one-half of woman's chronic diseases." * * * Hysteria is comparatively unknown in India, where it is a matter of religious feeling to procure a husband for a girl as soon as menstruation begins, but in this country, (England), whose customs enforce celibacy, no other disease is so wide-spread. * * * A happy sexual intimacy is the best remedy for hysteria.—*Elements of Social Science, pp.* 176–82. Thrown upon himself by the asceticism of our morality, the young man falls into solitary indulgence. Haunted by amatory ideas, and tormented by excitement of the sexual organs, the spirited youth wars manfully for the citadel of his chastity. * * * Night brings no consolation after the gloomy day, for he lives in constant dread of nocturnal discharges of semen, which weaken him so much, that in the morning he feels as if bound down by a weight to his couch. * * * He consults physicians, but, overawed by the general erroneous moral views on these subjects, they shrink from their duty to assert the sacredness of the bodily laws in opposition to preconception. * * * Rosseau was an instructive instance of a most noble mind, struggling under the inevitable ruin of a secret bodily disease. * * * Pascal also is thought to have had the disease, and probably Sir Isaac Newton, who is said to have lived a life of strict sexual abstinence, which produced before death a total atrophy of the testicles, showing the natural sin which he had committed. * * * It is a disgrace to medicine and mankind that so important a class of diseases have become the trade of unscientific men.—*Ibid,* 80, 81, 88, 102. See also Lewis' "Chastity," and Trall's "Sexual Physiology."

† The utility of the passions well directed has become a maxim in medicine as in morality; the fathers in medicine and their modern followers agree in this.— *Naphey's, p.* 76. Children should be the fruit of liberty and light; it is doubtless of the most elevated voluntary love that heroes have been born.—*Michelet.* The passions are the celestial fire that vivifies the moral world; it is to them that the arts and sciences owe their discoveries, and man the elevation of his position.-- *Helvetius.*

relations of private life. It will ere long be seen that a lady and gentleman can as innocently and properly occupy one room at night as they can now dine together.*

In the distorted popular view, Free Love tends to unrestrained licentiousness, to open the flood-gates of passion and remove all barriers in its desolating course; but it means   SEXUAL just the opposite; it means the *utilization of animalism*,   CONTINENCE. and the triumph of Reason, Knowledge, and Continence.

As is shown in the opening pages of this Essay, to say that every one should be free, sexually, is to say that every one's person is sacred from invasion; that the sexual instinct shall no longer be a savage, uncontrollable usurper, but be subject to Thought and Civilization. The damning tendency of marriage begins in giving the sexes "legal" license and power to invade, pollute, and destroy each other: and the immaturity of Science is painfully apparent, when it accepts the fatalistic theory of Love, and abandons the grave issues of coition to chance and "necessity." Though my experience is quite limited, facts within my personal knowledge enable me to affirm without fear of refutation, that Lovers' exchange, in its inception, continuance, and conclusion, can be made subject to Choice; entered upon, or refrained from, as the mutual interests of both, or the separate good of either, requires.†

Until Lovers, by pre-good sense, become capable of Temperance and Self-possession in sexual intercourse, it is an outrage on children to be begotten by them. Though Paul thought it "better to marry than to burn," it is best and feasible to neither marry nor burn; for, as in Plato's phrase, Lovers are persons in whose favor "the gods have intervened," sexual intercourse may be constantly under the supervision of both human and divine good sense. Since children are begotten by their parents, not by an act of Congress, or divine Providence, married people are forced to study methods of preventing conception; ‡ unnatural, disgusting, and very injurious means are frequently used, especially by some clergymen and moralists who, in their public teachings, hold that coition, except for reproduction, should be forbidden by law! From six or eight days before appearance of the menses to ten to

---

* The evils of celibacy I believe to be a fruitful source of uterine disease. The sexual instinct is a healthy instinct, claiming satisfaction as a natural right.—*Dr. E. J. Tilt, London.* Our appetites, being as much a portion of ourselves as any other quality we possess, ought to be indulged; otherwise the individual is not developed. If a man suppresses part of himself, he becomes maimed and shorn. The proper limit of self-indulgence is, that he shall neither hurt himself nor hurt others. Short of this, everything is lawful. It is more than lawful; it is necessary. He who abstains from safe and moderate gratification of the senses, lets some of his essential faculties fall into abeyance, and must, on that account, be deemed imperfect and unfinished. He may be a monk; he may be a saint; but a man he is not.—*Buckle.*

† I keep under my body, and bring it into subjection.—*St. Paul.* The discharge of the semen, instead of being the main act of sexual intercourse, is really the sequal and termination of it. Sexual intercourse, pure and simple, is the conjunction of the organs of union, and the interchange of magnetic influences, or conversation of spirits, through the medium of that conjunction. . . . Abstinence from the propagative part of sexual intercourse may seem impracticable to depraved natures, and yet be perfectly natural and easy to persons properly trained to chastity. . . . A very large proportion of all children born under the present system, are begotten contrary to the wishes of both parents, and lie nine months in their mother's womb under their mother's curse.—*Noyes' Male Continence, pp.* 12, 13, 15.

‡ When the health of the mother is doubtful, and the family cash box empty or a pre-disposition to some grave malady inherited, they will ask how conception may be prevented, or the next child postponed.—*Lewis' Chastity, p.* 89.

twelve days after their cessation occurs, conception may follow coition; * but intercourse at other periods rarely causes impregnation; if, however, it escapes control, it exhausts both persons, admonishing them to keep within the associative limit, which is highly invigorating, and not to allow themselves to gravitate to the propagative climax. To participate in *generative-sexual intercourse*, instead of dwelling so much upon it in thought and imagination, is Nature's own method to promote continence. The fact that those in whom the seminal nature is most repressed, — young male victims of sexual weakness, hysterical girls, hypoish boys and men, single women, priests, and poets, — dwell much in thought on social subjects, and yet, by unreasoning custom, are denied natural association with the opposite sex, is most disastrous to themselves and society. If persons do not acquire habits of conti-nence by force of will, Nature's method is sharp and decisive; she confronts them with a child, which effectually tames and matures both parents. Far better that their attraction lead to "illegal" parentage, than end in marriage, or by suicidal celibacy. The fashionable method of single persons, and of very many married people, is to get rid of the child before birth by abortion; but this murderous practice is unworthy of Free Lovers : they accept and rear the child, but take care that the next one be born of choice, not by accident. Since the increase of pop-ulation outruns increase in means of subsistence, Malthus urged that, unless people refuse to marry, or defer it till middle life, there will be too many consumers for the food grown; and that, if they do not heed this admonition, Nature sternly represses excessive increase of popula-tion, "by the ghastly agencies of war, pestilence, and famine." Ly-curgus favored destroying imperfect and sickly children; Plato, in his imaginative Republic, advises a similar weeding-out process; and, thinking sexual desire "a most enervating and filthy cheat," Shakerism endeavors to exterminate it — three popular devices to govern propaga-tion and Population : 1. The Shaker-Malthus method, which forbids sexual intercourse; 2. The abortion-child-murder method, which de-stroys life before or after birth; 3. The French-Owen method of barri-ers, withdrawal, &c., to arrest the process in its course; — but, since they are either unnatural, injurious, or offensive, all these devices are rejected by Free Lovers. Extending the domain of Reason and self-control over the whole human system, and believing that all things work together for the good of those that love good, they not only believe, but *know*, that, under self-discipline, "every organ or faculty in the body works invariably, in all cases, and at all times, for the good of the whole."

The thread of philosophy with which people connect scattered facts of their social experience, is religiously used to entangle
CAUSES OF   so-called "fallen women," in hopeless depression. But,
"PROSTITUTION." if each "common" woman entertains an average num-ber of five men as her customers, for every woman who "sells her virtue" there must be five "fallen" men who buy it. How

---

* Conception may take place from sexual union within six days before the be-ginning, to ten days after the cessation, of the menstrual evacuation.—*T. L. Nich-ols' Human Physiology p.* 271. M. Bischoff, the celebrated German physiologist, says that coition to be fruitful, must take place from eight days before to twelve after the menses cease. . . . Various unnatural means are employed to prevent the seminal fluid from entering the womb, thus preventing the union of the sperm and germ cell which is the essential part of impregnation; among these means are withdrawal before emission; the use of safes, or sheathes; the introduction of a piece of sponge so as to guard the mouth of the womb, and the injection of tepid water into the vagina immediately after coition. But these methods, except the latter, are injurious and disgusting.—*Elements of Social Science pp.* 348-9. See also Owen's "Moral Physiology."

came they to have money to buy it? How came she to be so dependent that she consents to sell the use of her person for food and clothing? Wine, women, and wealth are three prominent objects of men's desire; to be able to control the first two, they monopolize the third; having, through property in land, interest on money, rent, and profits, subjected labor to capital, recipients of speculative increase keep working *men* poor; and, by excluding woman from industrial pursuits and poisoning her mind with superstitious notions of natural weakness, delicacy, and dependence, capitalists have kept her wages down to very much less than men get for the same work.* Thus, men become buyers, and women sellers, of "virtue." But many women, not in immediate need of money, engage in "the social evil;" for, allied with this financial fraud is the great social fraud, marriage, by which the sexes are put in unnatural antagonism, and forbidden natural intercourse; social pleasure, being an object of common desire, becomes a marketable commodity, sold by her who receives a buyer for the night, and by her who, marrying for a home, becomes a "prostitute" for life.† The usury system enables capitalists to control and consume property which they never earned, laborers being defrauded to an equal extent; this injustice creates intemperate and reckless desires in both classes; but when power to accumulate property without work is abolished, the habits of industry, which both men and women must acquire, will promote sexual *Temperance*. In marriage, usury, and *the exceptionally low wages of women*, then, I find the main sources of "prostitution." Luckily the profit-system will go down with its twin-relic of barbarism, the marriage-system; in life united, in death they will not be divided.

In telling the woman of Samaria, who had just said to him "I have no husband," "Thou hast had five husbands; and he whom thou now hast is not thy husband," Jesus quietly recognized, without reproof, her natural right to live with men as she chose; and when a woman "taken in adultery, in the very act," was brought to him for criticism and sentence, he sent her accusers home to their own hearts and lives by the emphatic rebuke, "He that is without sin among you, let him first cast a stone at her." By the Mosaic Law she should have been stoned to death, and the lascivious ignorance of religio-"cultured" Massachusetts would imprison her; but wiser Love points her to the upward path of social and industrial liberty. Impersonal and spiritual, Love has also its material and special revelations, which make it a sacredly private and personal affair. Why should the right of private judgment, which is conceded in politics and religion, be denied to domestic life? If Government cannot justly determine what ticket we shall vote, what church we shall attend, or what books we shall read, by what authority does it watch at key-holes and burst open bed-chamber doors to drag Lovers from sacred seclusion? Why should priests and magistrates supervise the Sexual Organs of citizens any more than the brain and stomach? If we are incapable of sexual self-government, is the matter helped by appointing to "protect" us, "ministers of the Gospel," whose incontinent lives fill the world with "scandals?" If unwedded

SEXUAL RIGHTS.

---

* Sexual despotism, making almost every woman, socially speaking, the appendage of some man, enables men to take systematically the lion's share of whatever belongs to both.—*John Stuart Mill.* Working women, as compared with men, are defrauded of fifty per cent. of their rightful earnings.—*Amasa Walker.*

† It is a lamentable truth that the troubles which respectable, hard-working, married women undergo, are more trying to the health, and detrimental to the looks, than any of the harlot's career.—*Herbert Spencer.*

lovers, who cohabit are lewd, will paying a marriage fee to a minister make them "virtuous?" Sexual organs are not less sacredly the property of individual citizens than other bodily organs; this being undeniable, Who but the individual owners ean rightly determine When, Where, How and for What purpose they shall be used? The belief that our Sexual Relations can be better governed by statute, than by Personal Choice, is a rude species of conventional impertinence, as barbarious and shocking as it is senseless. Personal Liberty and the Rights of Conscience in Love, now savagely invaded by Church, State, and "wise" Freethinkers, should be unflinchingly asserted. Lovers cannot innocently enact the perjury of marriage; to even voluntarily become slaves to each other is deadly sin against themselves, their children, and society;* hence marriage vows and laws, and statutes against adultery and fornication, are unreasonable, unconstitutional, unnatural and void.

Against all repressive opposition, Individualism steadily advances to become a law unto itself; the right of private judgment in religion, wrested by Luther from Intolerance in continental Europe — later asserted in politics by Hampden and Sydney against the English Stuarts, and by Adams and Jefferson against British-American centralization — is now legitimately claimed in behalf of sexual self-government. Protestantism, Magna Charta, Habeas Corpus, Trial by Jury, Freedom of Speech and Press, The Declaration of Independence, Jeffersonian State Rights, Negro-Emancipation, were fore-ordained to help Love and Labor Reformers bury sexual slavery, with profit-piracy, in their already open graves. Thanks to the inspired energy of ancestral reformers, the guarantees of personal liberty, which we inherit from our predecessors, are all-sufficient in this Free-Love battle. Those who resist free tendencies to-day can read their doom in the prophetic wrath of Proudhon, who, confronting property usurpation and Napoleonic despotism in France, said, *He who fights against ideas will perish by ideas!* Yet not ideas, not intellect merely, but moral appeal, the might of Conscience, and the all-persuasive impulses of the human heart enter this conflict. Human nature may well blush if the *drama of deceit* enacted in the "Brooklyn Scandal" is to be taken as a fair expression of American thought and feeling. But the array of intellect, scholarship, and eloquence opposed in that struggle; the impressive pomp of courts, the

HEARTS,
TRUMPS.

---

* The Master said, "Swear not at all;" and no exception in favor of the marriage oath is made. Sacramental marriage is outside of the normal conditions of human society. . . . Under the Christian dispensation, no man can rightfully make himself, by any process cognizable before the civil courts, a voluntary slave. . . . No man can rightfully repudiate his own conscience; neither can he, by any foregone act, mortgage his own conscience in the future. . . . The 11th amendment of the Mass. Constitution says, "No subordination of any one sect or denomination to another shall ever be established by law." . . . If one sect believe on moral and religious grounds, that it is wicked to put all people under the alternative of not marrying at all, or of marrying for life, where is the constitutionality of the law which forces them to marry in a way against which they have conscientious scruples? With what show of justice could the courts punish, with fine and imprisonment, parties living in such a way that fornication and bastardy, through their example, becomes respectable?—*Greene's* "*Fragments,*" *pp.* 220-2. Those who marry as little intend to conspire their own ruin as those who swear allegiance; and as a whole people is to an ill government, so is one man or woman to an ill marriage.—*Milton.* Did South Carolina, which, before negro emancipation, had no divorces, present a better civilization than Connecticut and Indiana, in which divorces were readily obtained? Does the Romish Church, which opposes divorce, embody higher types of character than Protestant Churches favoring it?

mustering clans of ecclesiastical authority, the listening attitude of thousands of pulpits, and the recording pens of an omnipresent Press, — all these are for a day, fleeting and contemptible, when weighed against an honest heart-throb between one man and one woman! The loud clamor of words will cease, the majesty of courts fade, churches vanish, Christianity itself pass away, but the still, small voice of Love will continue to be heeded by Earth's millions gathering at its shrines! And as the dictation of statutes is increasingly resisted and the wrath of slave masters defied, more and more will the bonds of affection be welcomed, for the yokes which Cupid imposes " are easy and their burden light." I opened this Essay accepting Love as the *regnant* force in social life; I conclude it by emphasizing the same faith. Money, ambition, respectability, isolation, magnetic fervor, fascinating touch, glowing beauty, — whatever influences concur to induce social union, the nourishing power to continue and prosper it, is the attractive force of personal worth, the call to live and serve together, the impulse to defer self and partial interests to the welfare of the Being loved.* Sired by Wisdom, born of Truth, Love stimulates enterprise, quickens industry, fosters self-respect, reverences the lowly and worships the Most High, harmonizing personal impulse with the demands of morality, in a well-informed faith, which renders conventional statutes useless, where " the heavens themselves do guide the state."

---

* Judged by the final test, the chief thing, in life, is love.—*Theodore Tilton*. There must be a unitary passional code, enacted by God, and interpreted by attraction.—*Fourier*. Individuality, as the principle of order and repose, is directly opposed to promiscuity.—*Josiah Warren*. He whom love alone does not satisfy cannot have been filled with it.—*Richter*. No man is qualified to feel the worth of a woman who reverences herself. . . No woman shall receive an acknowledgement of love from my lips to whom I cannot consecrate my life.—*Goethe*. Let the motive be in the deed not in the event; be not one moved by the hope of reward; he who doeth what is to be done, without affection, obtaineth the Supreme.—*Kreeshna*.

☞ At this date June 1, Y. L. 8, Cupid's Yokes first officially assailed in Halifax, N. S., while being sold there by Josephine S. Tilton in Y. L. 5, though less than 4 1-2 years old, has been complained of or prosecuted a dozen times or more, twice burned in public squares by indignant city marshals, repeatedly " suppressed " by the United States and State Governments, meeting persecution which for superstitious rancor is unparalleled by any book since the appearance of Paine's Age of Reason that so shocked conservatives in America and Europe before the Revolution of B. L. 97. Sentenced to two years imprisonment at hard labor in Dedham Jail, June 25th, Y. L. 6, July 2.1 following I discarded the A. D. notation of time which recognizes a mythical God in the calender, puts Christian collars marked " J. C." on naturally free necks, and registers us subjects of the lascivio-religious despotism which the male-sexual origin and history of the cross impose,—dating instead, Y.L. in the Year of Love, from the formation of the New England Free Love League in Boston, Feb. 25th, 1873. Announcing the New Heavens and the New Earth, the Natural Society, foreseen by sensitives, poets and philosophers, Cupid's Yokes, after each " suppression," rises with new vigor to wrestle with benighted Irrationalism,—strong in the New Faith, the New Morality which is destined to supersede present religion, law and order. Like the " little book " spoken of in St, John 's Revelation (Chap. x, 2-10), sweet in the mouths but bitter in the bellies of vulgar bigots, explaining the mystery of Good as foreseened by its servants the prophets, pronouncing Christian " time no longer," this oracle of the banner State of Life, LOVE, now gives ideas and law to 40,000,000 American people. From Stephen Pearl Andrews, Mary Wolstonecraft and Charles Fourier, back to Plato and Jesus, Seers in all ages have favored Intelligence in Love and Parentage; and since Physiological information, " anything designed or intended to prevent conception " is the objective thought to be suppressed by Comstock's " laws " it is the imperative duty of citizens to proclaim it; for, not superstitious Nescience, but knowledge of ourselves as Human Bodies, naked truth between Man and Woman, SCIENCE is the right rule of faith and practice in Sexuality. More protestant than Protestants, yet essentially Catholic, Free Love proclaims the Right of Private Judgment in morals.—E, H. H.

LETTER TO A PROSPECTIVE BRIDE

Ida C. Craddock

···LETTER···

TO A

Prospective Bride

BY

IDA C. CRADDOCK

Lecturer and Correspondent on
Social Purity

Published by IDA C. CRADDOCK

P. O. Box 2093   PHILADELPHIA

1897

My dear Miss..................

Our mutual friend,   , has
asked me to write you a letter which will
be of help to you in your approaching
marriage. You see I do not even know
your name; nor do I know whether you
are a young, inexperienced girl, or a
mature woman. I know absolutely
nothing concerning you, except that you
are about to enter the sacred relation of
wedlock. If, therefore, I say some
things which startle or even shock you
by their frankness, I trust that you will
bear with me, remembering how entirely
in the dark I am as to your personality,
and remembering, also, that I write this
letter out of an earnest desire to enable
you and your husband to meet the
ordeals of the wedding night with dignity
and self-control and in aspiration to the
highest, and that in order to explain
clearly, it is necessary to be frank.

First of all, I wonder if you fully
understand just what it is you pledge
yourself to do, when you become legally
a wife ?

1

Speaking from a business standpoint, you engage to perform certain duties, in return for which your husband gives you a living. You will have, perhaps, to fill at various times the offices of companion, housekeeper, mother, governess and maid of all work in the house which his money supports—offices which, where there is mutual love and esteem, and where the work does not become drudgery, it is a joy to every true wife to fill. No doubt you have heard these matters discussed often enough. But there is one office in your husband's establishment which you will be called on to fill, year in and year out, and which is rarely—I may say, almost never—discussed beforehand with the woman. Yet it is the one of which she is the most ignorant. And it is also, next to motherhood, the most important. Indeed, upon its right performance all the other offices depend. And if she refuse to perform that one office—that office of which she knows so little when she takes upon herself the vows of a wife—there is not a court which would not free her husband promptly by divorce.

I refer to the duty of periodical co-habitation.

If you are a mature woman, you understand the meaning of this term, in at least a general way. If you are a young girl, and ignorant of its meaning, I beg that you will lose no time in making inquiries of some sensible, refined woman of your acquaintance. If you have among your acquaintances a woman physician whom you can ask to explain what is meant by cohabitation, it will be still better. But upon no account allow yourself to discuss the intimacies of the marital relation with a woman who considers that relation impure. She is not the proper person to instruct you in such matters.

Assuming that you do understand the meaning of this term in a general way, let us now consider what is the method which a refined gentlewoman should follow in performing this important function of her companionship with her husband.

The usual custom is to keep a woman as ignorant as possible in regard to this matter previous to her wedding night. She is expected to receive her instruction at the hands of her husband then. This custom, it seems to me, is something from which every decent, well-bred

young woman ought to shrink, as much
as she would shrink from asking her
husband upon the wedding night how to
regulate any other of her bodily functions.

There is, however, another and still
more important reason why the bride-
elect should be intelligently informed
upon her duties in this respect previous
to the wedding night. Man's strongest
passion is sexual; while the strongest
passion of woman is not, as a rule, sexual,
but maternal. Every normal woman
really mothers the man she loves. Upon
the wedding night, where there is any
romantic attachment, however slight, the
leading passions of both parties are
wrought up to a high pitch of intensity.
Not one man in a thousand has ever
been instructed in right marital living.
He finds his bride complaisant, yielding,
affectionately disposed to make him as
happy as she can because her own
passion of maternal fondness for him is,
all unconsciously to herself, so intensified;
and, too often, he behaves with a most
discreditable lack of self-control. The
brutalities of the wedding night are
ineffaceably stamped on the memories of
more wives than you imagine. And

these result mainly from the ignorance of the bride. Where the woman has obtained in advance an intelligent conception of right living in wedlock, and is imbued with a realizing sense of the importance of not allowing the man to make use of her as a convenience, the wedding night—instead of being a night of rape and torture to the woman, violating all her instincts of purity—may become a night of poetry and tender passion, of serene self-control, and exaltation of mystic rapture for both parties.

There are two functions which may be brought into use in the marital relation. They are:—

1. The love function.
2. The parental function.

Each of these functions is lawful and beautiful and pure at the proper time. Each of them is unlawful and debasing and impure at improper times.

The exercise of the parental function requires the ejaculation of creative fluid on the part of the man, which, uniting with the ovum within the woman, produces the germ-cell of the embryo.

The exercise of the love function apart from the parental function does not require such ejaculation.

This principle of the division of the
act of cohabitation into two separate
functions is known to comparatively few
men. In the well-nigh universal ignorance which prevails on the subject, the
majority have been accustomed to con-
found the exercise of these two functions
into one act. This custom is so general,
that it is difficult to make men understand that a sharp dividing line may and
should exist between the exercise of
these two functions. They mistakenly
imagine that the healthful exercise of
the love function should culminate with
an effort to bring the parental function
into the fullest possible activity.

Inasmuch as the wife cannot possibly
become a mother oftener than once in
nine months (and, if she is to do her
duty properly by her young children,
she ought not to become a mother oftener
than once in three years), it will be seen
that to men who follow the ordinary
custom, only three methods seem practic-
able :—

1. The wasteful scattering of creative
seed where no harvest can be reaped.

2. Random and wholesale creation of
children, including cohabitation and the
exercise of the parental function with an

already pregnant wife—which is an outrage upon the unborn child.

3. The frequenting of harlots.

Methods 2 and 3 need not be discussed
with a right-thinking woman. That a
husband ought to be loyal to his wife and
to his unborn child—this is self-evident.
Neither should he enter lightly upon the
office of fatherhood. But the evil of the
first method—the wasteful scattering of
the creative seed where no harvest is
intended—is not so well understood. It
is wrong for several reasons :—

It unfits the husband for the normal
use of the love function in prolonged
self-control.

It unfits him for fatherhood ; inasmuch
as the repeated ejaculation of the creative
fluid depletes his nervous strength, and
hence tends to render his children
weaker, more unbalanced, more lacking
in self-control than even himself.

It degrades the most sacred of human
relations into an act of selfish convenience
for the man.

These are a few of the arguments
against this habit. A volume could be
written thereupon.

I have said that it is very difficult to
bring men to understand these impor-

tant principles through argument and
reason.   But there is one way in which
the most selfish man can be brought to
an appreciation of this higher and purer
and nobler method of marital union ; and
that is, *through his own personal experience.*

Evidently, then, there is only one
suitable teacher for each man—the
woman whom he loves well enough to
make his wife.

Do you begin to realize now the work
which you, and only you, can do for this
man whom you love out of all the world
of men ?

And the time to begin is on the wedding night; for it is then, of all times in
his life, that a man will find no task too
difficult in seeking to please the woman
of his choice.   You can make of him
then what you please, if you have the
spirit to say "No!" to his selfish passion,
and to insist that he shall tread with you
the higher path of union in self-control
that night and ever after.   And when he
has once learned his lesson at your
hands, he will never wish to return to
the old way; for he will then know for
himself that the way which you have
taught him is more healthful, and far,

far more satisfying and uplifting physically, mentally and spiritually.

Last, but by no means least to a normal, right-thinking woman, this habit of
union in self-control on the man's part,
without the creative emission, renders it
possible, when the habit also of aspiration to the highest has become firmly
established throughout the union, to
choose the most suitable environments
of place and season in which to beget
children, and to make those children
ideals of physical perfection, of goodness,
intelligence and beauty. To create a
few, a very few children who shall be
an expression of the noblest thoughts of
yourself and your husband, and to give
those children all possible advantages of
education, travel and society, which shall
fit them to become honorable citizens of
the State, and bearers of the Divine
light into the dark places of the world—
is not this doing your duty as a wife and
a mother better than if you create chil
dren at haphazard and by wholesale to
such an extent that you can scarcely
secure for them a decent living?

And now, having thus outlined a suggestion of the teaching which I earnestly
hope you will impart to your husband,

let us consider a little the part which you yourself are to play, physiologically, in the marital union.

I have spoken of self control as something to be required from your husband. It is also something which you should require from yourself. Your final ecstasy should be completely under your control as to how and when it is induced. It should be induced coincidently with the ecstasy of your husband. As a woman is so constituted that, as a rule, she is very much slower than a man in coming to the climax, she should train him to wait for her, if her own natural functions are to be fulfilled healthfully. This may, and, indeed, should require from a half-an hour to an hour after entrance is effected, in order that each may exchange with the other, strengthening and uplifting magnetism. The normal, self-controlled use of the love function (when exercised in moderation) never debilitates, never enervates. It freshens both parties, and renews nervous energy for days thereafter.

The natural time for union is upon the day or days immediately following the menstrual period. It is then that a woman is most affectionate and most

passionate. Consequently, it is then
that a wife will respond most readily to
her husband. It is then, also, that a
woman most readily becomes pregnant.
The desire to create is working within
her, and all the energies of her life are
intensified. At that time she may create
a child or a picture or a poem; or plan
some philanthropic work; or reconstruct
her household along lines which, she will
probably find, if she examine carefully
into the matter, she began to plan out
just before her period, owing to the
peculiar nervous organization of a
woman, which is excited into activity
periodically as menstruation comes
round. Whatever she burns to do can
be done with especial vim and artistic
skill and spiritual insight upon those days
which directly follow the menstrual
period. And it is at this time, of all
times, that she longs, if she be happily
married, to interchange with her husband the creative, magnetic strength
which only they two can give to one
another.

Now, if she be a woman who is wise
in these matters, she makes of each of
these periodical unions a new wedding
night; and so she holds her husband by

ties of romance and passion and self-
control and spiritual union which no
power on earth can break. The honeymoon of such a couple is perpetual

Never, never, never allow yourself to
yield to your husband's request for
union unless you yourself desire it. For
a woman to consent when she does not
desire union, is to consent to unutterable
degradation; and it places her below the
harlot. Do not yield, at any place or
time, without preliminary courting on
his part—courting which you will probably find, from experience, ought to
continue for about twenty minutes or a
half-an-hour in order to awaken any
desire on your part for union. If your
desire do not arise through caresses,
kisses and embraces, without sexual
contact, the time for union has not yet
arrived for you. But you will find that
contact of the person at such times, either
with or without clothing, will often
furnish a means of the most satisfying
sort for exchange of magnetic strength,
without the least sexual excitement.

Right here, let me say a word or two
about the human form divine. The
living statue is far more beautiful to the
beholder who is in love with the soul

within, than any lifeless piece of marble
can be. There are times when to be
nude in one another's sight is to be
chaste. Men of the world nearly all
testify that it is the partially draped
form which is exciting to their animal
passion, and that this passion dies at
once at the sight of the entirely naked
woman. In the Bible story of the
Garden of Eden, you will remember that
it was the evident intention of God that
man and woman should walk together as
husband and wife, naked and not
ashamed; and it was not until they sinned
that their nakedness came to seem to
them a thing impure. Do you remember
the scathing question with which the
Lord greeted Adam's embarrassment at
being seen in a state of nudity—"*WHO*
told thee thou wast naked?" Certainly
it was not the Lord, in that case, who
put into the hearts of the man and
the woman the idea that nakedness was
a shameful thing. Whether the story of
the Garden of Eden be considered as
allegory or Oriental myth or historical
fact, the husbands and wives of to-day
can learn more than one lesson therefrom.

Women are usually taught that to ex-

hibit any sign of pleasure at being loved
by the man of their choice is, to say the
least, immodest ; and they too often
carry this false training even into the
intimacies of the marital relation, so that
they are unwilling to let their pleasure
be known by the slightest movement.
In behaving thus, they violate natural
law, and become abnormal and debased
conveniences for their husbands. It is
natural and right for a woman who is
uniting with her husband at a time when
she herself desires union, to execute
various movements of her pelvis during
the marital embrace; and the woman
who fails to do this, fails in a very important marital duty. The indifference
or unwillingness of wives to reciprocate
at such moments is one great cause of
the infidelity of husbands. In fact, a
woman who is thoroughly in love with
her husband and who unites with him at
the proper time in the month, can
scarcely help moving. This matter of
the pelvic movements of a wife during
union deserves a very careful study, if
one would attain to the highest ideal of
right living in the marital relation.

One reason why the wedding night is
so frequently attended with suffering to

the woman is, that the hymen has to be ruptured. This can be obviated if the membrane be snipped beforehand by the scissors of a surgeon. This is not at all a painful operation; and the membrane, which is attached to the walls of the orifice, will soon shrivel away, as does any other piece of dead skin. This advice is given upon sound medical authority. It is the tearing of the membrane from the walls which causes suffering upon the wedding night. However, the husband should be taken into confidence beforehand, and his acquiescence obtained. This, because of the prevalent superstition that a woman without a hymen is not a virgin. In point of fact, many women never had a hymen, and in many other cases, where they were born with one, they lost it in early childhood when romping. This is well attested by physicians. But the old superstition still obtains; hence the advisability of discussing the matter with the bridegroom-elect prior to the wedding night.

Indeed, I most earnestly advise you to discuss with your chosen husband, prior to the wedding night, this whole matter of your plans for right living in the marital relation. In so serious and so delicate a matter, he is entitled to know beforehand if you propose this radical departure from customary methods which I am here advising you to make.

Another reason why the wedding night is so frequently attended with suffering to the woman is, that the vaginal orifice is small. Like a glove which is a trifle small for one's fingers, it can be gradually distended, by successive attempts at coition, to a suitable size; but this requires patience and often considerable time. In the case of one young couple whom I had the great happiness to instruct, it was over two months before full entrance was effected; but the results were most satisfactory. In some cases, the bride has had to resort to a physician to secure the necessary distention by instruments. It is, of course, right to call in a physician for such a purpose where it is absolutely necessary, but it would seem as though the natural way, where possible, is preferable.

One effective aid to a painless first entrance is the anointing of the orifice with some harmless unguent, such as vaseline, cosmoline, etc. This is advised by physicians. In a normal union, where both parties to the act perform their parts properly, nature herself lubricates the organs of both with an emission which renders any anointing unnecessary; but this will probably not be the case at first, at least with the bride. To secure the natural lubricative emission, the pelvic movements referred to above will be usually found all sufficient. The lubricative emission in the man's case is non-creative and is not ejaculated, but simply exudes.

If the wedding day has been one of prolonged excitement, the most sensible thing that the bride and bridegroom can do upon retiring, is to go straight to sleep like two tired children. On waking in the morning, the first marital endearments may suitably take place, and will be found strengthening to both parties after the night's rest. Never, upon any account, allow sexual union to take place when either of you is physically weary or mentally fagged out. But the embrace of the entire person at such a time, either with or without clothing, and with no sexual contact, will often be found to satisfy and refresh.

So much for the physiology and hygiene of the wedding night. But do

not forget that ideal wedlock takes place
not merely upon the physical plane, but
also upon the mental and spiritual planes,
and in as nearly as possible an exact
equation. The amount of energy set
free upon any one of these planes should
not overbalance that set free upon any
of the others, if your wedded relations
are to be in conformity with the highest
standards of right living.

To appeal to God to sanction every
union is fitting; to consecrate the joys
and raptures of that union in thankful-
ness to Him is still more fitting; to ask
Him to share with yourself and your
husband those joys and raptures is to
rise into a oneness with the Divine
Heart of the Universe, which only they
who have known it can fully understand.
Not until you make God the third partner, so to say, in your unions, will you
and your husband understand the serene
and lofty enjoyment of the truly wedded,
whose marital embrace is blessed physically, mentally and spiritually by the
Power which upholds the universe.

IDA C. CRADDOCK,

P. O. Box 2093, Philadelphia.

June, 1897.

THE BARBARIAN STATUS OF WOMEN

Thorstein Veblen

THE BARBARIAN STATUS OF WOMEN.

IT seems altogether probable that in the primitive groups of mankind, when the race first took to a systematic use of tools and so emerged upon the properly human plane of life, there was but the very slightest beginning of a system of status, with little of invidious distinction between classes and little of a corresponding division of employments. In an earlier paper, published in this JOURNAL,[1] it has been argued that the early division of labor between classes comes in as the result of an increasing efficiency of labor, due to a growing effectiveness in the use of tools. When, in the early cultural development, the use of tools and the technical command of material forces had reached a certain degree of effectiveness, the employments which occupy the primitive community would fall into two distinct groups — (*a*) the honorific employments, which involve a large element of prowess, and (*b*) the humiliating employments, which call for diligence and into which the sturdier virtues do not enter. An appreciable advance in the use of tools must precede this differentiation of employments, because (1) without effective tools (including weapons) men are not sufficiently formidable in conflict with the ferocious beasts to devote themselves so exclusively to the hunting of large game as to develop that occupation into a conventional mode of life reserved for a distinct class; (2) without tools of some efficiency, industry is not productive enough to support a dense population, and therefore the groups into which the population gathers will not come into such a habitual hostile contact with one another as would give rise to a life of warlike prowess; (3) until industrial methods and knowledge have made some advance, the work of getting a livelihood is too exacting to admit of the consistent exemption of any portion of the community from vulgar labor;

[1] "The Instinct of Workmanship and the Irksomeness of Labor," September, 1898, pp. 187–201.

(4) the inefficient primitive industry yields no such disposable surplus of accumulated goods as would be worth fighting for, or would tempt an intruder, and therefore there is little provocation to warlike prowess.

With the growth of industry comes the possibility of a predatory life ; and if the groups of savages crowd one another in the struggle for subsistence, there is a provocation to hostilities, and a predatory habit of life ensues.   There is a consequent growth of a predatory culture, which may for the present purpose be treated as the beginning of the barbarian culture. This predatory culture shows itself in a growth of suitable institutions.   The group divides itself conventionally into a fighting and a peace-keeping class, with a corresponding division of labor.   Fighting, together with other work that involves a serious element of exploit, becomes the employment of the able-bodied men ; the uneventful everyday work of the group falls to the women and the infirm.

In such a community the standards of merit and propriety rest on an invidious distinction between those who are capable fighters and those who are not.   Infirmity, that is to say incapacity for exploit, is looked down upon.   One of the early consequences of this deprecation of infirmity is a tabu on women and on women's employments.   In the apprehension of the archaic, animistic barbarian, infirmity is infectious.   The infection may work its mischievous effect both by sympathetic influence and by transfusion.   Therefore it is well for the able-bodied man who is mindful of his virility to shun all undue contact and conversation with the weaker sex and to avoid all contamination with the employments that are characteristic of the sex.   Even the habitual food of women should not be eaten by men, lest their force be thereby impaired.   The injunction against womanly employments and foods and against intercourse with women applies with especial rigor during the season of preparation for any work of manly exploit, such as a great hunt or a warlike raid, or induction into some manly dignity or society or mystery.   Illustrations of this seasonal tabu abound in the early history of all peoples that have had a warlike or barbarian past.

The women,. their occupations, their food and clothing, their habitual place in the house or village, and in extreme cases even their speech, become ceremonially unclean to the men. This imputation of ceremonial uncleanness on the ground of their infirmity has lasted on in the later culture as a sense of the unworthiness or Levitical inadequacy of women ; so that even now we feel the impropriety of women taking rank with men, or representing the community in any relation that calls for dignity and ritual competency ; as for instance, in priestly or diplomatic offices, or even in representative civil offices, and likewise, and for a like reason, in such offices of domestic and body servants as are of a seriously ceremonial character — footmen, butlers, etc.

The changes that take place in the everyday experiences of a group or horde when it passes from a peaceable to a predatory habit of life have their effect on the habits of thought prevalent in the group. As the hostile contact of one group with another becomes closer and more habitual, the predatory activity and the bellicose animus become more habitual to the members of the group. Fighting comes more and more to occupy men's everyday thoughts, and the other activities of the group fall into the background and become subsidiary to the fighting activity. In the popular apprehension the substantial core of such a group — that on which men's thoughts run when the community and the community's life is thought of — is the body of fighting men. The collective fighting capacity becomes the most serious question that occupies men's minds, and gives the point of view from which persons and conduct are rated. The scheme of life of such a group is substantially a scheme of exploit. There is much of this point of view to be found even in the common-sense views held by modern populations. The inclination to identify the community with its fighting men comes into evidence today whenever warlike interests occupy the popular attention in an appreciable degree.

The work of the predatory barbarian group is gradually specialized and differentiated under the dominance of this ideal of prowess, so as to give rise to a system of status in which the non-fighters fall into a position of subservience to the fighters. The accepted scheme of life or consensus of opinions which guides the conduct of men in such a predatory group and decides what may properly be done, of course comprises a great variety of details; but it is, after all, a single scheme — a more or less organic whole — so that the life carried on under its guidance in any case makes up a somewhat consistent and characteristic body of culture. This is necessarily the case, because of the simple fact that the individuals between whom the consensus holds are individuals. The thinking of each one is the thinking of the same individual, on whatever head and in whatever direction his thinking may run. Whatever may be the immediate point or object of his thinking, the frame of mind which governs his aim and manner of reasoning in passing on any given point of conduct is, on the whole, the habitual frame of mind which experience and tradition have enforced upon him. Individuals whose sense of what is right and good departs widely from the accepted views suffer some repression, and in case of an extreme divergence they are eliminated from the effective life of the group through ostracism. Where the fighting class is in the position of dominance and prescriptive legitimacy, the canons of conduct are shaped chiefly by the common sense of the body of fighting men. Whatever conduct and whatever code of proprieties has the authentication of this common sense is definitively right and good, for the time being, and the deliverances of this common sense are, in their turn, shaped by the habits of life of the able-bodied men. Habitual conflict acts, by selection and by habituation, to make these male members tolerant of any infliction of damage and suffering. Habituation to the sight and infliction of suffering, and to the emotions that go with fights and brawls, may even end in making the spectacle of misery a pleasing diversion to them. The result is in any case a more or less consistent attitude of plundering and coercion on the part of the fighting body, and this animus is incorporated into the scheme of life of the community. The discipline of predatory life makes for an attitude of mastery on the part of the able-bodied men in all their relations with the weaker members of the group, and especially in their relations with the women. Men who are trained in predatory ways of life and modes of thinking come by habituation to apprehend this form of the relation between the sexes as good and beautiful.

All the women in the group will share in the class repression and depreciation that belongs to them as women, but the status of women taken from hostile groups has an additional feature. Such a woman not only belongs to a subservient and low class, but she also stands in a special relation to her captor. She is a trophy of the raid, and therefore an evidence of exploit, and on this ground it is to her captor's interest to maintain a peculiarly obvious relation of mastery toward her. And since, in the early culture, it does not detract from her subservience to the life of the group, this peculiar relation of the captive to her captor will meet but slight, if any, objection from the other members of the group. At the same time, since his peculiar coercive relation to the woman serves to mark her as a trophy of his exploit, he will somewhat jealously resent any similar freedom taken by other men, or any attempt on their part to parade a similar coercive authority over her, and so usurp the laurels of his prowess, very much as a warrior would under like circumstances resent a usurpation or an abuse of the scalps or skulls which he had taken from the enemy.

After the habit of appropriating captured women has hardened into custom, and so given rise on the one hand to a form of marriage resting on coercion, and on the other hand to a concept of ownership,[1] a development of certain secondary features of the institution so inaugurated is to be looked for. In time this coercive ownership-marriage receives the sanction of the popular taste and morality. It comes to rest in men's habits of thought as the right form of marriage relation, and it comes at the same time to be gratifying to men's sense of beauty and of honor. The growing predilection for mastery and coercion, as a manly trait, together with the growing moral and æsthetic approbation of marriage on a basis of coercion and ownership,

[1] For a more detailed discussion on this point see a paper on "The Beginnings of Ownership" in this JOURNAL for November, 1898.

will affect the tastes of the men most immediately and most strongly; but since the men are the superior class, whose views determine the current views of the community, their common sense in the matter will shape the current canons of taste in its own image. The tastes of the women also, in point of morality and of propriety alike, will presently be affected in the same way. Through the precept and example of those who make the vogue, and through selective repression of those who are unable to accept it, the institution of ownership-marriage makes its way into definitive acceptance as the only beautiful and virtuous form of the relation. As the conviction of its legitimacy grows stronger in each succeeding generation, it comes to be appreciated unreflectingly as a deliverance of common sense and enlightened reason that the good and beautiful attitude of the man toward the woman is an attitude of coercion. "None but the brave deserve the fair."

As the predatory habit of life gains a more unquestioned and undivided sway, other forms of the marriage relation fall under a polite odium. The masterless, unattached woman consequently loses caste. It becomes imperative for all men who would stand well in the eyes of their fellows to attach some woman or women to themselves by the honorable bonds of seizure. In order to a decent standing in the community a man is required to enter into this virtuous and honorific relation of ownership-marriage, and a publicly acknowledged marriage relation which has not the sanction of capture becomes unworthy of able-bodied men. But as the group increases in size, the difficulty of providing wives by capture becomes very great, and it becomes necessary to find a remedy that shall save the requirements of decency and at the same time permit the marriage of women from within the group. To this end the status of women married from within the group is sought to be mended by a mimic or ceremonial capture. The ceremonial capture effects an assimilation of the free woman into the more acceptable class of women who are attached by bonds of coercion to some master, and so gives a ceremonial legitimacy and decency to the resulting marriage relation. The probable motive for adopting the free women into the honorable class of bond women in this way is not primarily a wish to 'mprove their standing or their lot, but rather a wish to keep those good men in countenance who, for dearth of captives, are constrained to seek a substitute from among the home-bred women of the group. The inclinations of men in high standing who are possessed of marriageable daughters would run in the same direction. It would not seem right that a woman of high birth should irretrievably be outclassed by any chance-comer from outside.

According to this view, marriage by feigned capture within the tribe is a case of mimicry—"protective mimicry," to borrow a phrase from the naturalists. It is substantially a case of adoption. As is the case in all human relations where adoption is practiced, this adoption of the free women into the class of the unfree proceeds by as close an imitation as may be of the original fact for which it is a substitute. And as in other cases of adoption, the ceremonial performance is by no means looked upon as a fatuous make-believe. The barbarian has implicit faith in the efficiency of imitation and ceremonial execution as a means of compassing a desired end. The entire range of magic and religious rites is testimony to that effect. He looks upon external objects and sequences naïvely, as organic and individual things, and as expressions of a propensity working toward an end. The unsophisticated common sense of the primitive barbarian apprehends sequences and events in terms of will-power or inclination. As seen in the light of this animistic preconception, any process is substantially teleological, and the propensity imputed to it will not be thwarted of its legitimate end after the course of events in which it expresses itself has once fallen into shape or got under way. It follows logically, as a matter of course, that if once the motions leading to a desired consummation have been rehearsed in the accredited form and sequence, the same substantial result will be attained as that produced by the process imitated. This is the ground of whatever efficiency is imputed to ceremonial observances on all planes of culture, and it is especially the chief element in formal adoption and initiation. Hence, probably, the practice of mock-seizure or

mock-capture, and hence the formal profession of fealty and submission on the part of the woman in the marriage rites of peoples
among whom the household with a male head prevails. This
form of the household is almost always associated with some
survival or reminiscence of wife-capture. In all such cases,
marriage is, by derivation, a ritual of initiation into servitude.
In the words of the formula, even after it has been appreciably
softened under the latter-day decay of the sense of status, it is
the woman's place to love, honor, and obey.

According to this view, the patriarchal household, or, in other
words, the household with a male head, is an outgrowth af emulation between the members of a warlike community. It is,
therefore, in point of derivation, a predatory institution. The
ownership and control of women is a gratifying evidence of
prowess and high standing. In logical consistency, therefore,
the greater the number of women so held, the greater the
distinction which their possession confers upon their master.
Hence the prevalence of polygamy, which occurs almost universally at one stage of culture among peoples which have the male
household. There may, of course, be other reasons for polygamy, but the ideal development of polygamy which is met with
in the harems of very powerful patriarchal despots and chieftains
can scarcely be explained on other grounds. But whether it
works out in a system of polygamy or not, the male household
is in any case a detail of a system of status under which the
women are included in the class of unfree subjects. The domi-
nant feature in the institutional structure of these communities
is that of status, and the groundwork of their economic life is a
rigorous system of ownership.

The institution is found at its best, or in its most effectual
development, in the communities in which status and ownership
prevail with the least mitigation; and with the decline of the
sense of status and of the extreme pretensions of ownership,
such as has been going on for some time past in the communities of the western culture, the institution of the patriarchal
household has also suffered something of a disintegration. There
has been some weakening and slackening of the bonds, and this

deterioration is most visible in the communities which have departed farthest from the ancient system of status, and have gone farthest in reorganizing their economic life on the lines of industrial freedom.   And the deference for an indissoluble tie of ownership-marriage, as well as the sense of its definitive virtuousness, has suffered the greatest decline among the classes immediately engaged in the modern industries.   So that there seems to be fair ground for saying that the habits of thought fostered by modern industrial life are, on the whole, not favorable to the maintenance of this institution or to that status of women which the institution in its best development implies.   The days of its best development are in the past, and the discipline of modern life—if not supplemented by a prudent inculcation of conservative ideals—will scarcely afford the psychological basis for its rehabilitation.

This form of marriage, or of ownership, by which the man becomes the head of the household, the owner of the woman, and the owner and discretionary consumer of the household's output of consumable goods, does not of necessity imply a patriarchal system of consanguinity.   The presence or absence of maternal relationship should, therefore, not be given definite weight in this connection.   The male household, in some degree of elaboration, may well coexist with a counting of relationship in the female line, as, for instance, among many North American tribes.   But where this is the case it seems probable that the ownership of women, together with the invidious distinctions of status from which the practice of such an ownership springs, has come into vogue at so late a stage of the cultural development that the maternal system of relationship had already been thoroughly incorporated into the tribe's scheme of life.   The male household in such cases is ordinarily not developed in good form or entirely free from traces of a maternal household.   The traces of a maternal household which are found in these cases commonly point to a form of marriage which disregards the man rather than places him under the surveillance of the woman.   It may well be named the household of the unattached woman. This condition of things argues that the tribe or race in question has entered upon a predatory life only after a considerable period of peaceable industrial life, and after having achieved a considerable development of social structure under the régime of peace and industry, whereas the unqualified prevalence of the patriarchate, together with the male household, may be taken to indicate that the predatory phase was entered early, culturally speaking.

Where the patriarchal system is in force in fully developed form, including the paternal household, and hampered with no indubitable survivals of a maternal household or a maternal system of relationship, the presumption would be that the people in question has entered upon the predatory culture early, and has adopted the institutions of private property and class prerogative at an early stage of its economic development. On the other hand, where there are well-preserved traces of a maternal household, the presumption is that the predatory phase has been entered by the community in question at a relatively late point in its life history, even if the patriarchal system is, and long has been, the prevalent system of relationship. In the latter case the community, or the group of tribes, may, perhaps for geographical reasons, not have independently attained the predatory culture in accentuated form, but may at a relatively late date have contracted the agnatic system and the paternal household through contact with another, higher, or characteristically different, culture, which has included these institutions among its cultural furniture. The required contact would take place most effectually by way of invasion and conquest by an alien race occupying the higher plane or divergent line of culture. Something of this kind is the probable explanation, for instance, of the equivocal character of the household and relationship system in the early Germanic culture, especially as it is seen in such outlying regions as Scandinavia. The evidence, in this latter case, as in some other communities lying farther south, is somewhat obscure, but it points to a long-continued coexistence of the two forms of the household; of which the maternal seems to have held its place most tenaciously among the subject or lower classes of the population, while the paternal was the honorable form of marriage in vogue among the superior class. In the earliest traceable situation of these tribes there appears to have been a relatively feeble, but growing, preponderance of the male household throughout the community. This mixture of marriage institutions, as well as the correlative mixture or ambiguity of property institutions associated with it in the Germanic culture, seems most easily explicable as being due to the mingling of two distinct racial stocks, whose institutions differed in these respects. The race or tribe which had the maternal household and common property would probably have been the more numerous and the more peaceable at the time the mixing process began, and would fall into some degree of subjection to its more warlike consort race.

No attempt is hereby made to account for the various forms of human marriage, or to show how the institution varies in detail from place to place and from time to time, but only to indicate what seems to have been the range of motives and of exigencies that have given rise to the paternal household, as it has been handed down from the barbarian past of the peoples of the western culture. To this end, nothing but the most general features of the life history of the institution have been touched upon, and even the evidence on which this much of generalization is based is, per force, omitted. The purpose of the argument is to point out that there is a close connection, particularly in point of psychological derivation, between individual ownership, the system of status, and the paternal household, as they appear in this culture.

This view of the derivation of private property and of the male household, as already suggested, does not imply the prior existence of a maternal household of the kind in which the woman is the head and master of a household group and exercises a discretionary control over her husband or husbands and over the household effects. Still less does it imply a prior state of promiscuity. What is implied by the hypothesis and by the scant evidence at hand is rather the form of the marriage relation above characterized as the household of the unattached woman. The characteristic feature of this marriage seems to have been an absence of coercion or control in the relation between the sexes. The union (probably monogamic and more or less enduring) seems to have been terminable at will by either party, under the constraint of some slight conventional limitations. The substantial difference introduced into the marriage relation on the adoption of ownership-marriage is the exercise of coercion by the man and the loss on the part of the woman of the power to terminate the relation at will. Evidence running in this direction, and in part hitherto unpublished, is to be found both in the modern and in the earlier culture of Germanic communities.

It is only in cases where circumstances have, in an exceptional degree, favored the development of ownership-marriage that we should expect to find the institution worked out to its logical consequences. Wherever the predatory phase of social life has not come in early and has not prevailed in unqualified form for a long time, or wherever a social group or race with this form of the household has received a strong admixture of another race not possessed of the institution, there the prevalent form of marriage should show something of a departure from this paternal type. And even where neither of these two conditions is present, this type of the marriage relation might be expected in the course of time to break down with the change of circumstances, since it is an institution that has grown up as a detail of a system of status, and, therefore, presumably fits into such a social system, but does not fit into a system of a different kind. It is at present visibly breaking down in modern civilized communities, apparently because it is at variance with the most ancient habits of thought of the race, as well as with the exigencies of a peaceful, industrial mode of life. There may seem some ground for holding that the same reassertion of ancient habits of thought which is now apparently at work to disintegrate the institution of ownership-marriage may be expected also to work a disintegration of the correlative institution of private property; but that is perhaps a question of speculative curiosity rather than of urgent theoretical interest.

THE UNIVERSITY OF CHICAGO.   THORSTEIN VEBLEN.

Women in America

FROM COLONIAL TIMES TO THE 20TH CENTURY

An Arno Press Collection

Andrews, John B. and W. D. P. Bliss. **History of Women in Trade Unions** (*Report on Conditions of Woman and Child Wage-Earners in the United States,* Vol. X; 61st Congress, 2nd Session, Senate Document No. 645). 1911

Anthony, Susan B. **An Account of the Proceedings on the Trial of Susan B. Anthony, on the Charge of Illegal Voting at the Presidential Election in November, 1872,** and on the Trial of Beverly W. Jones, Edwin T. Marsh and William B. Hall, the Inspectors of Election by Whom her Vote was Received. 1874

The Autobiography of a Happy Woman. 1915

Ayer, Harriet Hubbard. **Harriet Hubbard Ayer's Book:** A Complete and Authentic Treatise on the Laws of Health and Beauty. 1902

Barrett, Kate Waller. **Some Practical Suggestions on the Conduct of a Rescue Home.** *Including* **Life of Dr. Kate Waller Barrett** (Reprinted from *Fifty Years' Work With Girls* by Otto Wilson). [1903]

Bates, Mrs. D. B. **Incidents on Land and Water;** Or, Four Years on the Pacific Coast. 1858

Blumenthal, Walter Hart. **Women Camp Followers of the American Revolution.** 1952

Boothe, Viva B., editor. **Women in the Modern World** (*The Annals of the American Academy of Political and Social Science,* Vol. CXLIII, May 1929). 1929

Bowne, Eliza Southgate. **A Girl's Life Eighty Years Ago:** Selections from the Letters of Eliza Southgate Bowne. 1888

Brooks, Geraldine. **Dames and Daughters of Colonial Days.** 1900

Carola Woerishoffer: Her Life and Work. 1912

Clement, J[esse], editor. **Noble Deeds of American Women;** With Biographical Sketches of Some of the More Prominent. 1851

Crow, Martha Foote. **The American Country Girl.** 1915

De Leon, T[homas] C. **Belles, Beaux and Brains of the 60's.** 1909

de Wolfe, Elsie (Lady Mendl). **After All.** 1935

Dix, Dorothy (Elizabeth Meriwether Gilmer). **How to Win and Hold a Husband.** 1939

Donovan, Frances R. **The Saleslady.** 1929

Donovan, Frances R. **The Schoolma'am.** 1938

Donovan, Frances R. **The Woman Who Waits.** 1920

Eagle, Mary Kavanaugh Oldham, editor. **The Congress of Women,** Held in the Woman's Building, World's Columbian Exposition, Chicago, U.S.A., 1893. 1894

Ellet, Elizabeth F. **The Eminent and Heroic Women of America.** 1873

Ellis, Anne. **The Life of an Ordinary Woman.** 1929

[Farrar, Eliza W. R.] **The Young Lady's Friend.** By a Lady. 1836

Filene, Catherine, editor. **Careers for Women.** 1920

Finley, Ruth E. **The Lady of Godey's:** Sarah Josepha Hale. 1931 **Fragments of Autobiography.** 1974

Frost, John. **Pioneer Mothers of the West;** Or, Daring and Heroic Deeds of American Women. 1869

[Gilman], Charlotte Perkins Stetson. **In This Our World.** 1899

Goldberg, Jacob A. and Rosamond W. Goldberg. **Girls on the City Streets:** A Study of 1400 Cases of Rape. 1935

Grace H. Dodge: Her Life and Work. 1974

Greenbie, Marjorie Barstow. **My Dear Lady:** The Story of Anna Ella Carroll, the "Great Unrecognized Member of Lincoln's Cabinet." 1940

Hourwich, Andria Taylor and Gladys L. Palmer, editors. **I Am a Woman Worker:** A Scrapbook of Autobiographies. 1936

Howe, M[ark] A. De Wolfe. **Memories of a Hostess:** A Chronicle of Friendships Drawn Chiefly from the Diaries of Mrs. James T. Fields. 1922

Irwin, Inez Haynes. **Angels and Amazons:** A Hundred Years of American Women. 1934

Laughlin, Clara E. **The Work-a-Day Girl:** A Study of Some Present-Day Conditions. 1913

Lewis, Dio. **Our Girls.** 1871

Liberating the Home. 1974

Livermore, Mary A. **The Story of My Life;** Or, The Sunshine and Shadow of Seventy Years . . . To Which is Added Six of Her Most Popular Lectures. 1899

Lives to Remember. 1974

Lobsenz, Johanna. **The Older Woman in Industry.** 1929

MacLean, Annie Marion. **Wage-Earning Women.** 1910

Meginness, John F. **Biography of Frances Slocum, the Lost Sister of Wyoming:** A Complete Narrative of her Captivity of Wanderings Among the Indians. 1891

Nathan, Maud. **Once Upon a Time and Today.** 1933

[Packard, Elizabeth Parsons Ware]. **Great Disclosure of Spiritual Wickedness!!** In High Places. With an Appeal to the Government to Protect the Inalienable Rights of Married Women. 1865

Parsons, Alice Beal. **Woman's Dilemma.** 1926

Parton, James, et al. **Eminent Women of the Age:** Being Narratives of the Lives and Deeds of the Most Prominent Women of the Present Generation. 1869

Paton, Lucy Allen. **Elizabeth Cary Agassiz:** A Biography. 1919

Rayne, M[artha] L[ouise]. **What Can a Woman Do;** Or, Her Position in the Business and Literary World. 1893

Richmond, Mary E. and Fred S. Hall. **A Study of Nine Hundred and Eighty-Five Widows Known to Certain Charity Organization Societies in 1910.** 1913

Ross, Ishbel. **Ladies of the Press:** The Story of Women in Journalism by an Insider. 1936

Sex and Equality. 1974

Snyder, Charles McCool. **Dr. Mary Walker:** The Little Lady in Pants. 1962

Stow, Mrs. J. W. **Probate Confiscation:** Unjust Laws Which Govern Woman. 1878

Sumner, Helen L. **History of Women in Industry in the United**

States (*Report on Conditions of Woman and Child Wage-Earners in the United States,* Vol. IX; 61st Congress, 2nd Session, Senate Document No. 645). 1910

[Vorse, Mary H.] **Autobiography of an Elderly Woman.** 1911

Washburn, Charles. **Come into My Parlor:** A Biography of the Aristocratic Everleigh Sisters of Chicago. 1936

Women of Lowell. 1974

Woolson, Abba Gould. **Dress-Reform:** A Series of Lectures Delivered in Boston on Dress as it Affects the Health of Women. 1874

Working Girls of Cincinnati. 1974